Anthropology's Politics

Anthropology's Politics

Disciplining the Middle East

Lara Deeb and Jessica Winegar

Stanford University Press
Stanford, California

Stanford University Press
Stanford, California

Printed in the United States of America on acid-free, archival-quality paper

Library of Congress Cataloging-in-Publication Data

Deeb, Lara, 1974- author.
  Anthropology's politics : disciplining the Middle East / Lara Deeb and Jessica Winegar.
    pages cm
  Includes bibliographical references and index.
  ISBN 978-0-8047-8123-7 (cloth : alk. paper) — ISBN 978-0-8047-8124-4 (pbk. : alk. paper)
  1. Anthropology—Political aspects—Middle East. 2. Universities and colleges—Political aspects—United States. 3. American Anthropological Association. Middle East Section.
I. Winegar, Jessica, author. II. Title.
  GN17.3.M628D44 2015
  301.0956—dc23
                        2015011164

ISBN 978-0-8047-9684-2 (electronic)

Typeset by Bruce Lundquist in 10/14 Minion

To our teachers, for our students

Contents

Preface

We never could have written this book before tenure. At least a dozen colleagues—across institutions, disciplines, and regional specialties—warned us that our project would take us into dangerous territory. One began an interview by first ensuring that we were tenured. Another cautioned, "Thank god you have tenure, but you will pay." A third emailed: "What sort of trouble do you get in for writing about one of the 9,000 pound elephants in the room? . . . Basically, I'd have to recommend you make sure this doesn't become dyna mite in a tenure fight or anything like that. Break the silence, but don't break yourself along the way." We were inspired to break our silence after giving a paper at a conference on the State of the Art of Middle East Anthropology. Our contribution diagnosed the experience of doing anthropology of the region immediately after 9/11, based on ethnography with scholars of our generation. The audience response was astounding. Afterward, senior scholars animatedly recalled similar experiences from earlier decades, and junior scholars encouraged us to further expose for them the minefields that plagued Middle East Studies and anthropology. We came away from the conference with the sense that we needed to explore the history of US empire's impact on scholarly practice, using anthropology of the Middle East and North Africa as a lens.

Infuriating experiences we shared nearly a decade earlier had primed us to expand our project in this way. At that time, we wanted anthropology to collectively respond to the horrors of escalating Islamophobia in the United States after the 9/11 attacks and the unleashing of the world's most powerful military on Afghanistan and Iraq. These wars, along with Israel's repeated assaults on Palestine and the US War on Terror's expansion across the globe, would result in colossal death and destruction. We wanted our discipline to speak out so that we could claim it with pride. But it didn't.

This experience marked the beginning of our scholarly and activist collaborations, as well as our ethnographic observations of these phenomena. Writing this book has taught us a great deal: much of what we have experienced during our careers is part of larger historically constituted challenges in academic practice. As anthropologists, we turned to ethnography to understand this terrain. And as with many ethnographies, our experiences as both researchers and subjects permeate the pages of this book.

We could not have written this without the generosity of our colleagues. Our most profound thanks and appreciation, first and foremost, go to everyone who allowed us to turn the ethnographic table on them. As anthropologists, they understand why we cannot thank them by name. This project has driven home how rich life experiences can never be fully captured in textual analysis. We hope that they enjoy reading this ethnographic analysis and that it resonates with their varied perspectives.

Susan Slyomovics and Sherine Hafez organized the original conference at UCLA that kicked off this project; we thank them as well as that conference audience for inspiring us to pursue it. Along the way, we received helpful comments from audiences at George Washington University, the University of Illinois at Urbana-Champaign, and the conferences of the American Studies Association and the American Anthropological Association (AAA). We appreciate the invitations and organizational work of Ilana Feldman, Jessica Greenberg, Nadine Naber, and Lisa Rofel that made those encounters happen.

Our institutions, Northwestern University and Scripps College, funded some of our research. Many undergraduate and graduate students helped us with transcription, data organization, internet research, and bibliographic searches: Lucienne Altman-Newell, Erin Berger, Amy Chang, Shanisha Coram, Sara Dada, Tim Garrett, Danica Harootian, Nedra Lucas, Soad Mana, Emily Matteson, Zaynab Quadri, Katherine Sobolewski, and Najeeba Syed. For their outstanding assistance with interviewing, archival research, and research into funding organizations, we are grateful to Vanessa Agard-Jones, Waqas Butt, Rachel Cantave, Andrea Elganzoury, Rachel George, Christine Sargent, and Claire Wilson.

Many colleagues helped us track down documents, searching old hard drives and file boxes, and sharing reams of virtual and literal paper with us: Lori Allen, Dale Eickelman, Carolyn Fluehr-Lobban, Suad Joseph, Barbara Larsen, Smadar Lavie, Sam Martinez, David Price, Victoria Sanford, Gregory Starrett, Daniel Varisco, and Jenny White. We especially thank Laurence Michalak for going above and beyond, excavating a storage locker to locate and scan *Middle East Research in Anthropology (MERA) Forum* issues and other materials for us. At the AAA, Kim Baker and Damon Dozier assisted us in locating documents, dates, and bits of information; we are also especially indebted to Executive Director Ed Liebow, for all of that plus his extraordinarily patient replies to seemingly endless email queries.

Our work was made easier by smart comments, useful references, or clarifications from Kamran Ali, Aslı Bâli, Kristen Brustad, Jessica Cattelino, Piya Chatterjee, Elizabeth Derderian, Micaela di Leonardo, Virginia Dominguez, Gretchen Edwalds-Gilbert, Ilana Feldman, Laura Ann Fernea, Jessica Greenberg, Simon Greenwold, Mark Hauser, Ghenwa Hayek, Katherine Hoffman, Elizabeth Shakman Hurd, J. Kēhaulani Kauanui, Tobias Kelly, Dima Khalidi, Nikolas Kosmatopoulos, Mark Mahoney, Amy Marcus-Newhall, Joseph Masco, Ellen Moodie, Nadine Naber, Esra Özyürek, Seo Young Park, Shira Robinson, Helen Schwartzman, Samuli Schielke, and Shalini Shankar. Chris Toensing generously dug up Middle East Research and Information Project (MERIP) history and helped us navigate a citational minefield.

We count ourselves particularly lucky to have received support and sage advice from Lila Abu-Lughod, Donald Donham, Daniel Segal, Andrew Shryock, Susan Slyomovics, and especially David Price, who has supported our project from its early days, answered numerous historical questions, and inspired us with his work. Donna Murdock, David Price, and Paul Silverstein read the manuscript in its entirety, and Corinne Kratz provided major insights along the way. We deeply appreciate their generosity and incisive interventions. Kate Wahl deserves special thanks for her brave and enthusiastic support. Her careful editorial expertise and intellectual acumen have made this book better, as have the diligent attentions of her team at Stanford University Press.

The founding members of the Task Force on Middle East Anthropology deserve a major shout-out for their inspiration and solidarity over the years: Fida Adely, Lori Allen, Amahl Bishara, Rochelle Davis, Ilana Feldman, and Laurie King. Another major shout-out goes to everyone currently working to bring discussion of Palestinian rights and the academic boycott of Israeli institutions to the AAA—we can't name them, for reasons that will become apparent in the coming chapters, but are honored to be working with them. Finally, gratitude and love from Lara to Qutayba, Hadi, Hera, and Ziad, and from Jessica to Hamdi and Zayd.

Anthropology's Politics

Introduction
Academics and Politics

The consummate image of the scholarly life is that it is defined by the free and impassioned pursuit of ideas. We conduct research and we teach; we produce, question, and impart knowledge. Yet all of us working in colleges and universities know that the life on which we once, perhaps naively, embarked is also filled with politics, much of it quite fraught. Early in graduate school, scholars get their first whiffs of tensions surrounding race, class, gender, and generation and learn which topics are open for discussion and/or research and which are subject to hegemonic silencing. The politics of the job market and tenure are particularly intense, in light of shrinking opportunities for tenure track jobs as well as high-profile cases of politicized unhiring and tenure denials and battles.[1] The classroom is another site of contested politics, in particular for junior scholars, women, and racial and ethnic minorities, as teachers must delicately manage controversial topics as well as students' prejudices against one another and against their professors. Committees, faculty meetings, administration and trustee decision-making processes, and the annual meetings of national academic associations are spaces where power is meted out and exercised. Learned and professional associations also often set the tone and agenda for what counts as legitimate disciplinary practice and academic concern. Of course, none of these politics are solely generated or contained within the brick and mortar of the academic institution itself. Larger social, economic, and political forces (national and international) play key roles in shaping academia and its politics, beginning as far back as the early life experiences of scholars—experiences that influence their decisions to enter the academy and work in particular disciplines and on specific topics.

This book examines the relationship between academics and politics in the United States after World War II (WWII), with an emphasis on the post–

Cold War period. It does so through a case study of Middle East anthropology,[2] because this field provides a particularly compelling lens through which to view some of the key stakes in the political struggles of academe as these articulate with broader forces of power. It is especially useful to investigate the convergence between this region and discipline because the Middle East and North Africa (hereafter MENA)[3] has been *the* primary geopolitical focus of US foreign policy during this era. In the immediate post-WWII period, the founding of Israel in 1948 sparked a decades-long process of wedding US foreign policy to Israeli state interests. US focus on the region was also fueled by the concomitant scramble to control access to newly discovered oil in the Gulf states. The fall of the Soviet Union essentially coincided with the first of three official wars in the region during which the United States has put hundreds of thousands of boots on the ground: the 1990–1991 Gulf War (the other two are the War in Afghanistan from 2001–present and the 2003–2011 Iraq War).[4] It also coincided with the peak of the first Palestinian Intifada, a period of mass resistance to the United States' main client state in the region: Israel. The end of the Cold War additionally saw the consolidation of a new canon—initiated two decades earlier—for graduate training in the humanities and social sciences in the United States. For MENA anthropology as well as other fields, two key tenets of this canon held that the "world areas" scholars researched had been set by colonial and Cold War powers[5] and that scholars could not ignore the subjective and political nature of knowledge production about, and representation of, so-called "others."

The politics of doing academic work related to the Middle East and North Africa in the United States grew especially fraught as the region took center stage in US imperial ambitions, paralleling the politics of doing academic work in Latin America in earlier decades when the Cold War was fought on those soils. On the one hand, over time we see significantly more interest in funding work on the region and hiring scholars to research and teach about it. Indeed, increased funding streams from the US government and private social research foundations helped to spur the post-WWII development of MENA anthropology in the first place. On the other hand, since at least the 1970s, academics who research or teach topics against the grain of dominant US national narratives about and interests in the region have faced the prospects of not having their research funded, not being hired, being accused—by parents, students, administrators, and people unassociated with academe or their campus—of bias and even treason in their teaching and public lectures, being targeted by blacklists and hate mail, and even losing their jobs. This is especially the case for those who teach about Palestinians and/or critical perspectives on Israeli state actions, and for scholars of Arab and/or Muslim descent, who face additional discrimination. Such challenges greatly intensified with the advent of the so-called War on Terror in the early 2000s, along with the increase in numbers and reach of right-wing "watchdog" organizations such as Campus Watch and the development of internet technologies that enabled greater surveillance as well as public targeting of MENA scholars.

Refracting US academic politics related to MENA through the lens of anthropology opens up analytic vistas that capture other kinds of tensions. The professional practice and demographics of anthropology embody both the post-WWII shift in US domestic politics toward an emphasis on civil rights and the inclusion of female and minority perspectives, and the backlash against these shifts and continued reproduction of structural inequalities. Many anthropologists view their discipline as one that champions (or should champion) the voices and perspectives of the marginalized, yet some of its practitioners have colluded with colonial and state power. Anthropology has become a heavily feminized discipline since the second-wave feminist movement and attracts many nonelite scholars (a number of whom are from working class backgrounds), yet it remains largely white, like academia in general. Anthropology is the most resolutely international of the social sciences in its breadth of research sites and privileging of fieldwork done "elsewhere," yet anthropologists based in the United States mainly cite the work of their colleagues in US institutions. And anthropologists frequently identify as politically left leaning and critical of capitalism, yet continue to work in increasingly corporatized university environments. Meanwhile, academics, politicians, and media pundits often characterize universities and colleges as bastions of liberalism that do not teach useful "skills" for social progress or economic success, often pointing to anthropology as a primary disciplinary example.[6]

Thus, our study of the politics of MENA anthropology as practiced in the United States during the apogee of the latter's empire reveals the politics of academia in multiple senses of the term "politics" and at different scales. In what follows, we examine the politics of governance and administration from the levels of departments to universities, disciplinary associations to the state, and the links in between. We uncover both assumptions and controversies about research, teaching, and extra-academic engagements, especially as these relate to the politics of class, gender, race, ethnicity, and generation. And we track the ways these forms of politics shape people's efforts to acquire and exercise power and authority in an academic environment that is utterly entangled with trends in US domestic and foreign policy. The result is a complex portrait of how the pursuit of ideas—that hallmark of scholarly practice—is never pure;

it is infused with tensions large and small. This is not to say that the lofty ideals of higher education have grown more tainted over time (surely the halls of medieval universities were host to many political machinations). Instead, it is to bring a key insight of post-WWII humanities and social science research—that knowledge and power are coconstituted—to bear not just on the scholarship we produce, but on *how* we produce it. This book thus concentrates on the *social practice* of being a scholar within an intricate and historically constituted set of power relations. It flips the ethnographic gaze onto us, something that (ironically) anthropologists rarely do, even in the historiography of anthropology.[7] We do this not to get a better view of our own navels, it must be said, but rather to expose important, yet often hidden, dynamics of higher education and knowledge production in the era of US empire.

We also write out of an ethical imperative, as scholars who have experienced firsthand the political strictures and costs of certain kinds of academic work and as US citizens with deep ties to a region that has borne the recent brunt of US intervention. Indeed, that imperative informs our approach to politics which we also, after indigenous anthropologist Robert Hancock, take to mean "a person's notion of the kind of world she or he wants to live in or seeks to create . . . to encompass all thought and action aimed at remaking or changing the world beyond the bounds of the individual." Many academics have these goals in mind when they teach and research; we call attention to how such thoughts and actions are deeply political and "necessarily tied to an ethics, which represents and demarcates the bounds of actions acceptable in the work of bringing these worlds into existence."[8] We acknowledge that we as authors have our particular notions of an ideal world and that these shape the ethics underlying our writing and analysis in this book. Some, no doubt, will charge us with bias; we reply that all knowledges are situated[9] and that for far too long this story is the one that has not been told. Telling it reveals the biases in the normative narratives surrounding anthropology, MENA, and academia in the United States.

Indeed, the central arguments of this book with regard to academic politics are relevant far beyond MENA anthropology. They reveal broader dynamics related to how the policies and actions of the US state, neoliberal economics, and domestic social movements deeply affect scholarly practice at multiple levels. In presentations of our research to interdisciplinary audiences as well as in our two decades of working in multidisciplinary academic contexts, we have heard strikingly similar discussions of academic politics. Our case study demonstrates several central aspects of them. First, while scholars may be drawn to their disciplines, regions, and topics out of personal interest, those interests are themselves shaped by larger social factors related to gender, social class, race, nationality, and the economic and political contexts in which one comes of age. The production of knowledge is political from its inception in a future academic's social life.

Second, substantial demographic shifts in the composition of some fields in the US academy have changed the nature of scholarship and particularly its relationship to political commitment and critique. The influence of various female and minority perspectives central to this process has, however, met with resistance from long-standing academic structures and hierarchies. This takes different forms depending on one's career stage or particular academic setting (e.g., classroom, job search, tenure and promotion, or publishing). We identify a major pattern that results from practicing scholarship in this environment: academics devise a number of strategies to preserve their scholarship, senses of self, and careers.

Third, as US empire has expanded and shifted geographic focus to MENA, so have the corporatization, militarization, and surveillance of knowledge production in the academy, increasing the risks and rewards for research and/or teaching about the region. Academia becomes a poison chalice—both a means to speak truth to power and a means to tether scholars to particular dominant structures of power.[10] These structures operate at different levels and include increasingly bureaucratic disciplinary associations, colleges, and universities, as well as the militarizing US state. Again we find that scholars' self-protection strategies are one of the important but understudied effects of this shift, including self-monitoring and sometimes even self-censorship when it comes to criticism of the US and especially the Israeli governments. These strategies are at odds with the ideals of the university as a space for the circulation of ideas, expanding human knowledge, or training future citizens and leaders. The case of MENA anthropology shows these general trends in heightened clarity and as such provides a lesson for all academics working in US institutions. If the United States is a nation in crisis, as analysts on both left and right tend to declare, and if colleges and universities are also at a tipping point, as a spate of recent books and articles suggest,[11] then the nation's 1.2 million postsecondary educators would do well to listen to this story.[12]

Economic Pressures Shaping US Academic Politics

Economics are a central component of these crises in the United States and academe. Indeed, the intensification of neoliberal capitalist globalization since the 1970s, and especially since the end of the Cold War, has affected scholarly practice considerably. Growing income inequality, declines in state funding for higher education, reductions in government (and sometimes private) research funding alongside increasing government regulations, and the infusion of a corporate ethos into the workings of colleges and universities have all led to budgetary pressures, a massive decline in the number of tenure-track faculty positions, and a huge growth in administrative positions.

In this climate, institutions increasingly rely on tuition dollars and donations, which means that boards of trustees, students, and alumni have greater power over what gets taught, how, and by whom.[13] Most recently, the University of Illinois at Urbana-Champaign exercised this power in unhiring scholar Stephen Salaita on the basis of his tweets critical of Israel during its 2014 assault on Gaza. In public institutions, we can add state legislatures to this list of stakeholders, whose interests are also bound up with those of business and sometimes the federal government.[14]

The vast administrative bloat across US campuses is in direct inverse proportion to the rise in contingent, non-tenure-track professorial labor.[15] The shrinking of tenure-line employment opportunities began in the 1970s and continued (with brief periods of respite) unabated into the Reagan era, during which only around 5 percent of new PhDs found tenure-track jobs, even though undergraduate enrollments rose by upwards of 40 percent.[16] With the rise in consumerism in American society as well as higher tuition costs, students became more avid consumers, and institutions responded. Money "saved" by reducing tenure lines has been redirected toward marketing, branding, and providing what administrations think consumers (e.g., students and parents) want: extracurricular perks such as state-of-the-art gymnasiums, successful sports teams, fancy dormitories, "foodie"-quality dining options, and services to help students gain lucrative careers.

Anthropology is no exception to this trend of tenure-track job loss; a 2009 report by the American Anthropological Association showed that the economic recession that began in 2007 resulted in at least a 22 percent drop in tenure-line job openings and the loss of seventy-five faculty lines (mostly in cultural anthropology).[17] And even faculty members in tenure lines are not secure— tenure denials happen (and not always due to poor scholarship or teaching), and, while still relatively rare, some institutions are firing tenured faculty and closing down whole departments, citing economic circumstances. Meanwhile, economic inequality in the United States has grown by such drastic proportions that very few Americans, budding professors included, can rest assured that they will be gainfully and consistently employed in their lifetimes.

Consequently, in order to get and keep good jobs, academics need to (or strongly feel they need to) shape their scholarly activities in ways that meet market demands without rocking any boats.[18] Taking MENA anthropology as a case study, this has meant, depending on the particular time period, avoiding critical approaches to US foreign policy, Israel-Palestine, Islamophobia, and hierarchies of race and gender—in research, teaching, public speaking, and collegial relationships. Various social and political forces over the past four decades have combined with these economic pressures—as well as with new funding opportunities—to determine which boats can safely be rocked.

Sociopolitical Forces and Academia's Changing Demographic Politics

Where once the US academy was mainly the province of white Anglo-Saxon Protestant men from middle- and upper-class backgrounds, a number of forces since WWII have produced demographic shifts in the professoriate. The growth in numbers of women, racial and ethnic minorities, and people of a variety of class and religious backgrounds (including Catholic, Jewish, and Muslim) has enabled scholars to challenge certain long-standing hierarchies and assumptions in both anthropology and MENA Studies. These demographic changes have also revealed politicized tensions and motivated new forms of discrimination rooted in those old hierarchies.

Federal legislation and mass social movements are key among the forces that have catalyzed these shifts. The G.I. Bill of 1944 opened the gates for non-elites, Jews, and Catholics to get college degrees and for some to eventually become faculty.[19] Many anthropologists of MENA are the children or grandchildren of those who benefited from the G.I. Bill, many of them are of Jewish or Catholic background, and in our sample roughly one-third of them are from the working classes or precarious lower-middle classes.[20] Title VI of the 1964 Civil Rights Act legislatively (at the very least) guaranteed that the G.I. Bill, and numerous other civil protections, would apply to racial minorities such as African Americans as well as anyone of any national origin. The Immigration and Nationality Act of 1965, which opened the doors for increased immigration from the MENA region, eventually led to major growth in numbers of region-related scholars (meaning those with heritage ties to MENA)[21] in the subfield of MENA anthropology. Our sample indicates an approximately 25 percent increase in region-related scholars since the late 1960s and that at least 40 percent of those in PhD programs in the United States today are region-related.[22] We also found a 26 percent growth in other racial and ethnic minorities in the subfield, though the number remains small, at 8 percent.[23] In addition to these laws and immigration patterns, various minority and immigrant rights movements in the United States and their associated institutions (e.g., the NAACP, B'nai Brith) helped to make *overt* forms of discrimination legally and socially unacceptable, which contributed to diversifying the academy—although it, including anthropology, remains very white. Title IX of the Educational Amendments in 1972, along with the women's movement, similarly paved the way for female scholars to enter academia in larger numbers. Within our sample, we see a 19 percent shift to more female than male anthropologists since the late 1960s. Today, the subfield is 61 percent female and 39 percent male, with a notable increase in the number of women since 1990.[24]

In 1990, Lila Abu-Lughod predicted that "feminist and halfie [e.g., region-related] ethnography are practices that could shake up the paradigm of anthropology itself by showing us that we are always part of what we study and we always stand in definite relation to it."[25] We argue that this massive influx of women and region-related scholars into the field altered its politics in fundamental ways, often by foregrounding serious critiques (both within the academy and beyond) of social inequalities based on race, gender, religion, and national heritage, as well as US empire, Israeli occupation of Palestine, and the inherently subjective nature of knowledge production. We find that over time it becomes less politically risky for female and region-related anthropologists to protest sexism and racism in the academy and in public outreach.

Anthropology was one of the early fields that region-related scholars, women, Jews, Catholics, and Muslims, as well as those of the middle to lower classes, perceived as a discipline that would simultaneously respect their experiences and provide them the tools to understand experiences of marginalization more generally. It helped them make sense of the tensions they experienced as the result of being in-between and/or excluded from various structures of power. These demographic shifts and anthropologists' narratives tell us that the discipline was and remains, for many of its practitioners, a powerful means of cultivating respect for subaltern experiences and galvanizing those experiences to speak back to power. Certainly the demographic shifts in the field stem not only from post-WWII sociopolitical legislation and movements, but also from beliefs that anthropology allows for diverse perspectives. Watershed theoretical moments in the discipline—and the academy—such as Marxism, poststructuralism, and postcolonial theory also fomented this shift.

This is not at all to say that anthropology is devoid of sexism, racism, classism, or prejudice against religious minorities.[26] Rather, our focus on the MENA subfield shows the complex transformation of these persistent problems over time. While demographically MENA anthropology (like the broader discipline) has become significantly more inclusive of Jews and Catholics, women, and racialized region-related minorities, frictions remain. There has been a decline in the more obvious forms of prejudice that our interlocutors experienced in the 1960s, 1970s, and 1980s, but increased hiring of underrepresented minorities[27] has also slowed considerably in recent years. The "presumed incompetence"[28] these scholars must confront on a daily basis in an academic environment that is far from color-blind has intersected in nefarious ways with the overall decline in tenure-track jobs.[29] Furthermore, less overt stereotyping of women, nonwhites, and those of Muslim background occurs regularly. Region-related anthropologists in particular must constantly fight assumptions that they are oppressive Middle Eastern men, oppressed Middle Eastern women, un-American patriots, or virulent anti-Semites. Their research and teaching about the region are monitored more closely than that of other scholars. They must also deal with a range of microaggressions, "subtle and commonplace exchanges or indignities (both conscious and unconscious) that . . . convey demeaning messages."[30] This term aptly describes the persistence of subtle, and quite insidious, expressions of bias that our interlocutors described, in the (relative) absence of more overt forms that are now (mostly) illegal.[31] These dynamics are directly related to US foreign policy and engagement in the MENA region.

United States-MENA Engagements and an Unevenly Expanding Academic Field

US global engagements are the third factor contributing to the production of academia's politics, especially how and why people research in and teach about MENA and which issues they might experience as too risky to confront. US involvement in the region has drawn people to MENA anthropology, intimately shaped research, teaching, and public engagement, and created politicized minefields and pressures on scholars to conform to normative US perspectives on the region, particularly Israel-Palestine.

Understanding this process requires situating it within dominant US encounters with MENA since WWII, as marked by dramatic moments of militarized violence and supposed peacemaking. As Melani McAlister argues, these encounters coalesced around the politics of oil (i.e., maintaining American access to Middle Eastern oil reserves) and religious origins (i.e., jockeying for claim to the Holy Land). We update McAlister's pre-9/11 study by adding the interrelated politics of courting and fighting various so-called "Islamist" groups. All of these US encounters with the region "vacillate between two poles: distance, othering, and containment" and "affiliation, appropriation, and co-optation."[32] Orientalism and its variant in Islamophobia also shape this vacillation by positing a "style of thought based upon an ontological and epistemological distinction made between 'the Orient' and . . . 'the Occident'" in which the Orient is rendered an alluring and mystical, yet uncivilized, backward-thinking, irrationally religious other which must be saved (or conquered) by Western progress and enlightenment.[33] Additionally, as McAlister noted, domestic racial politics intertwine with international politics to shape these two poles—for the case in this book, particularly the politics of being Arab, Muslim, or Jewish in America.

This discord between fascination with and repulsion from MENA influences anthropologists' initial attraction to discipline and region, as well as audience reactions to their teaching, research, and public lectures. How all of this happens depends in large measure on the nature of US engagement with MENA at specific historical moments. The 1948 founding of Israel and the rise of American Jewish Zionist groups eventually interwove with escalating US evangelical Christian support of Israel,[34] and, even more importantly, with US foreign policy to protect oil interests and combat resistance to the US state and its allies in the region. This configuration of factors shaped our interlocutors' interests in working there—whether via a nascent Orientalist fascination (common among white scholars) and/or a desire to get to the bottom of dominant negative narratives and eventually show the humanity and complexity of MENA social life (common among region-related scholars, as well as some white scholars). Anthropology was attractive for both these modes of engagement—as the discipline that traditionally studied (and sometimes romanticized) the other, and as the discipline whose methodology and theoretical approaches were viewed as most apt for accessing on-the-ground complexity and using it to talk back to dominant narratives about the region.

Specific events within this long US political engagement affected scholars' access to research sites as well.[35] On the one hand, US state legislation and funding did not guarantee such access, even as studying the region became a state priority.[36] The 1978–1979 Iranian revolution against a US-backed dictator essentially prohibited generations of US scholars—with a window of exception for Iranian Americans—from doing research there.[37] So did the 1975–1990 civil war for Lebanon, where the United States was intimately involved—not least by shelling Beirut from the USS New Jersey and vetoing a UN resolution calling for the end of Israel's 1982 invasion of the country. Attacks on the US embassy and Marine barracks in Beirut led to a decade-long travel ban for US citizens, and since its lifting in the 1990s a general increase in access has been disrupted by periodic Israeli attacks, most seriously in 2006. The same was the case for Libya, due to a series of bombings and hostage takings in the 1980s in protest of US military aggressions, primarily the 1981, 1986, and 1989 US attacks on Libyan planes and ships in the disputed waters of the Gulf of Sidra. Similarly, for over thirty years Afghanistan has not been a safe research site due to violence and instability instigated by US-Soviet Cold War military confrontations, which continued during the twenty-first-century US war there. Algeria's civil war led to a travel ban that prevented US anthropologists from conducting research there from 1991 until 2002. This civil war began when the ruling Algerian political party, in coordination with the military, annulled the first multiparty elections in 1991 after the first round would have brought an Islamist political party to power—an annulment the United States supported in line with its Pax Americana designs on the region, even though in other contexts it supported similar Islamist actors. Ethnographic research in Iraq was first curtailed by the protracted and US-fueled Iran-Iraq War in the 1980s, then the US Gulf War of 1990–1991 followed by extremely destructive US sanctions on the country, and most recently the US-led Iraq War that began in 2003 and continues to reverberate despite officially ending in 2011. And Syria has been a black box for contemporary ethnographic research, first due to problems obtaining research permission and engaging ethically with interlocutors under the Asad regimes and now also due to war. [38]

On the other hand, the presence of US diplomatic ties and/or economic aid to a country has eased access in some places, as these relationships carry with them both stated and unstated obligations to grant visas and permissions to researchers carrying US passports. Yemen's popularity for many years, including during the Cold War, was at least partly due to the fact that it was, in the words of a Yemen scholar's mentor at the time, "beholden to the U.S. government because of all the foreign aid given to them" and therefore accessible to US researchers. While US scholars had great difficulty doing fieldwork in Egypt during the Nasser period (particularly after 1967), it became the most popular MENA fieldsite after the Camp David Accords in 1978 and subsequent aid from the United States. The 1993 Oslo Accords between Israel and the PLO, which for a brief period decreased the "overt violence of the occupation,"[39] enabled a critical mass of scholars to conduct research in the occupied Palestinian territories for a time.[40] Generally decent diplomatic relations with Morocco, Turkey, Jordan, and some Gulf countries have also facilitated access to fieldsites.

The events that instigated ebbs and flows in fieldsite access not only motivated scholarly interest in working in specific parts of the region but also molded the content of that interest as it evolved through academic careers. Violence in particular created and cemented stereotypes of Middle Easterners, especially men, as terrorists, which anthropologists then sought to complicate, if not outright combat, drawing on both their knowledge that miniscule numbers of Middle Easterners actually engaged in violence against Western or Israeli interests and their knowledge that US and Israeli aggression in the region was concealed from public view and whitewashed as a possible motive for such violence. This image of the Middle Eastern man as terrorist came to the fore in the 1970s with the emergence of militant Palestinian resistance tactics against Israeli killings of Palestinians and colonization of Palestinian land (such as hostage taking on planes and at the 1972 Olympic Games in Munich). The stereotype (and its mirror in the image of the "oppressed Muslim woman") then solidified over time with the 1979–1981 US-Iran hostage crisis, the aforementioned Lebanese and Libyan bombings of the 1980s, the first Palestinian intifada against Israeli occupation (1987–1991), the 1990–1991 Gulf War, the 1993 World Trade Center bombing, the second intifada beginning in 2000 during which Palestinians began to refuse Oslo's disastrous effects, the September 2001 attacks on the United States, and the subsequent violent opposition to US wars and imperial designs in the region.[41] Interlocutors who experienced any of these events in their formative years (e.g., in college and early adulthood) were likely to recall them as motivating a set of questions about the region and a desire to answer those questions and counter those stereotypes. And those region-related scholars who experienced racism as a result of these events were also sometimes drawn explicitly to anthropology in response.[42]

Several of these events also stimulated broader academic and government interest in MENA scholarship such that greater scholarly engagement with the region has been enabled by increases—at certain points in time—in both state and private funding for MENA research. After WWII, United States–based area studies programs and departments swelled, bolstered by the National Defense Education Act of 1958 and its accompanying programs like Fulbright-Hays and Title VI funding for languages (including Arabic).[43] Both federal and private foundation funding for MENA research increased again after 9/11. The Fulbright program funded an average of three additional MENA anthropology projects per year after 2001.[44] And funding for MENA projects from both the Social Science Research Council's International Dissertation Research Fellowship (IDRF) and the Wenner-Gren Foundation increased during this time.[45] However, with the exception of Wenner-Gren (an anthropology-specific organization), very little of this new funding was directed toward anthropologists.[46]

And all funding was subject to political constraints: federal funding was never available for countries with active travel bans and rarely for those with travel warnings. While a scholar might instead receive private foundation funding, academic institutions (especially public ones) sometimes refused research permissions for faculty or graduate students planning projects in places with federal warnings or bans.[47]

An additional troubling tension appeared during the War on Terror. Federal research funding has always reflected national security and political concerns, and policymakers have used resulting knowledge to their own ends.[48] But the twenty-first century brought new government efforts to use funding to shape scholars' research topics and frameworks.[49] These efforts range from the Minerva Consortium's Department of Defense funding for research on specific topics of national security interest;[50] to the Pat Roberts Intelligence Scholarship Program, which funds students in certain language and area studies programs in exchange for a commitment to serve in a US intelligence agency;[51] to the National Security Education Program's Boren fellowships, which require a one-year commitment to work "in the Federal Government in a position with national security responsibilities."[52] The latter two are examples of what many scholars describe as "strings-attached" funding: grants that include a clause requiring recipients to serve in some (often intelligence or security-related) government capacity after completing their degree.[53] By and large, MENA anthropologists refused to apply for this type of funding, and many also advised their students to avoid it.

In addition to funding increases at certain points in time and despite these constraints, we also see an overall increase in academic jobs in MENA anthropology. By most interlocutor accounts, the discourse of the "peace process" produced by the nonetheless deeply problematic Oslo Accords made it more politically acceptable to do research in Palestinian communities, opening new potential job possibilities for Palestine experts. As with funding, 9/11 and the subsequent US wars in the region provided the biggest boost to the job market—although once again, anthropology saw relatively less growth in MENA positions than did fields like political science, history, and Islamic Studies.[54] And this jump in employment possibilities was to be short-lived, as the financial collapse of 2008 precipitated a decline in the entire academic job market.[55]

These shifts in funding and job possibilities since 2001 reflect the ways that global politics have intertwined with the university's corporatization to create instrumental, and sometimes militarized, academic interest in the region— ultimately creating another kind of friction between knowledge production and US state interests. As funding to produce expert knowledge about MENA increased, students demanded more classes (often believing that MENA expertise would help them find jobs), precious tenure-line positions with foci in the region opened, and media outlets (connected with new university media relations offices) sought academic pundits on MENA affairs. But these various entities desired specific kinds of knowledge, and some disciplines were seen as more important to understanding the region than others (especially from a nationalist foreign policy perspective). Patterns of funding and job growth suggest that anthropology is not often seen as a "useful" discipline in that regard. Our research shows how anthropologists navigate this terrain, where certain topics (and positions on topics) are in particular demand.

Within anthropology as well, one can see geopolitical interests—sometimes refracted through cultural assumptions—instigating scholarly interest in topics like Middle Eastern Muslim women's agency, violence, and Islam.[56] Scholars who work on such matters must navigate all sorts of assumptions about them; those who do not must be able to speak to these topics in order to demonstrate their relevance. It remains to be seen how continuing political developments, including the uprisings that began in various countries in 2011 and the growing movement in academia to boycott, divest from, and sanction (BDS) Israel, will influence access, funding, and job prospects in the field. Certainly, ongoing US state involvement in the region nearly guarantees that the academic minefields created by all of these economic, social, and political forces will persist, but not without protest.

Academic Minefields

This book provides overwhelming evidence of pressures and attacks on scholars for teaching, research, and public lecturing that offer a critical perspective on the actions of the United States—and especially the Israeli—governments in the region or that offer a humanizing perspective toward Palestinians, Arabs, and Muslims. Three key points stand out in our analysis of how the aforementioned trends shape scholarly practice vis-à-vis academic minefields. First, Orientalism remains one of the central frameworks underwriting and legitimating the actions—both belligerent and benevolent—of these states in MENA.[57] It is a mode of "dominating, restructuring, and having authority over the Orient" and "the whole network of interests inevitably brought to bear on" any discussion involving the so-called Orient.[58] Academia is a key part of this network of interests, and as such, certain players in it produce Orientalist knowledge about MENA and/or Muslims in the forms of scholarship, teaching, public speaking, administrative decrees, and everyday conversation. Although many of our interlocutors argued that they work in a theoretically "post-Orientalist" anthropology,[59] their narratives suggest that many MENA scholars encountered Orientalist attitudes at a variety of levels of academic life (including among colleagues who do not see themselves as aligned with US and/or Israeli state interests). Most frequently, this took the form of comments or positions on Palestinians, Islam, and Muslim women, especially—though not exclusively—when expressed to region-related scholars. Of course, such encounters also drew on long-standing histories of US racism, sexism, and xenophobia.

Second, the degree to which academics are able to take critical scholarly approaches to US nationalism or foreign policy, in both research and teaching, shifts with the dominant political winds of the day, with some variation based on the location and type of institution in which one works. And taking a critical scholarly approach to Israel-Palestine has always been risky—but the contours of that risk have changed as more Palestine scholars entered the field alongside more concerted and broadly public campaigns against them by activist Zionist organizations; these became especially virulent with the rise of the internet and War on Terror discourses. Nonetheless, we are starting to see cracks even in that most intransigent area of academic censorship and suppression. We join scholars such as Piya Chatterjee and Sunaina Maira in arguing that "what is really at work in these attacks are the logics of racism, of warfare, and of nationalism that undergird U.S. imperialism and also the architecture of the U.S. academy. . . . These logics shape a systemic structure of repression of academic knowledge that counters the imperial, state building project."[60] And lastly, we provide ethnographic data to further support insights that such attacks are frequently racist, sexist, and homophobic[61] and/or target those who are on the political left. What Chatterjee and Maira call "academic containment"—that is, "stigmatizing an academic as 'too political,' devaluing and marginalizing scholarship, unleashing an FBI investigation, blacklisting, or . . . not granting . . . tenure," "is marked decisively . . . on specific kinds of bodies whose presence is definitively marked as 'Other.'"[62]

We need to understand these academic minefields in relation to the broader loss of professorial legitimacy in the United States. The "culture wars" that came to the fore in the 1980s (but were brewing much earlier) were part of a larger backlash against the greater inclusion of women and minority voices in US higher education[63] and the growing criticisms—from within and outside academia—of the politics of representation.[64] These culture wars created an image of the US academy as a bastion of "unpatriotic, politically correct, and radical

faculty members" who did not value the supposedly true brilliance of the Western canon,[65] a claim that bolstered the rising movement of right-wing political
Christianity in the United States and served to quell criticisms of Reagan-era
economic attacks on the poor and working classes that disproportionately affected racial and ethnic minorities. Ellen Schrecker argues that "this damaging
stereotype deprived the academic profession of its previously respected voice
within American political discourse, thus clearing the way for further attacks
on academic freedom in the aftermath of 9/11."[66] This context was and is vital
for our interlocutors; the following chapters deepen our understanding of its
ongoing effects on academic work in general by concentrating on the critical
role of MENA scholarship in eliciting attacks and stereotyping.

The most difficult period for critical academic work other than the McCarthy era was in fact the few years following 9/11. While academics did not face
direct attacks from the federal government as they did in the 1950s, they now
had to contend with smear campaigns that were quickly mobilized over the
internet. Over a decade later, after public opinion swayed against the US war
in Iraq, it might seem as if academics (generally viewed to be liberals) and anthropologists (many of whom think of themselves as being left of the liberals)
had always vocally opposed that war and other post-9/11 US actions in the region. Yet in addition to ample evidence of assaults on the academic freedom to
conduct a critical appraisal of US government policies and actions in the wake
of 9/11, we also see examples of a more general reluctance to support those
who were speaking out against those policies and actions. While our research
suggests that taking this sort of critical position was more difficult in majority
Republican "red" states and in larger universities, we also see problems faced
by people working in New York and Washington, DC (the sites of the attacks),
and note professors' appreciation of the openness of students in ROTC or from
military families to criticism of US actions, often because they had first-hand
experience with the wars in question.

Overall, our interviews add richly varied ethnographic support to arguments that the post-9/11 period was both part of a longer history of assaults
on academic freedom dating back to at least the McCarthy era and also different from that time—due to new media technologies, the Patriot Act, the rise
of private advocacy groups (especially right-wing and Zionist political organizations), the narrowing and militarization of government-academic funding relationships, and the concurrent shifts in university economic practices.[67]
This ethnographic perspective shows how these developments affected scholarly practice on multiple levels, ranging from the selection of research topics

to experiences in the classroom to feeling compelled to do public outreach. MENA anthropologists, and MENA scholars more generally, constitute a bell-wether for the degree to which such national and global politics affect daily academic work at any particular moment. As Sherine Hafez and Susan Slyomovics observe, "anthropologists who have dedicated what is now an overwhelming corpus of work to understanding the MENA have been faced with the very challenging task not only of conducting fieldwork in a region that is commonly linked to war and terrorism but also of contending with the need to constantly work against the grain of . . . normative knowledge."[68]

As we write, we are in an era when it is more acceptable—to other academics, administrations, students, and certain private advocacy groups—for scholars to publicly present scholarship or teach critically about the US state, an era pre-figured by earlier moments in the US academy, such as the anti–Vietnam War and anti–South African apartheid movements. We are also in a moment that is seeing more widespread scholarly criticism of Israeli state policies and actions, a point elaborated in the following chapters but especially in our conclusion, where we discuss the movement to boycott Israeli academic institutions. None-theless, the vast bulk of our research shows that for decades, to critically exam-ine Israeli policies and practices and/or simply work in Palestinian communities has been a major (and since the 1980s *the* major) political risk in the academy.[69] When it comes to academic politics, Israel-Palestine is central and exceptional. We are not the first to make this argument, but we offer ethnography to show just how deeply Israel-Palestine politics have affected scholarly practice, in ways at odds with the very definition of what scholarship should be.[70]

The Israeli-Palestinian conflict—as it is understood in the United States—has impinged on a wide range of scholarly activities from at least 1969 to the present. This period coincides with the widespread expansion and deepening of ties between the United States and Israeli governments, the success of pro-Israel lobbying groups in aligning US foreign policy with Israeli state interests, and the deliberate extension of those groups' activities into academe.[71] We have concrete and specific evidence, going back decades, of a number of politically motivated criticisms of and attacks on scholars who research and/or teach about Palestinians, and/or present a critical perspective on Israeli state policies (even when those same scholars also criticize the policies of other states in the region). These instances include threats to deny tenure, actual denial of a con-tract renewal, refusal to hire, revocation of a research grant, physical and verbal altercations at public lectures, public media shaming, internet slander, and the placement of student informants in classrooms by external organizations.[72]

In addition, we have widespread evidence of more subtle, but no less effective, pressures on scholars to adopt the "compulsory Zionism" that has become normative and institutionalized in the United States.[73] That is, scholars, academic administrators, and students are expected to support the specific political and positive view of Israel as a Jewish state that should serve as the designated and rightful homeland of the Jewish people. In large measure, this requires accepting a particular contemporary version of Zionism as a nationalist ideology that supports "the national movement for the return of the Jewish people to their homeland and the resumption of Jewish sovereignty in the Land of Israel" and typically (though not always) also implies "protection of the Jewish nation in Israel through support for the Israel Defense Forces."[74] However, historically there have been multiple versions of Zionism (including versions that did not hold that the solution to the oppression of Jews should be "Jews' achievement of sovereign political power in their own land").[75] Our research shows the everyday ways in which this version of compulsory Zionism is executed and enforced within academia.[76] These small, unspectacular incidents can be understood as microaggressions, if we expand that term to include scholars who do not adopt (or are seen as potentially threatening) positive views of Zionism.[77] Everyday encounters with compulsory Zionism include such things as faculty members trying to ascertain a job candidate's Israel politics during campus visits (whether or not the person works in that part of the region), colleagues making assumptions about a scholar's personal politics because of their background, and colleagues making prejudicial comments about Palestinians (often while sympathetic faculty members remain silent).

When added to the more dramatic threats to employment or blacklisting (first in print form and now on watchdog websites), such everyday encounters make very clear the assumptions underlying the practice of academia and just who holds the authority and status to bolster those assumptions and principles. Although criticism of the state of Israel exists in the humanities and social sciences, it remains contested in these areas of the academy and rare in the hard sciences and professional schools. Our interlocutors often experienced this exceedingly politicized academic environment as threatening, opposed to the principles of critical thinking and scholarship, and a major drain on time that would be better devoted to teaching and research. In response, many anthropologists avoid Israel-Palestine in their teaching or research. Those who do not spend considerable time proactively preventing problems and managing those that do occur.

Over time, the specific effects of Israel-Palestine politics on scholarly life have varied. The aforementioned brief window that the Oslo Accords created facilitated more scholarship on Palestine, and some anthropologists within the newest generation of scholars seem significantly less trepid (although still cautious) about teaching and research on the topic. That window seems to have closed with the dawn of the second Intifada in 2000, and attacks on scholars critical of Israeli state policies have grown more organized, public, and deliberate in the ensuing years.

It has become commonplace to assert that 9/11 is the origin point for Islamophobic attacks and other pressures on those who teach and lecture about MENA and US involvement there. Our research emphasizes that these attacks have a far deeper history. Yet they have intensified alongside general attacks on academic freedom in the post-9/11 period. This escalation is also a response to increased student campus activism for Palestinian rights in the wake of Oslo (e.g., the establishment of many Students for Justice in Palestine and Jewish Voice for Peace chapters) and greater monitoring of that activism.[78] And it is related to growing pro-Israel student activism, pressures from private donors in the neoliberal educational environment,[79] and private Zionist and right-wing organizations' deliberate targeting of academe as a key site for their interventions. The internet has also greatly facilitated the goal of these off-campus groups to, as one group words it, "positively impact the campus discourse towards Israel."[80] Using internet and on-the-ground mobilization, such groups seek to counter any campus discourse, including scholarly perspectives, that is critical of the Israeli state,[81] even if these perspectives are based on solid research (as determined by the main arbiter of scholarly quality: peer review). They regularly target scholars they view as too "liberal" or "radical" on MENA politics, including anthropologists.[82] As Schrecker notes, such campaigns aim to "delegitimize the work of mainstream scholars, especially those in Middle East Studies who do not support the Israeli hard line."[83] Many of the writers are students sent to events to "report back" on the supposed anti-Semitism, anti-Israel, anti-US, or pro-Islam statements of professors.

Examples of such groups include Campus Watch, Scholars for Peace in the Middle East, Discover the Networks, and The David Project, all founded in the early 2000s.[84] In 2012, The David Project published a white paper that argues that universities and colleges are especially important targets because they represent the future leadership of both the United States and the Zionist movement and therefore need to be exposed as the last bastion of discourses criticizing Israeli policies.[85] Other organizations dedicated to Zionist interventions on campuses and in academe include the Israel on Campus Coalition, the AMCHA Initiative, Hasbara Fellowships, and StandWithUs,[86] while broader groups like the "unabashedly pro-America and pro-Israel" think tank Endowment for Middle East Truth take frequent public stances on campus matters.[87] Such organizations are lobbying the US government to revoke Title VI funding for MENA area studies centers that they deem to be against their interests—and some people believe that they played a role in successfully defunding UCLA's Center for Near Eastern Studies in fall 2014.[88]

We emphasize that Zionism and Judaism and Israel are not one and the same and that to assume they are leads to gross misunderstandings of history and makes it more difficult to call out actual forms of anti-Semitism when they occur.[89] For example, some academics opposed to Zionism occasionally assume that all Jewish and/or Israeli students will be Zionists and act on that basis (often by treading extra carefully in the classroom). But there is much evidence, among our interlocutors and beyond, of both Jewish and Israeli opposition to Zionism as well as nonnormative and critical views of Israel.[90] Some of these perspectives have emerged with force on the US academic scene in recent years, especially in concert with the campaign to boycott Israeli academic institutions.[91] We also emphasize that academics regularly critique the assumptions, hierarchies, politics, and practices of social movements, philosophical traditions, and nation-states. To do so with Zionism and/or Israel is becoming increasingly more acceptable, though still an uphill battle, among younger generations. Understanding how this has come to be requires attention to generation as an analytic.

A Generational Approach to Track Changing Politics

We add generation to our considerations of how gender, class, race, ethnicity, and national heritage shape how and why scholars are drawn to MENA anthropology,[92] as well as whether and how they experience and respond to discrimination and attacks. We do this by tracking how anthropologists conceive (or not) of themselves as part of an academic and/or social generation and by tracing patterns in academic cohorts (as defined by year of PhD) over time. By taking generation as both a "native" and an analytic category, one can better understand how people experience academia's tensions and integrate presentist and historicist approaches to politics, as the anthropological historian George Stocking argued we must do.[93] This allows us to uncover (often previously hidden) genealogical sources for today's predicaments as well as try to understand past actions in their historical contexts. As another of our forebears in anthropological historiography Regna Darnell wrote, "presentism in [a] reflexive sense, choosing issues for historical attention because they still matter today, is fully commensurable with historicism."[94]

In his classic 1952 essay "The Problem of Generations," Karl Mannheim argued that generational groups (as defined in social rather than solely biological terms) share "a common location in the social and historical process" and that this "thereby limit[s] them to a specific range of potential experience, predisposing them for a certain characteristic mode of thought and experience, and a characteristic type of historically relevant action." This "common location" gives members of a generation "certain definite modes of behavior, feeling, and thought."[95] Recent works in anthropology have built upon these insights to show that generations are both produced by and defined through experience of *and* response to particular social events.[96] All of our interlocutors who expressed feeling part of a specific generation did so by reflecting on an academic, national, and/or global political awareness that was awakened sometime between their late teenage years and early graduate school.[97] Mannheim posited that generational consciousness emerges during formative years because as youth reach adulthood (which in academic terms can mean entering graduate education and the professoriate), they experience a "fresh contact" with the "accumulated heritage" of the discipline such that they bring to it "a changed relationship of distance from the object and a novel approach in assimilating, using, and developing the proffered material."[98] Scholars have used this insight to emphasize that youth are often crucial to social change, but must—as both category and actors—be understood in conversation with older generations,[99] an imperative we follow by tracing how people understand their formative years (often in graduate school training) as constitutive of their academic identities and practices. Adopting a generational perspective allows us to better understand a major force in how academic research and politics shift (or not) over time: scholars themselves, whose agency is both constrained by "accumulated heritage" but also enabled by "fresh contact."

Most of our interlocutors narrated generational sensibilities formed in relation to key theoretical moments in anthropology and MENA Studies (often experienced when they were students) and/or major political events.[100] We identify roughly five generations based on patterns in their perspectives and experiences. The earliest received their PhDs before 1980 and trained between the late 1950s and the early 1970s.[101] While clearly there were significant theoretical shifts during those decades, it makes sense to consider this a single *academic* generation because anthropological study of MENA remained rare in this period; the demographics of academia were still overwhelmingly white and male; and all of these individuals were trained before the watershed publication of Edward Said's *Orientalism* in 1978, which radically changed scholarship about MENA. Some of our interlocutors in this group identified with what they called "the sixties generation," and the Vietnam War and/or the feminist movement figured prominently in their senses of generational belonging, with several describing themselves as activists. While some also pointed to 1970s Marxist and/or feminist theoretical interventions as foundational, more commonly members of this group defined themselves as theoretically opposed to postmodernism and poststructuralism.

Anthropologists who obtained their PhDs in the 1980s form a bridge generation. They initiated the shift toward the theoretical "posts" as assistant professors newly influenced by Foucauldian approaches as well as *Orientalism*. This is the generation that saw significant numbers of female and region-related scholars enter the field, many of whom were keen to deconstruct the relationship between power and knowledge production. Yet some members of this group felt pressure (from themselves and others) to keep anthropology empirical and scientific in earlier senses of those terms. Politically, members of this cohort highlighted the tail end of the anti–Vietnam War movement and the women's and civil rights movements, as well as decolonization and liberation movements (especially those of Palestinians), as triggers for the formation of generational consciousness.

This sense of generation related to larger social movements faded for people who received their PhDs in the late 1980s or very early 1990s, the group that also expressed the least generational cohesion. Perhaps this is related to the disillusionment with the US Left and the increasing co-optation of radical politics by individualizing consumer logics that were ushered in by the Reagan era.[102] And while people in this cohort described theoretical interests in nationalism, feminism, and area studies, most did not experience theory as defining them as a generation, perhaps because they were in graduate school at a time of theoretical upheaval (e.g., the emergence of the "posts").

Scholars trained in the 1990s constituted a major generational formation. The decade saw a huge increase in the number of MENA anthropologists entering graduate school, which more than doubled from previous generations. For the first time in anthropology, there existed a critical mass of MENA specialists to drive region-related issues to the forefront of disciplinary discussions.[103] Most of our interlocutors in this group expressed strong generational identity.[104] They mentioned the Iran hostage crisis, the anti-apartheid movement, the end of the Cold War, the Reagan era, the Oslo Accords, and especially the 1990 Gulf War as formative political moments, with one explaining that their generation saw "the Middle East emerge as the new enemy." Theoretical trends motivated further generational identification for this group. Trained by scholars who had embraced postcolonial and poststructuralist critiques, they were the product of what had become a new anthropological canon, what one person described as "a post-Orientalist academia," and tended to emphasize discipline over area studies.[105] And many in this generation embraced activist anthropology and a social justice focus; some even thought that their generation was especially and uniquely politicized—an assumption that likely stems from factors including the relative lack of activism in the immediately preceding cohort, the internet's new facilitation of generational awareness, a lack of intergenerational communication, and the burnout and busyness that accumulate as careers advance.

Finally, anthropologists trained in the 2000s—a group that also nearly doubled in number after 9/11—expressed an almost universal sense of generational belonging in relationship to politics, mainly in response to 9/11 and the subsequent wars in Iraq and Afghanistan. Unlike earlier generations, many of these scholars experienced 9/11 as a foundation for their academic relationships to MENA. Others defined their cohort as the one "during which the world went to hell." Expanding capitalism also factored into this group's generational identification; one explained their generation as having "endured the very severe consequences of the discrepancy between the promises of neoliberal politics and the limitations of what that meant for social mobility, integration, employment, and so on." There was less agreement on the importance of theory to generational identity; the most common themes included interdisciplinarity and being "post the posts." Two people summed this up with variations on the question, "What's after Foucault? What's after that guy when these kinds of interventions have become a staple?" And once again public and/or activist anthropology, especially in its relationship to technology, was important to many in this group. Overall, different generations of scholars hold varying understandings of anthropology's proper role in public debates and political activism. The similarities and differences between cohorts create both alliances and tensions within the subfield (often along demographic lines) that then mirror similar ones in the broader fields of anthropology and Middle Eastern Studies, and indeed in the academy at large.

The Political Academic Landscape

Each of this book's chapters examines an aspect of this political academic landscape as different cohorts of scholars experience its transformations and resulting frictions. Our analysis is based on ethnographic interviews with over one hundred anthropologists, participant-observation in the field for over twenty years, and archival and media research (for more, see Appendix A). Chapter 1 addresses how individuals become scholars. Through analysis of life histories, we track patterns in how people chose anthropology and the Middle East as fields of study and discuss the gendered, racialized, classed, and generational aspects of these patterns, especially as these result from scholars' efforts to navigate tensions emerging from national and global politics. Chapter 2's focus is academic professionalization and socialization. Using interview and other data related to graduate school and job market experiences, we show how anthropologists of MENA learn to navigate gendered and racialized disciplinary and academic frameworks for legitimizing (or delegitimizing) scholarly work. Such frameworks are fraught with pressures that lead to the development of strategies of self-preservation, including self-monitoring and self-censorship, that persist across generations. The fact that for decades MENA anthropologists have censored themselves to preserve their ability to do academic work is especially apparent in Chapter 3, which focuses on how scholars engage different publics, including students and lecture audiences, as well as publishers, in both academic and nonacademic venues. Again we find that MENA anthropologists face racialized and gendered challenges and attacks influenced by national and global politics, and that college and university administrators cannot be counted on to support them. Scholars thus find themselves carefully enacting the self-protection practices into which they were socialized as graduate students. When colleges and universities let external pressures affect the learning process, many faculty become reluctant to share their expertise on the region. Yet they also find ways to push against this silencing. US involvement in the region has created an opportunity and imperative to share academic knowledge, juxtaposed with the recognition that doing so may come at serious cost to one's professional life.

Chapters 4 and 5 look at how anthropologists created institutional scholarly communities as part of the process of embracing the poison chalice and navigating academic tensions more broadly. These institutions were essential to create networks for advancing scholarship, gain colleagues who shared one's commitment to the peoples of the region, claim expertise as MENA became critical for US foreign policy, and, more generally, build a collective voice on matters of larger import. Institution building also served as a powerful means to educate MENA colleagues in other disciplines about the value of anthropology, and, perhaps more important, to educate anthropologists about MENA—something that MENA anthropologists still feel is critical given the intransigent biases and ignorance that some non-MENA anthropologists have about the region. This has been a heavily gendered process, and one where bureaucratic proceduralism has often stifled quick action and noncentrist voices. And as we come to the twenty-first century, MENA anthropologists' academic institutional commitments face new challenges—from the discipline's expanding relationships with the US state, including in the government, intelligence, and military realms. We find that in large measure MENA anthropologists have been excluded from the discipline's discussions about anthropology's engagements with various military conflicts in the region—from Israel-Palestine to the Iraq War, from whether or not to condemn state violence against civilians to whether or not to participate in clandestine and/or military research.

We conclude by reflecting on the fate of these academic politics through the lens of the current movement to boycott Israeli academic institutions complicit in the oppression of Palestinians. This campaign will not be easily silenced. Indeed, if the group of academics that views itself as very progressive, but that has had a conservative impulse at its core on a range of matters, thinks that the boycott is something to be discussed, the politics of US academia may well be shifting in the most substantial way since the end of World War II. It remains to be seen how this will affect scholars' abilities to produce vital and innovative scholarship, teach critical thinking skills, and address other pressing political issues within and beyond academia.

1 Becoming a Scholar

Budding scholars do not just pick their discipline and regional focus out of a hat. Nor do they end up studying what they study solely as the result of personal choice, as dominant US ideologies of individualism might suggest. Rather, national and global politics interweave with specific life trajectories and academic trends to shape the process of becoming a certain kind of scholar, across the humanities and social sciences. US global dominance since World War II, shifting demographics in US society, and social movements alongside changing academic and theoretical responses to these conditions—influenced decisions to choose anthropology as a disciplinary home. Growing US engagement with MENA led more scholars to focus on the region. Such forces, and the tensions they produced in life trajectories, were a common thread through a range of experiences, any of which could be a primary force shaping a person into an anthropologist and a MENA scholar: from living through the Vietnam era to witnessing racist backlash during the 1990 Gulf War; from participating in the 1960s feminist movement to protesting apartheid in the 1980s; from growing up bicultural or in a diverse immigrant community to partaking in Orientalist popular culture; from hearing Zionist discourse at the family dinner table to traveling to the region for work, religious, or personal reasons; and from experiencing 9/11 during one's college years to living in a country saturated with the effects of the War on Terror's intensified military interventions.

When experienced during formative periods in nascent scholars' lives, these events not only shaped subsequent career foci, but also contributed to feelings of generational belonging, often sparking shifts in approaches to anthropology as well as to academic, national, and global politics. Race and gender intersect with this generational variation, as political forces affected region-related and white scholars differently. A majority of white scholars were initially drawn to discipline and region through dominant US Orientalist frameworks of demonization and/or co-optation, often via fantasy or ideas about anthropology as the exoticized study of the other. In contrast, most region-related scholars were attracted to anthropology and MENA as a result of immigration experiences that included intensified othering and surveillance of their communities across the decades. They tended to view anthropology as the discipline most suited to simultaneously understanding their cultural background and critiquing dominant US narratives about the region and its peoples. As white scholars were trained in critical approaches to imperialism within anthropology, they came to hold similar views of the discipline's potential to unpack both their own and dominant US ideas about MENA.

The idea that anthropology is conducive to political engagement, even activism, has also pulled people into the discipline differently across generations. At first, female as well as region-related scholars saw anthropology as useful for analyzing and fighting structures of inequality. This perspective grows increasingly common among all scholars who enter the field after the end of the Cold War, a shift that parallels theoretical shifts (from Marxism to poststructuralism) that deconstructed homogeneous, bounded notions of the culture concept and focused more concertedly on formations of power. Over time, Palestine becomes the main lens through which this overt political pull into discipline and region is expressed (or refused) in anthropologists' narratives—no matter where in the Middle East or North Africa a scholar works.[1] Certainly, deepening US state involvement in MENA, together with escalating neoconservative approaches and the rampant stereotyping and warmongering of right-wing media, pushed people not only to want to use anthropology's critical tools to understand the region better, but also increasingly toward a more politicized anthropology. These conditions also contributed to the creation of a set of funding and institutional structures, as well as social networks, that enabled people to become anthropologists of MENA and sometimes motivated the social production of such scholars.

The Role of Funding, Institutions, and Networks

It would be impossible to pursue a burgeoning interest in anthropology or MENA Studies without funding for language training and fieldwork, departments with faculty interested in mentoring promising undergraduate and graduate students, broader academic networks, and institutions with which to affiliate in the field. Across generations, these factors molded the ways that all our colleagues committed to their scholarly interests, especially as these support structures increased in tandem with both US interventions in the region and MENA anthropology itself.

Language training was usually necessary for field research, and the availability of funds for this training frequently drew people into specific regional foci within anthropology. Prior to the 1970s, language study was often funded by National Defense Foreign Language (NDFL) Fellowships, which later became the Foreign Language and Area Studies (FLAS) Program grants. The Middlebury Summer Immersion Program in Arabic and the Center for Arabic Study Abroad (CASA) at the American University in Cairo have emerged as two of the most popular programs since that time.[2] CASA was founded in 1967, the year of the second Arab-Israeli war and the height of the Cold War, in which Egypt was a strategic site. The program has been funded by the US Department of Education, Fulbright (run through the US Department of State), and the Ford and Mellon Foundations. Students have also received FLAS funding to attend CASA as well as other programs in the region and summer language schools in the United States. The same is true for Middlebury; that Arabic program launched in another significant year: 1982, on the heels of the US-Iran hostage crisis and the Israeli invasion of Lebanon. In 2006, a few years into the War on Terror, the US Department of State's Critical Language Scholarship, funded by its Bureau of Educational and Cultural Affairs, began funding participation in Arabic immersion programs in Egypt, Tunisia, Morocco, Jordan, and Oman. Residential language immersion programs like Middlebury and CASA have done more than teach anthropologists language. They have nurtured their interest in the region by linking them with other graduate students and future MENA specialists, creating interdisciplinary academic cohorts. For one of our interlocutors, Middlebury triggered interest in the region because "it was always a human and personal and contemporary thing that brought [other students] to the study of Arabic."

The greater availability of US government and private foundation funds for language learning as well as area studies research more broadly—beginning with the 1958 National Defense Education Act and continuing with Fulbright, the Wenner-Gren Foundation, and Social Science Research Council, among others—has strengthened some scholars' interest in particular regions, if not motivated them. One senior colleague discussed benefiting from the big boons in funding right after the 1973–1974 oil embargo and then again in 1979 because of the Islamic revolution in Iran and the war in Afghanistan:

> There was no real reason necessarily within the discipline to pick that area of study and, to tell you the truth, I think it was largely the fact that the U.S. government at this time . . . poured in a lot of money into the study of the Middle East. . . . So I think that politics had a lot to do with it. Cold War politics, but also the politics of the region of the Middle East to encourage the formation of this field and to put real money into it. . . . And I was the beneficiary of one of these National Defense Language Fellowships . . . and I took Arabic, which I learned to love. . . . But there was no a priori reason to think this would be the language I would choose.

Likewise, someone who entered the field more recently said she was drawn to the region because of the immense funding (much of it nongovernment related) that was available after 9/11.

Other institutional structures were also important. In the 1960s, 1970s, and 1980s, when MENA was frequently associated with archaeology (a subfield of anthropology that already had an institutional apparatus there) some new scholars became interested in the region's contemporary cultures through initial work on excavations. Jon Anderson has noted how anthropologists also used the resources of archaeological institutions to conduct their studies.[3] Similarly, participation in the editorial collective of the Middle East Research and Information Project (MERIP) fostered interdisciplinary connections to the region and its scholars, especially for people trained in the 1970s and 1980s before there existed a critical mass of MENA anthropologists.

As with any academic specialization, the subfield of MENA cultural anthropology grew when established scholars began recruiting new ones. More people teaching MENA cultural anthropology meant more students delving into it, a reflection of both intergenerational inspiration and the greater availability of MENA-related undergraduate courses. These additions to college curricula across the country jumped considerably once again after 9/11. The narratives of people trained in the 1990s and especially the 2000s contain mentions of particularly memorable readings, professors, and classes (e.g., the professor who walked into lecture, held up a tampon, and asked why it was taboo. Our interlocutor said, "That was it. She had me at hello.") Mentors supported undergraduate study abroad in the region, which grew ever more popular in the 1990s and after and was another key means by which some people cemented their interest in MENA and anthropology.[4] Increased integration into disciplinary networks in particular highlighted for new scholars the attraction of anthropologists' forms of sociability. A senior female scholar recalled someone asking her, as she tried to decide on a field, "Who do you want to talk to for the rest of your life? Anthropologists or nurses?" And in a delightfully funny example (that might not be that unusual), another told us: "I was studying chemistry . . . and the year I was to graduate, I was hanging out with a bunch of anthropologists because they had better chemicals than the chemistry group!"

Nonacademic institutions and networks sometimes cultivated developing scholars' interests in discipline and region as well and were often themselves part and parcel of dominant US encounters with MENA. Before graduate school, some anthropologists joined the Peace Corps, while others worked in the region through development NGOs, high schools, or oil companies. In some cases, intimate partners or friends related to either the region or discipline piqued nascent scholars' interest. A few white anthropologists had traveled to MENA as part of their (or their family's) participation in religious organizations, or their parents had hosted church friends who had spent time in the region and regaled them with stories about it. Not only did these early experiences with institutionalized religion spark interests in MENA, but they could also lead a person to anthropology (which served, as one person put it, as "an intellectualized response to a set of personal conflicts" involving religion).

Making Sense of Discomfort: Finding Anthropology

A vast majority of our interlocutors expressed something akin to this "set of personal conflicts" as an impetus to joining the discipline. A circulating folk theory holds that people who end up as anthropologists grew up feeling like outsiders in their own society, which makes them curious about otherness in general.[5] Addressing this idea, Steven Caton writes,

> Like the bohemian artist, the anthropologist has been constructed in various
> discourses as an individual who as a child felt alienated or even excluded from
> . . . certain norms or conventions. If they have any genuinely artistic talents,
> these individuals might become artists; or if inclined to scholarly pursuits,
> historians, and when combined perhaps with a yearning for adventure, an-
> thropologists. . . . Anthropology, or so it is maintained, is one of the vocations
> an alienated individual in society might imagine himself or herself pursuing
> because its practice—known as fieldwork—has, however temporarily, taken
> the person out of his or her own milieu.[6]

This folk theory, like all folk theories, reflects many anthropologists' lived experiences. Senses of personal conflict, alienation, and liminality often stemmed from feeling at odds with the modes of othering or co-optation that dominated US encounters with the Middle East, and/or dissonance with the prevailing social or political forces in one's environment writ large.

Our interviews began with an open-ended question about why and how scholars came to the field of anthropology. For some, anthropology was not a conscious choice. It instead felt like a random confluence of events or circumstances. Nonetheless, most people constructed their responses in relation to their life histories, beginning with stories of discomfort with dominant social contexts in early life.[7] In the manner of Edward Said's intellectual exile, they described themselves as "individuals at odds with their society" whose marginality contributed to their desire and ability to see the familiar as unfamiliar and grapple with questions of difference.[8] This sense of not (quite) belonging, as they narrated it, was experienced in ways notably marked by race, ethnicity, religion, social class, and the location and/or movement of one's family home.

Many scholars were drawn to anthropology because they felt othered as young people—whether they lived in contexts of significant diversity or they felt out of place in relatively homogeneous places. They viewed the discipline as a way to make sense of diversity and difference and their consequences in the world. One senior anthropologist told us:

> I was an anthropologist long before I knew there was such a thing, before I could spell it. . . . I grew up in an Orthodox Jewish family in a Catholic neighborhood with a father whose small business employed guys in the shop who were Black, Hispanic, and Appalachian, so I grew up with their otherness as well as my own. When a teacher would ask me to write an essay in grammar school about a religious holiday, I always wrote about somebody else's. At [my undergraduate school] then, I majored in anthropology.

A midcareer scholar reflected that a sense of uncomfortable disjuncture, related to growing up middle class in a small town with farming and working class families, led them to anthropology's focus on difference and inequality. Another who grew up in a mixed-ethnicity family in the Middle East described similar feelings leading them to the field.

The sense of feeling betwixt and between is, not surprisingly, most pronounced for anthropologists whose families immigrated to the United States. Many people, of a variety of backgrounds and across generations, detailed experiences of never quite feeling at home due to the movement of their family.

In addition to immigration, this movement could be related to international or domestic travel for work. Several spoke about moving frequently while growing up, sometimes due to a parent who worked for the military or a church, and how this involved, in the words of one, having to constantly "learn the local scene." This created both an interest in new environments and embryonic ethnographic skills for understanding them. Immigrants tended to express a more pronounced discomfort with movement as an unsettling process, but also commented on the kinds of ethnographic aptitude it eventually provided. A mid-career scholar displaced by regional wars said that frequent displacement "had a lot to do" with the decision to become an anthropologist and that "it gave me skills that were useful for an anthropologist, [such as] shifting registers."

Caton has written eloquently about his immigration to the United States from Germany at age nine as a "formative experience" that in part brought him to anthropology. He, like other anthropologists who immigrated, described the "adjustments, linguistic and cultural" as "difficult, at times traumatic."[9] Like so many others who describe their discovery of the discipline as a moment when things "clicked" or "made nothing but sense" in relationship to early life experiences, Caton writes: "In [cultural anthropology] courses it seemed that I had found a professionalization (through fieldwork) of the predicaments of cultural liminality and travel that had been part of my childhood. Their subject matter seemed painfully self-evident to me: there were norms of behavior and symbols and fairly stable patternings of both that differed from place to place. Hadn't I hit my head against that wall before? Now in my academic major I had a name for it: cultural relativism."[10]

When immigration situated a scholar as a racialized ethnic or religious minority in the United States, the experience of liminality was compounded. For many region-related anthropologists, family movement produced a struggle to understand both their difference within US society and the non-US parts of their backgrounds, and they recognized the discipline as a good way to do that. A senior anthropologist who immigrated to the United States as a child described the culture concept as particularly useful to that process: "The concept of culture opened up all kinds of doors and windows to my own engagement with the experience of being bicultural. Having come here as a child but being treated by my family as though I was still in [the Middle East], and never really fully navigating that entry into American society . . . I'd always felt . . . marginal to American culture, but I didn't have that word [culture]. I didn't have that way of understanding it." Another slightly younger scholar explained that returning to the United States after spending most of their childhood in the region made them feel "different, marginalized." They described always being "slightly an outsider" and, in the same sentence, being "in love with understanding the ways people behaved with each other." And another trained in the 2000s remarked that anthropology is a "refuge" for minorities growing up in the United States because it helps people to find "a space [for] questions that is very open to this drawing from very different traditions and backgrounds, and being very kind and thoughtful about what our relationship as a nation or as citizens is to both individuals within our own country who are different from us and also across the sea."

Overall, people in younger generations described this feeling of being "slightly an outsider" in far more explicitly politicized terms. For some region-related scholars trained in the 1990s and after, the theme of discrimination and racism in the United States was central in their narratives about why they were drawn to anthropology. There are several possible reasons why those trained prior to the 1990s did not mention these themes as readily or frequently. Their formative youth lies further in the past, and any such experiences from that life stage may be less fresh in their memories or seem less important with the passage of time. Such experiences may also have been taken for granted or less politicized for people who grew up prior to the identity politics debates of the 1980s.[11] It is also, of course, possible that older anthropologists were less likely to experience—in their formative youth years—the kinds and volume of explicit anti–Middle Eastern prejudice that accelerated after the Islamic revolution in Iran and the specific anti-Arab racism that grew exponentially after both the end of the Cold War and September 11, 2001.

In addition, our older Arab American interlocutors grew up during a period of US history when Arabs were considered and often categorized themselves white, which may also shape their interpretations of experiences of discrimination. Younger Arab American anthropologists are more likely to think of themselves as nonwhite, reflecting the increased racialization of Arabs and Muslims in the United States.[12] They described experiences of racism—and labeled them as such—far more frequently and explicitly in our interviews. Two, for example, discussed painful experiences in high school during the 1990–1991 Gulf War. One remembered being called "sand n*****" for the first time in their life. They said that at the time they were realizing that "there's a gap between what I think my identity is, and how I'm situated, how I'm placed by bigger society" and that "anthropology is the most useful tool, intellectually, to try to deal with that kind of experience." Another recalled that the entire war was televised in common areas of their high school, and that "99 percent of the school was standing in front of the television cheering the US. At the time I thought I was the only Arab student. All these white people literally cheering every time a bomb hit. And then me, watching that."

Our interlocutors narrated all these youth experiences of dislocation as vital to their attraction to anthropology, reflecting a disciplinary self-representation that is likely not limited to scholars working in MENA. They may have been socialized within the discipline to narrate their development within it in this manner (because marginality holds a certain currency in the field) or have come to recognize their own marginality in the process of becoming anthropologists. Or anthropology may indeed lure people for whom such experiences are central to their scholarly formation. It is notable that neither marginalized experiences of gender nor sexuality were mentioned as draws to the field in our interviews and that social class and religion were not discussed nearly as much as (im)migration, race, and national heritage.[13] Class—along with the region of the United States where one was raised—appeared in a few interviews with lower-middle class and working class white anthropologists as something that contributed to their feeling isolated from knowledge of MENA and less cosmopolitan than others, though they did not necessarily articulate this as either marginalization or a motivation towards anthropology. Indeed, the folk theory of marginality, while bolstered by our data, does not fully capture the myriad reasons why people choose anthropology as a lifelong commitment.

Finding Ethics through Disciplinary Focus

Our conversations revealed another equally if not more important way that local, national, and global politics led people to the discipline. Many of our interlocutors expressed being attracted to anthropology because they thought it provided an ethical way of engaging and understanding the world because it foregrounded on-the-ground experience—experience whose complexity inherently challenged the dominant narratives and structures of power around them.

Scholars of different generations and backgrounds also said that anthropology was flexible enough to allow them to study anything and everything they wanted and to study it in a way that encouraged this critical questioning of societal norms. As a senior anthropologist explained, anthropology appealed to him as an undergraduate "because it looked like I could do everything I ever wanted to do by doing an anthropology major." A female scholar trained four decades later noted, "I ended up deciding that anthropology would be a good major for me, precisely because I had such a hard time figuring out what I—well, I was interested in too much actually and anthropology kind of gave me that flexibility to . . . explore a lot of things at once." Given our interlocutors' general aversion to structures of power and discomfort with social pressures to conform, it is not surprising that they found a discipline whose own structures of power could be interpreted as open to criticism—especially after postmodernist and poststructuralist critiques of disciplinary formation and representations emerged in the late 1980s.[14] An anthropologist trained in the early 2000s put it succinctly when they said, "I decided to be an anthropology major rather than a lawyer, which my parents would have preferred me to be. [The] style of reasoning seemed more diverse and lateral than the kind of one-directional side of legal reasoning." This discourse of freedom through flexibility reflects a desire to hold open the possibility of researching *any* topic that might emerge as important as experiences accrue during one's career. Anthropologists appreciate that their discipline allows for the study of anything—be it politics, art, engineering, biology, literature, and so forth—as social processes and objects, and believe that other disciplines do not afford that opportunity to the same extent. Some people understood this as the inherent "interdisciplinarity" of the discipline. As an anthropologist trained in the 1990s said, "with anthro you can study anything . . . it's much more about the way you study than the subject you study."

The "way you study" in anthropology resonated with both the sense that this was an ethical discipline and early feelings of insider-outsiderness. Anthropologists who grew up with the aforementioned feelings of marginality or disjuncture had to pay close attention to social interactions in order to make sense of the world and found the discipline's methods appealing. Participant-observation made especial sense to them because it is a methodology of the in-between. One is simultaneously an observer of the strange (or of that which is purposefully rendered unfamiliar) and a participant struggling to listen to people and apprehend their experience on their own terms—activities many of our colleagues were already doing before they knew to name it "participant-observation."

Several people spoke of the sheer pleasure of the method of fieldwork, of being able to talk with what one anthropologist called "real human beings" from a range of different communities and hear from them in their own words. A scholar trained in the 1980s told us, "Anthropology was just the right thing for me. I have to admit, I just love human stories. I don't know what to say. I love listening to people's stories. . . . I really feel at some level that I love the ethnographic enterprise. I love doing ethnographic fieldwork." Another, from a later generation, said of their initial introduction to anthropology in college, "I was just fascinated by the engagement with the rich detail of people's lives."

The fieldwork requirement for a PhD in anthropology was an explicit draw for many, with one person going so far as to say that it "sold it" for them: "I always wanted the in-the-field-ness, the being-there-ness." Some had discovered how much they liked interacting with people through earlier work with NGOs or other applied or development work.

The pleasure of fieldwork, and perception of it as somehow more "real" than other research methods, was linked to a positive view of microanalysis as compared to macroanalysis. In other words, many anthropologists enjoyed fieldwork because they valued inductive, ground-up approaches to both generating and answering questions. Beyond viewing the micro level as advantageous for scholarship, many people saw attention to it as enacting a particular ethics: an ethics of listening to people on their own terms and/or an ethics of destabilizing dominant, Euro-American ways of being in and understanding the world. These were often intertwined and, for some scholars, associated with particular aspects of their identities. Most of our female interlocutors of all generations connected ethnography directly to feminist praxis. Additionally, region-related anthropologists trained from the mid-1990s through the 2000s were more likely to emphasize an ethical project of provincializing Euro-American power and perspectives as an advantage of anthropological methods.

Scholars also frequently coupled the ethics of listening and critique with particular geopolitical and theoretical moments. An anthropologist trained in the late 1960s to early 1970s explained this ethical stance: "I just always saw things from other people's perspective and their experiences. . . . And I remember my mother saying, why are you so critical always of everything in the US?" For this scholar and some others of her generation, the countercultural, antiwar environment of the 1960s magnified the appeal of a discipline that attempted to understand how dominant cultural patterns form. A few decades later—after the Cold War played out in Vietnam, Afghanistan, and across Latin America, and the Middle East replaced the USSR as the United States' primary enemy—new scholars continued to be attracted to anthropology for its ethics of listening to people and contesting Euro-American hegemony and particularly US imperial ambitions. This sense remained important through the first decade of the twenty-first century, as an anthropologist trained in the 2000s noted: "There's something about anthropology that felt like, at its best . . . [it] allowed one to sort of stretch one's thinking beyond you know, Euro-American canons of political thought."

In this new century, some (especially region-related and lower or working class scholars) were also drawn to anthropology because they saw it as a way to ethically make sense of 9/11 and its aftermath. One clarified the discipline's pull in this way: "I think 9/11 maybe heightened feelings of me as a minority in the United States, and as a Muslim. And so it was very, very important to my thinking about anthropology and working with it as a discipline and figuring out my place as a minority and how was anthropology really useful to me in terms of allowing me to be a minority and to accept that and to think through it by looking at other cultures that are even more minorities in relationship to American culture." A region-related anthropologist also trained in the 2000s explained how 9/11 shaped their decision to go to graduate school for anthropology as their discipline of choice in order to counter polarized binary discourses like that of the clash of civilizations:

> 9/11 was shocking, it was tragic, it was heartbreaking. I was a senior in high school and, like everybody else, I saw images of people jumping out of the windows, and it was absolutely horrific. And then [pause] it becomes apparent that most of the hijackers are Arab . . . and then you suddenly have the War on Terror . . . and so the relationship between the United States and between the Middle East . . . becomes of very strategic importance, and everyone begins to discuss it and analyze it. . . . And I felt a real investment in having a stake in these discussions, but also in making sure that we do not fall into the trap of playing into Bin Laden's rhetoric of the jihad against the "evil, American empire" and Bush's rhetoric of "You're with us or you're against us," and Samuel Huntington's discourse of the clash of civilizations, etc.

And a white anthropologist from a working class background of this same generation described their trajectory to the discipline as a way of making sense of a confusing and "convoluted" international political scene at the time. They switched from international relations to anthropology to understand 9/11 because the latter's approach was to "ask questions about why things were happening . . . what's going on, what are people's perspectives on this" as opposed to "the why do they hate us question."

Discipline switching (and sometimes even career changes) due to ideas about anthropology's perceived ethics was not unusual. One scholar left comparative literature for anthropology in the 2000s because of their "belief in empirical knowledge and my sense of ethics that imbues this method and that kind of wish to multiply the conversation, and to parochialize what is a very confident kind of Western narrative about how things work." Another began a graduate program studying international relations but then discovered that "anthropology had a lot more depth and a lot more to offer than international affairs. I was *really* frustrated with surface level, macro, let's study the whole world . . . from an American hegemonic perspective." Two others switched from development work to anthropology for, as one put it, the latter's "methodology" and "an ethical approach to the way I see the world." A third opined that the discipline has "the best set of tools . . . for understanding the world in a meaningful way" and actually "engage with the world," because it asks "you to leave your comfort zone and . . . think about the world and see things from different perspectives." And another switched to anthropology after completing an MA in political science because she "realized that comparative politics is a very Eurocentric field and . . . I wouldn't be able to ask the questions I was interested in asking."

When we asked one of these anthropologists to expand on this idea of "ethics," they explained that it was in part about the way that anthropology "connects to the struggles we all have" and lays bare the complexities of people's lives through engagement with interlocutors. For this person, traveling abroad was the moment at which they "realized that much of the information that we (or at least I) were getting was through the press and was like cake frosting—yet there was a whole cake underneath it. You didn't know what flavor. . . . I suppose getting to know contexts, individuals and countries in more depth made me realize the contingencies and complicated mess that gets glossed over."

Our interlocutors' articulations of an ethics of anthropological method, engagement, and critique are not unique to scholars working in MENA. One can trace the idea of fieldwork as ethical to a sensibility that continues to infuse anthropological training and the discipline's identity. The idea that anthropology provides critical perspectives on dominant discourses within the United States hearkens back to Boasian critiques of racialism.[15] Also reflecting US anthropological history, a handful of our colleagues mentioned exposure in youth or college to Native American cultural practices (often initially in exoticized ways) as a factor that led them to anthropology. For them, anthropology initially represented or defined itself as the discipline interested in Native Americans.[16] That interest was then extended, often through undergraduate courses, into a desire to understand difference and critique colonial histories and relationships more generally.[17]

Increasing numbers of anthropologists understand this ethics as deeply political and shaped by the feminist and antiracist perspectives that resulted from the greater inclusion of women and minorities in the academy and the theoretical challenges they brought to the canon. Many new anthropologists felt that this ethics was especially necessary in approaches to MENA, as the region and its people were progressively targeted by the US and stereotyped in US discourses. In order to understand how ethics and politics are interwoven over time for MENA anthropologists, we need to explore how they were drawn to the region as a research site in the first place.

Finding Regional Focus through Self/Other

Scholars' race and national heritage were the most significant factors in this process. With few exceptions, white American anthropologists and nonwhite scholars without Middle Eastern heritage were originally drawn to the region by a fascination with its otherness—sometimes shaped by Orientalism—and/ or through what they thought of as a series of "accidents" or "random" events and experiences. Building on the discourse of attraction to anthropology as a way to grapple with discomfort, travel to MENA sometimes facilitated the discovery of an "other" place: a place where a white person either was "allowed" to be uncomfortable when confronted with difference or was in fact comfortable because they were expected to be different (unlike their experiences in the US). Conversely, region-related anthropologists mostly reported wanting to study MENA as a way to understand their origins or aspects of their families or as a way to make sense of difference at home. As Lila Abu-Lughod has noted of "halfie" anthropologists, "their agony is not how to communicate across a divide but how to theorize the experience that moving back and forth between the many worlds they inhabit is a movement within one complex and historically and politically determined world."[18] This striking variance between scholars is likely applicable to the discipline as a whole in its engagement with other world regions. It also raises the question of the degree to which this is a feature of anthropology in the United States in particular.[19] Certainly, this pattern stems from the specifics of US engagement with the so-called Orient as an object of empire at various times in post–World War II history[20] and the ways this history intersects with US racial politics and constructions of whiteness, as well as histories of white privilege related to travel and tourism.[21]

However, there are four important twists to this variation that may shed light on MENA anthropology in particular. First, none of the (very few) region-related anthropologists trained prior to the 1970s originally intended to work in MENA. That shifted radically in the 1970s, although at times such anthropologists recalled concerns about whether or not working specifically in their country of origin might compromise their scholarly legitimacy. We suggest that this change resulted from the diversification of the academy and massive transformations in social theory following the civil rights, second-wave feminist, and gay liberation movements, as well as the subsequent identity politics movements of the late 1980s. Second, region-related scholars were not necessarily immune to Orientalist fascination with the region or to desires to seek out the "other," particularly in relation to rural and/or desert areas. Third, this general pattern of fascination with the other persists among some anthropologists trained in the 2000s, but it is not as prominently articulated. This may be because these scholars are so fully embedded in the post-Orientalist, feminist, and antiracist paradigms that became the norm in anthropology (and some other disciplines) in the wake of the late 1980s culture wars that to admit to an Orientalist fascination with MENA, even in youth, would be too compromising, especially to tenured scholars such as ourselves.[22] Yet this phenomenon could just as easily be related to the fact that increased global technological circuits connect this generation to the region in multiple ways, or by the fact that international travel has become increasingly easy for the US middle class. Both these changes have the potential to disrupt stereotypes. And finally, in a fourth twist, people's attraction to conducting research in MENA—whether it arose from a desire to understand the other or one's own background—sometimes started as deeply politicized or quickly became so.

It is notable that white anthropologists often framed their arrival to the region as a series of coincidences. While there is a grain of truth to this interpretation, closer examination of their narratives reveals patterns of early fascinations with travel and discovery and the enticement of mass media representations of MENA as an exotic place. Our analysis also shows that social networks created many of the so-called random accidents that led to their study of the region. This misrecognition of patterns as accidents may be how the unmarked dominant in the field (whiteness) is expressed—for to mark (and claim) the dominant as exoticizing, Orientalist, or having what are often privileged connections would be to delegitimize one's standing as an anthropologist ill at ease with norms and conventions.[23] It would be to recognize a form of race and class privilege with which anthropologists are uncomfortable, for in many of these cases the connection to MENA was forged through college (which often, it bears reminding, is a privileged space), the Peace Corps, development organizations, or family and friends who had the resources to travel or work outside the United States.

In fact, one could argue that it is the privilege of living as the unmarked category in the center of empire that enabled an attraction to MENA for white anthropologists, for empire shaped a geography of non-Western sites of imagination. White scholars mentioned the allure of seeing *Lawrence of Arabia*, reading Paul Bowles, reading *The Source*,[24] viewing family tourist photos, and

encountering Middle East archaeology, whether via a fascination with the biblical or with ancient Egypt.[25] A significant number were entranced by travel tales
told by missionaries or other members of their churches, tales that inspired
their explorations of anthropology and/or MENA. Several interlocutors ranging from working class to middle-class backgrounds were enchanted via jaunts
to Morocco during study abroad or postcollege travel stints to Europe—rites of
passage for relatively privileged youth in the United States. Morocco entranced
another person on a trip there during his military service. Some people from
towns, rural areas, or smaller cities spoke of MENA holding a special fascination
for them because of their own geographic background. For these scholars, the
region served as a way to both experience difference and become cosmopolitan.
As an anthropologist who grew up in a rural area explained, "We didn't even
have TVs. . . . I mean we had two radio stations in town. I knew nothing about
anything." Another, who is from a small Midwestern city told us, "I'd never been
outside the United States before. . . . Modern society in [a major Middle Eastern
city] just seemed so much more interesting and totally incomprehensible."

And many were quick to admit the absence of real substance in these early
interests. Someone who applied to the Peace Corps after college said, "The recruiter said [North African country] and I thought to myself, okay, . . . North
Africa, former French colony, Arab country . . . I bet the food there is really
good! It was that superficial." Clearly this is not simply a story of white privilege and empire, for anthropologists' varied social class and geographic backgrounds within the United States also structured desires to travel to places
viewed as exotic. Nonetheless, a relatively unprivileged person in the United
States still has the world made available to them by US power in particular
ways. Whether or not white anthropologists originally thought their discomfort at home could be remedied by finding a new "home" in MENA remains
an open question precisely because, as Caton writes, "the naïve hope harbored
by many first-time fieldworkers that the group into which they have been 'adopted' can become another home" is so "unacknowledged."[26] At least one of our
colleagues—a working class anthropologist who felt alienated from other students in their graduate program due to class differences—"felt so much more
at home" during fieldwork in the region. And overall, the joy and excitement
white anthropologists expressed while narrating their first exposures to the region contrasted significantly with the apprehensive and discontented tones that
characterized many of their descriptions of the places where they grew up.

Attraction to the region as a potential home, or as a way of "coming home"
metaphorically, sometimes appeared more explicitly in the narratives of

region-related anthropologists. It is not that these anthropologists wanted to return home to some imagined origins, but that they had personal, intellectual, sometimes political puzzles that they felt they needed to solve by working in the region.[27] This project could simultaneously bring them, in the words of one, "closer and closer to my heart." It is important to keep in mind that such scholars were increasingly racialized and discriminated against in the United States. For region-related anthropologists who grew up primarily in the United States, choosing to work in MENA was often a way to make sense of these painful experiences, as well as of growing up bicultural more generally. In addition to dealing with racism, these scholars were motivated to focus on the region because of visits to family there while growing up and/or efforts to understand their own parents. As one person put it, reflecting on how an attempt to understand their Arab parents led them to anthropology: "My parents were weird. Is that because of their culture? In their culture, would they still be weird?"

Anthropologists with bicultural families often articulated especially complex relationships to the region. One noted that studying MENA was about "unfinished family business" to "resolve standing issues" coming from having one parent from the region and one from the United States. Another who grew up in a working class "multicultural" area with a large Arab American community and who was deeply aware of the discrimination experienced by their Arab American parent explained, "So I was on this weird borderland, like I sort of identified with it but somewhat didn't identify with it. My grandfather spoke to me in French—he didn't speak to me in Arabic—and in English, of course. So I had this weird set of questions like what does this all mean?" And the desire to study the region as a way to make sense of it as part of "home" was, for many region-related anthropologists, also a project of coming to ethnographically understand the political conflicts that had so affected their lives as bicultural youth.

Generational differences further complicate this trend in ways that correlate with shifts in anthropology's own identity politics and the growing presence of nonwhite scholars within the discipline and academia. Region-related anthropologists trained prior to the 1970s did not want to work in MENA, and one was even explicitly told not to, in order to be a "good anthropologist." This fit with the methodological emphasis at the time on what this person described as "maximizing detachment from the home culture for perspective." Yet every region-related scholar trained in the 1970s wanted to work there because it was what made sense both to them personally *and* to their graduate programs. This newly welcoming attitude toward "studying one's own" was likely related to the interventions prompted by feminist and anticolonial scholarly approaches that problematized notions of objectivity in research and highlighted the ways that subject position and research agendas could be (and for some feminists necessarily were) related. At the same time, anthropology's fascination with the exotic, still acceptable to articulate at that time, led a few anthropologists of this generation to try to understand "home" by constructing difference from it in a romanticized way. Often they turned to people or geographies that were unfamiliar from their childhood experiences. A senior anthropologist reflected on this quite explicitly: "My mother was working with UNESCO in [North African country], and her colleagues . . . would go into the desert in jeeps, you know, with goat skins for water. It just seemed like the most romantic thing in the world. This is what I wanted to do. They were my heroes." Another person also trained in the 1970s, a child of professionals, spoke of originally wanting to work with the traditionally nomadic Tuareg because they seemed so exotic.

By the late 1980s and early 1990s, region-related anthropologists who wanted to work in MENA began experiencing backlash or expressing ambivalence about their personal relationship to the region-as-fieldsite. Those trained during this period described having to confront the idea that working in MENA (and especially in one's country of origin) could mean being taken less seriously by other scholars. One person explained their decision to work on a different MENA country than where they grew up: "If you were a foreign student and you wrote your dissertation on your own . . . you ended up being identified as someone who . . . clearly can't talk about other things." Several of these scholars consciously refuted assumptions about some inherent similarity between researcher and interlocutors based on national or ethnic context. It is quite likely that their careful distancing from their interlocutors was related to entering the field at the height of identity politics and the culture wars; in other words, they experienced the academy during a period of significant transition and backlash against the interventions that feminist and critical race studies had instigated.

Scholars trained in the mid-1990s expressed far more comfort with choosing to work on one's home country and/or the region more broadly, even though racialized accusations of bias continued in some quarters. The greater presence of strong region-related faculty mentors contributed to this shift. It also stemmed from the acceptance, in anthropology, of those influential critiques of the gendered and racialized construction of "objectivity" that began in the 1970s. Indeed, by the mid-1990s, the idea that "studying one's own" could produce insights and "situated knowledge"[28] that were not possible under frameworks that claimed "objectivity" through distance was broadly accepted in anthropology as well as some other disciplines like gender studies and literary criticism.[29] Yet pushback persisted. One scholar remembered having "many grad school conversations about whether one can work legitimately in one's heritage country" and the "relief" of their doctoral committee when they decided to work on a community other than their own in their country of origin. Equally pernicious was the idea that region-related anthropologists could *only* work in the region. At least one such scholar was told that they had to work in MENA—partly because faculty thought they could produce knowledge about the region from a privileged position but also due to ideas about language skills.

Those who entered graduate school in the twenty-first century, no matter what their positionality, continued to have mixed feelings about whether or not being from the region was (or would be viewed as) an advantage or disadvantage. For region-related scholars, the new century ushered in another moment of heightened concern that if they chose to work in MENA they would not be taken as seriously as a white anthropologist. In a key example of how strong the backlash has been against these radical transformations in anthropology, knowledge production, and the academy more broadly, consider this quote from an anthropologist who received their degree near the end of the first decade of the 2000s: "I didn't want to study [my country of origin] because I would hate to have anybody look at me (a) as a native anthropologist and (b) I would never want somebody to look at me as if I had worked less. This would drive me crazy. So the only way I made it okay for myself was to decide to work on something that I had no knowledge about whatsoever." We also spoke with a region-related scholar who thought that some white anthropologists' work, while insightful, was hampered by significantly less time spent in the country. One white anthropologist said that they were afraid of being called an Orientalist, while another spoke about how being white gave them advantages in terms of making connections in the region. Others suggested that region-related researchers "had it easier"—making erroneous assumptions about linguistic capabilities or personal connections facilitating fieldwork. These disagreements over positionality and knowledge production are far from over, and they are often tangled with broader patterns of discrimination against Middle Easterners linked to US imperial interventions in the region.

Discipline and Region as Means to Political Engagement

Escalating US involvement in MENA has directly and explicitly led growing numbers of scholars to do anthropology of the region because of what they describe as political concerns and/or activism. Specific events and social movements have acted as "crystalizing agents" that contribute to generational formation.[30] This was especially the case for women and for region-related anthropologists across generations, as well as for most people trained after the Cold War. We suggest that this increase is largely due to the fact that it has become clearer to anthropologists that the United States is the main global hegemon and that its expanding economic and military activities in the Middle East, as well as its support of the Israeli state, are central causes of hardship for the communities in which they work. Many scholars with US citizenship expressed an added sense of responsibility to engage with and communicate about the region in a way that speaks back to US empire's effects at home and abroad.

Every female anthropologist we interviewed who was trained prior to the mid-1970s described coming to anthropology and MENA as part of a rising political consciousness associated with the civil rights movement, the anti-Vietnam war movement, the second-wave feminist movement, and/or decolonization movements. Several were drawn to Arab socialism; most described a concern for Palestinians' right to self-determination. And most were themselves activists, especially in student movements. During this era of social upheaval, these possibilities were fully intertwined. As one senior female scholar told us, "1968 still lives with those of us who are its children. It was globally informative and transformative. Out of 1968 there emerged urban anthropology, Marxist anthropology, feminist anthropology—the three key anchors that shaped my intellectual development."

Comparatively few male anthropologists of this generation described a strong history of activism and radical political consciousness that related to their disciplinary and regional interests. Indeed, a greater number of male anthropologists did not spend as much interview time, if any, articulating their politics in this period as part of their path to anthropology or MENA, although some noted that graduate school was a way to avoid the draft. In fact, these male scholars tended to delineate a separation between their academic work and the political atmosphere at the time. One told us, "I'm afraid I just wasn't very politicized. I mean I was interested in what was going on in general in the political world, but I just didn't see how that translated into stuff on campus, and I didn't feel obliged to. I was there and active in the broader anti-war movement, but integrating activities like this into our academic training concerns was problematic and difficult." Another related his disapproval of the American Anthropological Association's political stances against Vietnam.

We suggest that women drawn to academia in this era were more overtly politicized towards the left than their male colleagues partly because the academy was well over 90 percent male when they began graduate school, including in anthropology. The experiences of gendered marginalization that these female pathbreakers shared with us necessarily made their academic choices—including those related to discipline and region—part and parcel of a larger feminist political consciousness, and many highlighted the critical importance of both the feminist movement and feminist scholarship to their academic formations. These scholars were also more likely than most of their male peers to take public stances on MENA-related political issues throughout their careers. Men had greater choice about whether or not to be as explicitly political and about whether or not they should relate broader structural inequalities to their studies. From this early period, this sense of choice was overlaid by a discourse that attempted to construct anthropology as an objective science,[31] a discourse that continues until today and is gendered and racialized in accusations that female scholars and scholars of color who attend to their positionality in relationship to their research are not objective.[32]

Moving forward in time, doing anthropology and/or working in MENA became an unequivocal way for people of all genders to express, address, question, complicate, and sustain political commitments. Most scholars who obtained their degrees in the 1980s discussed their political activism as part of their academic life story. One person described it as being "a question of how I could realize what I believed then," while another said she was drawn to anthropology through her political activism in the United States because the discipline spoke to her as being "more interested in social movements, feminist movements, political movements." Other anthropologists described early adulthood experiences with politics in the region (ranging from meeting Algerian revolutionaries to encountering Marxist student movements while studying abroad to experiencing the Islamic Revolution in Iran), and several noted the centrality of meeting Palestinian national liberation activists or their own Palestine activism to their decisions to focus on MENA anthropology. A colleague described studying in the region this way: "Decolonization was still in the air. And [university in the region] had students from all over Africa, from Afghanistan, Pakistan, the Arab world, the U.S. It was just a very exciting place to be." This experience combined with feminism to shape her topical focus and solidify her desire to work in a majority-Arab society. The few anthropologists trained in this interstice between the Vietnam era and the end of the Cold War who deliberately disavowed a relationship between their scholarly desires and political perspectives were primarily white and tended to reiterate the separation between scholarship as objective and leftist politics as subjective that we heard from white male scholars trained in earlier decades.

Most anthropologists who came of academic age around the end of the Cold War drew an explicit connection between their political positions and their disciplinary and regional choices. This is hardly surprising, because this generation's consciousness was formed at the moment not only when the Middle East became the United States' primary enemy, but also when US neoliberalism was cementing its creation of drastic classed and racialized inequalities. A white working class anthropologist who grew up during the Reagan era reflected: "And I remember my mom, telling me . . . gosh, if I could do anything, I'd be an anthropologist. You know she had sort of discovered Margaret Mead when she was a young woman in some crappy place in Indiana, and it just sort of . . . held up this possibility that you could get out of this American nightmare. So I'd always had that in the back of my head."

Over 60 percent of anthropologists trained in the 1990s cited personal political commitment as a key aspect of their decisions to enter anthropology and/or focus on MENA, including all scholars with family ties to MENA and half without. This political engagement was not necessarily MENA-related, at least initially; for several people, coming of age during the era of global activism against apartheid in South Africa was important for their own politicization.[33] No matter what initiated political awareness, a political impetus to study MENA formed during many individuals' undergraduate years—whether through coursework, study abroad, or campus activism around key events such as the first intifada. As one anthropologist said, "[my topic] was unfolding before my eyes," and another, "Palestine was an easy choice [of fieldsite]." Frustration with increasingly negative media images of Middle Easterners in the 1980s and 1990s, including stereotypes about Muslim women,[34] also played a role, with one region-related interlocutor stating that her personal mission was to show that "there's much more in the Middle East than images of Islamist militants."

For half of the non-region-related scholars trained in the 1990s, the decision to work in MENA began with what was variously termed an academic, random, aesthetic, or romanticized interest that later became definitively politicized. Colleagues described coming to political consciousness during initial trips to the region, in conversations with friends and family in the United States, through activism for Palestinians and against US and Israeli wars in the region (frequently as undergraduates), and through the theoretical emphasis of graduate work. Especially crucial to their theoretical foci were engagements with South Asian and Middle Eastern Studies historians, political scientists, and anthropologists around questions of postcolonialism, as well as poststructuralist theory, especially Foucault.[35] Mobilization against the 1990–1991 Gulf

War was critical in inspiring quite a few people of this generation to work in MENA. One white anthropologist described a mood felt by many after hearing about the invasion:

> I was immediately outside. There was a call that came around . . . on our automatic phone system, and it said "demonstration." I went, immediately. It was the first demonstration I was ever in. . . . It was thrilling to be [part of] such a massive number of people, um, rejecting something that was being done. But, and then I also realized I know nothing about that area. How could we be killing people I never even knew about except as like, well, I wasn't even thinking about it as if it was real at all. So I enrolled [in my first Middle East anthropology class].

It is impossible to overemphasize the centrality and dominance of Palestine in a majority of the narratives of people trained in the 1990s about how they came to MENA anthropology, even the narratives of those who do not work on Palestine or in Palestinian communities. Coming to understand Palestine politics—and often embracing an anti-Zionist political position—was a critical moment in one's academic coming of age. This manifested in a variety of ways: making a political choice to study there or not; generating new or intensified interest in the region; or in the words of one, marking "a new sense of the urgency of political realities." The decisive importance of Palestine politics for this group of anthropologists can be directly traced to the timing of the first intifada and the post-Oslo period in relation to their formative academic years.

As one might expect, the events of September 11, 2001, sparked a political consciousness for a new generation of scholars. Several of our interlocutors remarked that they decided to go to graduate school for anthropology and/or to study MENA as a result of their experiences and questions around 9/11 and its aftermath. "It was hard to not feel somehow affected by the event in the sense of just being saturated by all kinds of media," explained one. The specifics of how 9/11 affected people's decision making varies by race and ethnicity. A region-related anthropologist highlighted the significant role he thought those like him could play in "bridging the gap" between "lived experience" in places like Palestine and "what sort of mainstream Americans are hearing in their churches and on the news and in the classrooms." Another region-related scholar nuanced this idea of "bridging the gap" after reflecting on how living with an Arab partner dealing with major visa problems in the immediate post-9/11 dragnet finalized their commitment to work in the region: "I felt like the role I could play was in bringing these two things together. Bringing, not bridging the gap, but at least bringing . . . the United States into conversation with the Arab world in a more responsible [way]—and the opposite, also. In a more ethical, responsible, deep way."

White scholars' narratives about the effects of 9/11 on their political and academic commitments were somewhat different. They were more likely to speak of 9/11 as motivating anthropological study of MENA in order to "open one's eyes" to government actions, to a region stereotyped as "Other" in the media, and to contradictions. Reflecting on their experience as an undergraduate that fall, a white anthropologist said, "I definitely think [9/11] shaped my decision to go to the Middle East. I think with seeing all the media coverage and also . . . [a person I knew] was deployed to Afghanistan. And so I also had his accounts of what was happening there, so . . . that combined with the media coverage, combined with being in college . . . [where] we didn't have a lot of students from the Middle East . . . so to me it was like an eye-opener." Another explained that their interests stemmed from going to college in a Patriot Act climate, which "puts you in this really paranoid view of the world and politics in general. . . . That makes you . . . want to figure something out, right?"

With the exception of some region-related scholars, anthropologists trained in the 2000s did not mention political engagement with Palestine politics nearly as frequently as those in earlier generations when describing how they came to anthropology of MENA. Their focus was instead directed to these specific features of the post-9/11 domestic and geopolitical landscape of war. The fact that the largest attack on US soil occurred during their college years may explain why 9/11—combined with the subsequent US wars in Iraq and Afghanistan and the curtailing of US civil liberties—overshadowed the Palestinian struggle in their political consciousness. It is also possible that they are a generation that takes the presence of anti-Zionist political perspectives on their campuses for granted in ways that scholars who attended college prior to the late 1990s do not and that they have been more regularly exposed to both books on Palestine in their classes and activist groups like Students for Justice in Palestine. It remains to be seen how the MENA uprisings that began in 2011 create new interest in anthropology of the region. A colleague who began graduate school just after 9/11 mused on a shift that might be occurring for those following them: "The newer, younger generation is not as affected viscerally by the actual event [of 9/11] itself, and so that conversation [about 9/11-related US engagement with the Middle East] is going to take on a different tone because that immediate gut reaction is not going to be there. . . . And so I think actually, the revolutions . . . have actually been . . . one of the more radical shifts away from that conversation of 9/11 because they have really painted the region in a very positive, interesting light." Another potential shift may emerge from the twenty-first-century US wars in MENA: we might see more anthropology graduate students focusing on the region as a result of experiences there during military service. Bethany Kibler, profiled in Harvard University's graduate school bulletin in 2012, when she was a first-year PhD student in anthropology, is one example. The article notes that her interest in the region "arose directly from her military service, during which she learned Arabic;" her military service also led her to anthropology in order to address "the pressing need to understand societies that are different than our own."[36]

. . .

A constellation of factors goes into the making of a scholar who focuses on a particular discipline and region. This does not mean that intellectual questions are of less or no significance; topical choice certainly led some people to MENA. A person might enter a PhD program in anthropology knowing that she wants to study something related to Islam, but solidify her fieldsite based on the specific kinds of questions in which she is interested. Or a person might begin graduate work interested in questions of ecological change and political infrastructures—questions that might lead him to work in particular Middle Eastern countries. Or an interest in particular questions about postcoloniality, or pluralism, or social movements could lead a scholar to fieldwork in the region, much in the way that earlier anthropologists interested in certain forms of kinship and descent tended to conduct research there. These kinds of intellectual considerations are true for anthropologists across world regions; research questions are developed in the intersections of theoretical frameworks, regional features, and methodological pragmatics. Transformations in theoretical and topical trends in anthropology related to specific regions, including MENA, are also important, and we have written about those elsewhere.[37]

Our focus here has instead been on how broader social and political institutions, networks, and local, national, and global forces—and the tensions they produced—pull people into their academic specializations. Once people commit to discipline and region and enter graduate school and then the professoriate, they come to realize more fully how these institutions, networks, and forces hamper the promising allure of anthropology as a critical and ethical discipline that can provide ways to tell other stories about a much-maligned region. Working in neoliberalizing institutions of higher education in the United States has for decades been fraught with politicized pressures. While many still consider anthropology the best discipline for critical ethical engagement, the glow fades for MENA anthropologists as they face sexism and racism from the overt to the microaggressive and as they contend with colleagues' prejudices regarding the Middle East, Islam, and, most importantly, Israel-Palestine. These prejudices knit with academia's changing economics, US militarization in MENA, and right-wing and Zionist pressure groups to produce a toxic environment for these scholars wishing to speak truth to power.

2 Making It through Graduate School

Steven Salaita. Nadia Abu El-Haj. Joseph Massad. Norman Finkelstein. Thomas Abowd. These names signal to many scholars the potential consequences of writing and teaching about the Middle East and North Africa in the United States. External community organizations, sometimes cooperating with people on campus, targeted these academics for taking anti-Zionist political positions, being assumed to take such positions, being Palestinian, simply asking scholarly questions that call Zionist assumptions into question, or some combination thereof.[1] Two of these scholars are anthropologists. Tom Abowd was denied a routine contract renewal after being attacked for speaking at a campus event related to Palestine. Nadia Abu El-Haj faced significant public pressure on her (eventually successful) tenure case because her scholarship asked questions that threatened Zionist nationalist truths. Both these cases highlight the ways in which academics' backgrounds, scholarship, and politics converge, especially around Palestine. They are also, to our knowledge, the only two cases where anthropologists have come under such pronounced, persistent—and in Abowd's case—successful, assault.

Despite the fact that the vast majority of our interlocutors have not personally experienced such menacing opposition to their tenure or retention, they still expressed apprehension, a sense that working on the region was a "minefield," and fears that they *could* easily be targeted by right-wing and/or Zionist organizations because of their teaching, public lectures, or research, and that their institutions would not necessarily protect them.[2] These stories are enough to send chills down a graduate student's spine. One person described this fear as "knowing that people who fall on the wrong side can suffer in their careers." The few scholars who have not had any difficulties on the job market or been harassed for their scholarship or teaching know of others who have had these experiences. Situations like those of Abu El-Haj or Abowd exacerbate those fears in part because anthropologists believe that anthropology is different from other fields. Many anthropologists view themselves as progressive, if not at least liberal, and are consistently surprised when their disciplinary colleagues present (perhaps unwittingly) conservative positions on the region. This is especially true for scholars who espouse anti-Zionism as part of their progressive outlook. So it was particularly disturbing to many MENA anthropologists when politically motivated charges arose from intradisciplinary contexts. We expect such allegations from people in other disciplines, the common phrasing goes, but not from our own. Indeed, anthropology is not immune to compulsory Zionism in the academy,[3] and many fear that if they criticize Israel, they will be called an anti-Semite and/or a self-hating Jew and/or suffer career consequences.

The fact that levels of apprehension are greater than actual experiences of job denial or loss does not mean that our colleagues are imagining things. Less dramatic but pervasive experiences impacted career trajectories. Abowd and Abu El-Haj are important not because they are exceptional, but because they represent extreme versions of common experiences. Global politics have combined with national, local, and institutional forces (including sexism, racism, and economic pressures on higher education) to affect careers materially in terms of access to the discipline and regional fieldsites, relationships with advisors, experiences on the job market, tenure battles, and ability to obtain research funding. These material effects had significant consequences for many anthropologists' professional lives, as did politically motivated complaints and attacks against their work in the classroom or in public lectures.

The general climate of fear as well as racist and sexist pressures impacted scholars during periods of career vulnerability such as graduate school and the job market, the focus of this chapter, and the tenure process, a subject of the next. In these moments, academics learned that they must cultivate various modes of self-protection in order to continue their work without major conflict or upheaval. Throughout their careers, they then apply these strategies, which include self-monitoring and self-censorship. From graduate school onward, many MENA scholars decline to research, lecture, write, teach, or speak to colleagues about certain topics or do so only in ways marked by extreme politesse and a set of precautionary measures. They politely navigate faculty sexism and racism in graduate school and on the job market, add preemptive clauses on syllabi about unauthorized recording or the academic benefit of encountering opposing perspectives, ghostwrite when addressing sensitive topics, and avoid communicating personal views on social media. These practices contradict the principles of both the First Amendment and academic freedom as colleges and universities claim to promote them.[4] Furthermore, they are at odds with producing scholarship and cultivating critical thinking skills in our students. By examining the case of MENA anthropology, we see very clearly a set of key tensions at the core of anthropology and academic practice more generally.

Graduate School Discriminations

Anthropologists who were graduate students during different time periods emphasized the relative impact of sexism and racism on their experiences in ways that correlated with major demographic shifts toward more women and minorities in the field. Sexism marked the first entrée of women into anthropology.[5] One of our female interlocutors who entered academia in the male-dominated 1960s told us that when she sought graduate school advice from prominent anthropologist Marshall Sahlins, he said to her, "Women shouldn't be in anthropology; they should be home." When she walked out of his office visibly upset, the department secretary redirected her to another professor; when she spoke with him, he said "Yeah, good, that's great, come study the Middle East . . . but don't get pregnant." She recalled, "This was *one day* [her emphasis]. I was getting all this crap. I said, 'I'm not married . . . I don't plan to get pregnant. I wanna do my graduate work!'" It is a good thing that Title IX was passed in 1972, because by the 1990s, such overt sexism was widely recognized as illegal.

Nonetheless, until the 1990s, some advisors discouraged students from working on women's communities. For example, a female MENA anthropologist told us that even into the late 1980s her male MENA anthropology advisor denigrated research on women as unimportant and "womby." Furthermore, moving into the 1990s, female students still sometimes found themselves being treated differently. Quite a few of them reported being warned to avoid marrying in the field. They heard advice like "You're not going to be one of my students who marries one of those Arab guys, are you?" or "Just don't come back with an Arab husband" from advisors who were mostly female and both white and region-related. This sentiment reflected negative stereotypes about Arab men, second-wave feminist anxieties about their female students starting families during graduate school, and an idea (derived from both identity politics and anthropology's self-critique) that anthropologists should not cavort with the natives.[6] Yet we have no evidence of male scholars being advised to avoid relationships with women from the field, despite Paul Rabinow's famous published account of his evening with Moroccan prostitutes during fieldwork.[7]

At the same time, many of our female interlocutors fondly recounted the support they received from their female mentors. And scholars of all genders often expressed deep appreciation for the feminists ahead of them in the field. In the words of a recent PhD: "I feel like women anthropologists who work on the Middle East have been really great mentors to a number of generations of anthropologists . . . No one's territorial about things, so even if you have another ethnologist who works [on your area or topic], but she's more senior— she will help you, she'll give you advice, she'll mention your name to somebody to write a review or to publish in something. And it's all the women who tend to do that. I haven't been seeing men doing that, which is interesting." Despite supportive feminist networks, region-related and other nonwhite scholars of both genders described feeling that they had to negotiate professors' and peers' racialized assumptions about them in graduate school. These experiences grew more prevalent over time, perhaps because before the 1980s, conversations about race remained latent in anthropology and there were relatively fewer scholars of color in the discipline. As more minorities entered the field in the late 1980s and critiques of anthropology's whiteness circulated more widely, more region-related scholars realized that they were often racialized as non-white and judged according to a binary of good versus bad Middle Easterner.[8] Our interlocutors' narratives are related to the increasing racialization of Arabs and Muslims in the United States,[9] as well as a scholar's social class, religious background, appearance, and linguistic practices, (including whether or not they are perceived to have a non-American accent when speaking English).[10] A nonreligious junior anthropologist of mixed Euro-American and Arab heritage from an upper-middle-class background noted: "Honestly I feel like I'm seen as so white most of the time. I mean my language, my appearance, my dress to a certain extent. . . . Whatever it is, I look like such a white, middle-class [person]. . . . And in some ways I almost feel like that's a betrayal to my students of color. But then on the other hand . . . it is kind of who I am. I mean I grew up in quite a white, middle-class suburban setting and so . . . it's a strange thing."

Geopolitical events and US foreign policy had a direct bearing on these experiences. This same scholar noted how 9/11 affected her relationships, as a graduate student, with non-Arab faculty, "who would just kind of get into freak-out mode and they would just see me as the sort of closest person they could talk to about these things. . . . You know, honestly I think they just wanted to talk to an Arab who they could sort of get along with. It was a little bit like that, where I was the sort of token person, you know what I mean?" Another region-related scholar similarly noted that non-Arab faculty "liked me as a person but that was to validate their weird anxieties about Arabs and Middle East-erners, like their view of the Middle East was a group of angry Jew-haters, and I was the enlightened exception because I was their student."

Across the decades, the degree to which region-related (and especially Arab or Arab-American) students felt discrimination also depended on the visibility and intensity of Israel-Palestine politics at their graduate institution. Palestinian scholars were most likely to discuss how faculty (and sometimes other students) were uncomfortable around them and sometimes perceived them as a problem. An anthropologist trained in the 1990s reflected on this situation, saying, "The fact that I'm Palestinian, it's worse than [the fact that] I'm from the Middle East. . . . A few times just like in conversation and stuff like that, it's the big elephant in the room, if you say you're a Palestinian. People don't feel comfortable."

In fact, Israel-Palestine politics affected anthropologists' experiences as students regardless of their race or ethnicity. While region-related students were caught up in these dynamics due to racist assumptions about their political proclivities, white students experienced negative reprisals when they expressed anti-Zionist or other political positions that were viewed as pro-Palestinian. At least three of our interlocutors had faculty withdraw from or refuse to serve on their dissertation committees for reasons they attributed to political disagreements on Israel-Palestine; they either suspected this strongly or had learned of a situation's political undertones from a classmate or another professor. Regardless of whether or not political disagreement was at the root of the matter, these incidents contributed to an environment of suspicion and fear of political reprisal.

The Political Intersection of Discipline and Region in Graduate School

Along with racism and sexism, US relations with the Middle East and North Africa have shaped dissertations for anthropology graduate students in ways ranging from access to fieldsites and funding to advisors' demands. Nearly every major granting agency in the United States has, at various times, allowed funding decisions to be influenced by Israel-Palestine politics. A senior scholar told us that when he was on the board of the Middle East Studies Association (MESA), he dealt with a situation in which a MESA member complained that Israeli government officials were inappropriately involved with the Fulbright selection process, derailing any proposals they deemed politically problematic. He reported that an inquiry indicated that this was not the case. An anthropologist who applied to the Social Science Research Council for funding to work on Palestinians in the early 1980s was advised by someone on the review panel to avoid mentioning the Israeli occupation because this reviewer thought other members of the panel would reject the proposal on that basis. The National Science Foundation *withdrew* funding originally awarded for a Palestine-related project in the 1990s from a scholar who interpreted that unusual move as the result of political pressures. And when a Palestine scholar in the mid-1990s called a representative of the Guggenheim Foundation seeking insight as to why their application was rejected, they were told, "There's someone on the committee that was not going to let this happen. I'm telling this to you, but I'm not going to name names." For the 2000s, we heard two accounts of Islamophobia on a National Science Foundation review panel. Since 9/11, funding for graduate training in MENA Studies programs has also been targeted. As late as 2014, a group of conservative pro-Israel organizations lobbied the US government to revoke Title VI funding to MENA Studies programs that they considered to be against their interests "by using amendments . . . to the Act . . . that were originally created to police programs deemed too critical of U.S. foreign policy following 9/11."[11]

Beyond the obvious issues of access and funding, there remained the necessary hurdle of convincing one's faculty mentors to support a project. Faculty advice and pressures regarding where and where not to work complicated the politics of navigating graduate school and contributed to students' impressions of how fieldsite choices might affect their careers. Anthropologists mentoring graduate students who wanted to work in MENA before 1980 often discouraged them from doing so on the grounds that the region was "unimportant," "theoretically uninteresting" to the discipline, or unworthy of study because its societies were literate and "complex"—the latter view reflecting the biases of a previous era in anthropology that favored work on nonliterate, small-scale societies.

One of our interlocutors recalled that professors "told me over and over, 'You will never get a job'" because they focused on the region. Another said:

> When I told [a well-known anthropology professor] that I wanted to work in the Middle East, he said, "Well that's a big mistake." And I said, "Why?" And he said, "Well, the body of literature on that area was not very rich," as a result of which there was not much of a basis on which to form any long-lasting theory. And he said "Yes, it's true that we don't know much about the Middle East, but that's not a reason necessarily to fill in the light spaces on the map." I think he actually used that term.

Several people also told us that MENA was not taken very seriously as a regional subfield in cultural anthropology before the late 1980s because it was associated with the ancient world and therefore viewed as archaeology's domain. This particular disciplinary blinder in American anthropology is likely related to the fact that for decades, dominant US public discourses and popular culture figured the region and its inhabitants as directly linked to a biblical past.[12] Furthermore, anthropology as a discipline had, in those earlier years, tended to portray its non-Western subjects as vestiges of an earlier era; this was acute in relation to MENA due to these religious associations.[13]

By 1980, the reasons mentors discouraged students from focusing on the region began to change. MENA transformed from an archaic place best studied by archaeologists to a backward, threatening place populated by primitive and violent sexists. A male anthropologist who was in graduate school in the 1980s described the complicated gender politics of these new forms of devaluing the region in cultural anthropology, which extended beyond dissuading white female students from "putting themselves at risk" by cavorting among Middle Easterners:

> There were some professors [who] wondered why you would want to work in the Arab world. One professor actually said to me, in public, in front of other students, "I don't understand why you would want to study a culture that fetishizes violence." I mean, she actually said that. And I didn't know how to respond. . . . Among feminist anthropologists, there was the insinuation that "Arabs and Muslims are primitive." They wouldn't say it that way exactly, but it was a strongly held kind of thing. So, if you studied these people and you weren't an Arab or Muslim yourself, if you were just white, the question would be, "Well, what draws you to that culture? What draws you to those kinds of people?"

This considerable shift in some US anthropologists' attitudes towards MENA was likely related to representations of Middle Easterners' reactions to US (and European) involvement in the region at the time. The news was replete with stories about the escalation of violence as a tactic of Palestinian liberation and the related oil embargos of the 1970s, the 1979 Islamic revolution in Iran and concomitant hostage crisis, the 1983 bombing of the US and French military barracks in Beirut, the series of Libyan attacks on US and European targets in the 1980s, and the growing Islamic revival with its associated increase in urban women's "veiling." With little extant ethnographic research on the region, sparse anthropological work on violence, and the dominance of a second-wave feminist approach that could not account for the headscarf as other than oppressive, it appears that anthropologists were vulnerable to US public sphere discourses that still framed MENA's residents as stuck in the past, but now also as barbaric, greedy, sexist desert-dwelling sheikhs or uncivilized violent Muslims.[14] Yet alongside the development of this more virulent strain of prejudicial attitudes towards MENA, more anthropology students began working in the region, in part as a personal response to intensified US involvement there and the resulting stereotypes.

Partly for these reasons, Palestinian communities were just emerging on students' radars as potential research sites at this time, and our interlocutors recalled that faculty systematically discouraged this choice. One of the pioneering Palestine anthropologists described the struggle to find a PhD advisor willing to work with students aspiring to conduct research among Palestinians: "They would tell you, 'No. Why do you want to do that? You don't ever want to get a job? Why do you want to do that? I will not work with you.'" Indeed, the sentence "you will not get a job" came up consistently in interviews not only with scholars who forged ahead with Palestine-related research, but also with people working across MENA. Many recalled friends or colleagues who had been "punished" on the job market for working with Palestinians and people saying, "Look what happened to so-and-so." As one person put it, "Palestine simply couldn't be touched then." Working on it was "political suicide" or "asking for trouble." Another, who defied this dispiriting environment to work with Palestinians, said, "Nothing could be done, and we thought we could sort of push through." The resilience of these anthropologists who persevered despite discouragement—and despite facing many of the job market struggles about which their professors had warned them—truly paved the way for future scholars.

This generation of scholars also experienced the potency of identity politics in the 1980s, which prompted some of our white interlocutors to consider issues of representation and defend their interest in studying cultural "others" when choosing MENA as a focus. One such scholar spontaneously made this argument in defense of a nonnative perspective in anthropology: "I believe that no matter who you are and where you're from . . . you can be a good scholar. . . . I don't believe as anthropologists we can only study that which is closest to us. I don't believe that's true at all. I think sometimes if you're coming from a very different place, sometimes you see things that a person from that place might not be able to see, and so I don't believe in the whole thing about positionality that you can only represent the place from where you come." The fact that these anthropologists often felt obliged to make such arguments underscores the extent to which several critical shifts in the discipline impacted graduate students at the time. These changes included critiques of anthropology as a colonial enterprise, critiques of anthropological representations of "the other," debates about feminism's relationship to anthropology that highlighted the ways scholars were implicated in their research, and more prominent region-related voices within the subfield. As someone who began graduate school at the end of the 1980s described that period, it was "the height of identity politics, when everyone was *supposed* to work on themselves."

Region-related anthropologists who were also students at that time did not agree as to whether or not "working on oneself" was advisable; they saw having a personal relationship to the field as everything from a strength to a major career liability. A few scholars reacted to the idea that working on their community of origin was "what one should do" by deliberately framing projects to upend identity politics' assumptions. As one person commented, when describing people's surprise at the idea that a scholar from one MENA country would conduct research in another, "It's like, wait, would you ask that to [a white] American anthropologist? *No*, because the assumption is that there is a particular flow of research." This assumption—that white scholars study the other and native scholars study themselves—was a relic of earlier racialized understandings of anthropological research that lost sway after both the critique of representation and the demographic changes in US higher education instigated by the 1965 immigration reforms.

Beginning in the 1980s, the debates over knowledge production also intersected with Israel-Palestine politics, shaping ideas about what constituted an acceptable fieldsite or topic for Jews and non-Jewish Arabs. Arabs were told that they could not study Jewish communities in MENA, whereas we have no evidence of Jewish scholars being told that they could not study Arabs.[15] The 1990s witnessed a major shift in research among Palestinians: graduate students of a range of backgrounds began to ignore the warnings and work in the occupied Palestinian territories as well as in Palestinian refugee communities in significantly greater numbers; as we write, Palestine scholarship is one of the three top areas of research in MENA anthropology.[16] But the warnings persisted. Over half of our interlocutors trained in the 1990s noted that (in the words of one) "word on the street" during graduate school was still that if you worked with Palestinians you would never get a job. This, another said, "was the common wisdom; it was in the air." And quite a few people paid attention; they revised—essentially self-censored—their initial desires to work in the occupied Palestinian territories into dissertation projects focused on other places in MENA. In one case, a professor successfully scared a student away from doing their dissertation research there by telling them they had to "be willing to be crucified by Zionists. If you do research in that area, you have to be willing to spend your academic career fighting all the time, just fighting, you know?" Several people observed that even supportive professors "wouldn't touch Palestine [themselves] with a ten-foot pole" (an oft-repeated phrase about the issue). For a few others, faculty admonitions that Palestine was a "political hot potato" and to be "careful about that" combined with pragmatic concerns about living in the occupied Palestinian territories after witnessing and experiencing checkpoints, tear gas, and Israeli state violence. One person decided against working there after an experience on a pre–field trip to the West Bank, during which "there was tear gas all over the place. . . . [The Israeli army] get us out of the taxi, they start beating everybody with clubs. And, you know, I got whacked a little bit on the arms, like, you know . . . this shit, you know, and my friend's like, 'Oh yeah, we've all been in jail. It's just life.'"

Yet some students in the 1990s pursued their interest despite the challenges. The first Palestinian intifada often sparked that interest, while no doubt also fueling faculty advisors' wariness. Their research was facilitated by the political opening created by the 1993 Oslo Accords, after which, as one anthropologist explained, "the word Palestine became palatable to people in the US in a new way." The occupied Palestinian territories' growing popularity as a fieldsite also reflected the ways that graduate students may be more attuned to changing academic trends, or how faculty advice may be predicated, with the best of intentions, on their own past experiences (or those of colleagues and friends) that may no longer be as pertinent. In other words, mentors' advice may lag behind shifting political landscapes. A professor who had herself been cautioned for her protection to avoid her university's Middle East Center in the 1970s because it was controlled by Zionists, who had watched other students researching Palestine in the 1980s not get jobs, and who had (in her view responsibly) cautioned her own students in the 1990s to find other fieldsites noted, during our 2012 interview, that working on Palestine had gained a "cachet" it did not have in the past and that it might even have a "radical chic."

Critically important here is the fact that by the 1990s several Palestine scholars held tenured faculty positions and served as direct or indirect role models for graduate students. A new critical mass of MENA anthropology professors and graduate students also provided a community of support for emerging scholars. In interlocutors' reflections on this period, we started to hear cracks in the discourse of avoidance and a reframing of the occupied Palestinian territories as an ideal site to ask certain anthropological questions. Most notably, an anthropologist trained at this time said she thought working there was an advantage because it was outside the then-dominant "prestige zones," so it was "easy to contribute something because it wasn't an overly saturated field." This seemingly exceptional statement prefigured both the growing acceptability in the discipline of Palestine-related research and another moment of change when some scholars began to describe MENA—though usually *not* Palestine— as a positive career choice.

By the mid- to late 1990s, discussions of positionality and representation were a regular part of curricula in most anthropology graduate programs, and our interlocutors who trained at that time often spontaneously reflected on these issues in our conversations. No longer was it a given that the anthropologist was better off as an "outsider;" rather, white scholars were more likely to articulate concerns that their work would be open to marked criticism from region-related scholars. Several expressed their own insecurities or hesitation to make claims or take stances on issues when there were, in the words of one person, "plenty of people of Arab descent . . . who have much more say on the issues than I do."

This reversal in assumptions about the location of ethnographic authority— combined with the still extant idea that region-related scholars would be biased in studying "their own"—led to complex pressures on region-related students to find "an other" to study in their countries of origins, such as a different sub-national group. Of these then-graduate students, approximately two-thirds did so, for reasons of personal or political interest, or due to faculty insistence. The other third worked in other countries in the region. Only one region-related graduate student in the 1990s was strongly discouraged from working in their parent's home country: an anthropologist of Jewish origin whose parent immigrated from MENA was advised by a non-MENA anthropologist, "You don't want to be a professional ethnic." In contrast, a different region-related anthropologist was pressured in graduate school to work in MENA because their mentors found impossible and ludicrous the idea that they (a nonnative English speaker with language skills for MENA research) would go study a part of the world where they would need to learn a third or fourth language. Notably, we have no evidence that graduate students of Ashkenazi Jewish background were discouraged from studying Palestinians or had their objectivity about the conflict questioned.

By the 1990s, we also see pressures on region-related students to study topics prevalent in the US popular imaginary of MENA. Most overtly, the "problem" of women's "veiling" pervaded public discourse on the region, and feminist-of-color critiques of second-wave feminism were inspiring new scholarly interest in "figuring out" Muslim women. In a sign that ongoing stereotypes dominated some precincts of the discipline, faculty directly pressured a region-related student to focus her dissertation on women and Islam although she had mentioned neither topic in her graduate school application. She told us, "I was like, 'Fuck women and Islam, I don't want to work on Islam, I got away from Islam!'" Such demands were common, especially for female anthropologists who could be read as "Arab" or "Muslim."

During this time, as anthropology overall grew more diverse, non-region-related scholars of color, especially those from the global south, encountered enduring assumptions about appropriate fieldsites. As one such scholar explained,

> There are certain things that I don't think are going to change any time soon, which are grounded in [anthropology's] own philosophy. One is the idea that you should study where you come from if you're not white American. And of course I don't do that, so there's always certain issues there, right? Often my first question at job interviews is, "Why did you end up studying the Middle East?" usually asked with wide, confused eyes. So that's often something I have to explain. I kind of appreciate it when I'm not asked to explain it.

This limit on the disciplinary lessons learned following anthropology's self-critiques continued into the twenty-first century.

In the new millennium, graduate students continued to confront conversations about authority and knowledge production, as well as concerns about working with Palestinians, as they determined where to locate their dissertation projects. A recent PhD described being in graduate school just after 9/11 as her "coming of age" because she was consistently cautioned by those ahead of her who were "trying to inform me of what's out there" to "teach me about what's to come." In addition, the second Palestinian intifada brought the relative opening of the Oslo period for Palestine studies to an end. Overall in the 2000s, with few exceptions, faculty no longer warned students away from Palestine-related research. However, many students continued to self-censor by suppressing their initial desires to work there because of a general sense that, as one put it, "If you can, you probably want to stay away from the whole Palestinian thing because it's too politically sensitive and it might hurt you, it might hurt your career." Some of these scholars planned to work on Palestine issues later in their careers, perhaps after securing a job and tenure. As one explained, "It was like, put that [desire] away until after you do your dissertation and so on, so that you don't have to deal with all the kinds of issues that people who work in Palestine have to go through."[17]

Scholars trained in the 2000s maintained concerns about ethnographic legitimacy in relation to racial or ethnic background. The contours of these conversations had changed, both because the height of identity politics had passed and because institutionalized ethnic studies programs had altered campus dynamics. More region-related scholars—especially women—articulated discomfort or anger at being tokenized and asked to "represent" the region or Islam due to racialized assumptions rather than their research. It was also primarily *female* region-related scholars who voiced anxieties about their authority, whereas a number of region-related males suggested that they were better able to access and understand dynamics in their "home" fieldsites. One of the latter explained that he thought his colleagues of similar backgrounds had an important "unique role" to play in the discipline: "I think that our voices can really enrich the scholarship of the anthropology of the Middle East. I don't believe that you have to be from the region to be able to work on the region. Not at all! I think anyone who wants can work on the region. But I think it would be a tragedy if . . . none of the voices included people from the region, then we'd have a problem." But region-related women of the same career stage expressed feeling that they had to work harder to prove their "anthropological credentials and commitments" than other scholars, because of assumptions that they had relied on kinship or other connections in the field. This gender difference in constructions of authority reflects enduring hierarchies within the academy, particularly for female region-related scholars.[18] One person, for example, explained that she had not wanted to study her country of origin because she did not want people to think that she had somehow labored less than they had.

This particular scholar was justified in her concern that she would not be taken as seriously as others, because in *every* cohort of anthropologists, we heard some white scholars suggest that region-related anthropologists had it easier. These suggestions were built on frequently inaccurate assumptions that those colleagues had personal connections that facilitated entrée into fieldsites and/or faced fewer linguistic challenges.[19] We suggest that this white discourse about region-related scholars having it easier might be a reaction to the loss of ethnographic authority that came with the major theoretical shifts of the late 1980s and early 1990s or at least a reaction to the claim that native scholars have greater representational authority. To assert, as several white anthropologists did, that one had to work harder to learn a language or access a new place is to claim another kind of authority—that of diligence—which can perhaps replace the now contested authority of outsider objectivity so often adopted by senior white men.[20] Nonetheless, most anthropologists (of all backgrounds) would likely argue that there is scientific benefit to crossing boundaries of knowledge and attempting to understand individual and group logics other than one's own—which is what happens even when region-related anthropologists work in their countries of origin. No matter what one's relationship to their fieldsite, fieldwork itself was another complex process during which graduate students had to manage political entanglements.

The Politics of Getting through Fieldwork

Scholars who did conduct their research in places where they had personal connections did not necessarily experience those connections as an advantage. One person explained that she had to learn to switch into and out of "active research mode" and that topics close to one's heart meant that one had to "learn to sort of distance, like keep my own feelings about [a topic] out of it." Having family and other relationships in one's fieldsite could also create social obligations and, especially for women in some contexts, expectations about social propriety that could complicate the research process. At least one anthropologist changed her fieldsite to avoid such expectations when it became clear that access to the public sphere in which she was interested was going to be impossible in a place where people knew her. Our female interlocutors, like female anthropologists more generally, frequently described encountering sexism in the field.

Anthropologists who were neither white Americans nor of Middle Eastern background described the complex ways that race, region, and sometimes religion affected their field experiences. They noted that some of their interlocutors saw them as "people from the third world working in other third world places," forcing them to justify their interest in MENA once again, during fieldwork itself. Because they could rely on neither of the two dominant paths to authoritative knowledge—whiteness or Middle Eastern background—they sometimes faced the additional challenge of being taken less seriously as scholars of the region, both during fieldwork and at their academic institutions.[21]

The benefits of being perceived as an outsider or insider were never clearcut as US involvement in MENA deepened. While white scholars trained before the 1980s sometimes viewed their outsider status as a research advantage, this perspective was sporadic in subsequent generations, due to both disciplinary changes and growing hostility toward US foreign policy in MENA, which made fieldwork a challenge for many US-based anthropologists (including some region-related scholars). In addition, our interlocutors were sometimes entangled in local or national political conflicts in their fieldsites. Some white anthropologists perceived their outsider status as protection from these situations, while others were pulled into local political struggles precisely because they were viewed as external observers. Some region-related scholars described navigating the national politics of their fieldsites as a challenge equal to, if not greater than, that posed by Israel-Palestine politics in the United States. And when the various sets of politics were intertwined—for example, if an Arab American scholar were to conduct research with Jewish interlocutors, which some people viewed as turning the colonial table around—the combination could be toxic, because, as one person put it, "It comes with bad luggage." Affiliation with US institutions and funding always underlay field issues in both negative and positive ways. As Nadia Abu El-Haj told Jane Kramer in an interview for *The New Yorker* about the controversy over her tenure: "Part of the affront for all those people who attacked me was that I was a 'Palestinian' doing the kind of field work I did. . . . But make no mistake about this: my ability to do it was that I was an American. I had grants. I had access. How many Arabs do you think would have that?"[22]

There have been countless occasions in which academic researchers are not allowed into countries or have been harassed for hours at borders and airports, including in the United States. A scholar's passport frequently made all the difference. People who held non-US passports could sometimes skirt US travel bans and access sites that were off limits for those who travelled as US citizens. Lacking a US passport could also be a major liability, as citizens of other countries in MENA or the global south often struggled to obtain visas.[23] After 9/11, region-related anthropologists (even US citizens) also had to contend with the problems of flying while Arab or Muslim, and all scholars traveling to places "of interest" could be hassled by TSA agents (one white interlocutor described deliberately dropping his institution's well-known name at borders to facilitate his entry). As recently as 2011, several anthropologists were questioned at US airports; their emails were read and their documents, books, and belongings sifted through in detail. As one person who has had TSA agents ask them about "every single thing in my suitcase" put it: "You kind of get used to it, and it becomes just a matter of everyday life and academic practice."

Obtaining necessary security clearances or research permissions can also be difficult, especially when projects address topics governments find problematic. An anthropologist who was initially denied clearance for her project went to the American Research Center in Egypt (ARCE)—which has direct ties to both the US and Egyptian governments—to inquire why. A program employee told her, "My dear, you mention social class. You know we haven't had social class in Egypt since Nasser." She deleted the reference to social class and quickly received clearance despite ARCE's knowledge that her project's content had not necessarily changed. Scholars have also been forced to cut their dissertation research short, as in the case of Aseel Sawalha, a Palestinian graduate student at the City University of New York who was deported while conducting fieldwork in Beirut—and lost much of her data—because Lebanon rescinded residency permission for some Palestinians in the country. It did so just as the US State Department lifted its travel ban to Lebanon; apparently, it was dangerous for US citizens to have any contact with certain categories of Palestinians, including an anthropology graduate student from a US institution.[24]

Difficult conditions in many MENA sites were an intimate component of the politics of fieldwork, especially in the occupied Palestinian territories. Here we quote a colleague's eloquent and raw written response to our question about the problems scholars faced accessing their fieldsite and conducting their research there:

> You could point out that one scholar was questioned for hours, not allowed into Israel, held in a cell (that's a room with a door with no handle on the inside) for some hours, and sent back to [her country of residence] (there goes the money for that flight; there goes that research trip; there goes the next two months spent in a deep depression, sad about not seeing friends, worried about not pursuing research), with no explanation. And then on a second occasion, the same scholar, who had been assured by the Israeli embassy in her home country that there was no security case against her and that she should have no trouble getting in to do her research, was told at the airport by the Ministry of the Interior that she would not be allowed to go into country unless she gave them $5,000 (as a kind of deposit, which she didn't have), and then told that she would not be allowed to go into the West Bank at all, and if she did, they would find out and bar her from the country for ten years. This, of course, is a serious and real violation of academic freedom, of freedom of expression.
>
> You could talk about being stopped and questioned at the airport for an extra special long time because you're carrying out Arabic magazines that the security people don't like—magazines that show pictures of the effects of occupation. So much for the great democracy of the Middle East.
>
> My house was ransacked by the Israelis. Along with the houses of all of my neighbours. Better than having it demolished, as has been the case with hundreds of Palestinian homes.[25]
>
> You could tell stories about what it's like to watch your friends, your adoptive fieldwork family suffer when their children, nephews, sons are shot, arrested, beaten, tortured, shot, beaten, arrested, tortured.

You could tell stories about what it's like hearing someone get shot and die in the alley way outside your house.

You could tell stories about what it's like when helicopter gun ships shoot at your house and how you calculate, without a very good sense of geometry, what the various bullet trajectories through various doors and windows might be.

You could tell stories about what it's like to hear bullets bounce off the brick walls of the house of your friends with whom you're staying, and about trying to persuade your zealously *sumud-y* [steadfast] host that it would be better to go onto the ground floor, where there are fewer bullets bouncing, even if she doesn't like her brother who lives there.

You could tell stories about the shame one feels when an impending Israeli army invasion drives you to leave your field site, and a friend says, 'I wish you wouldn't go or that you could take me with you, but you go anyway, by yourself.'

You could tell stories about what it's like to find that the checkpoint to your town is shut, with no one being allowed in, and having to figure out where to spend the night until the occupation forces decide whatever it is the fuck they want to decide.

You could tell stories about what it's like to sit at a checkpoint in the baking heat for hours, along with everyone else, or bounce over bone-rattling detours through fields and be stuck for some time next to a stinking chicken coop, just trying to get to your next interview.

I watched young [Palestinian] men being harassed in Jerusalem, tried to confront the soldiers, and recognized there was nothing that I could do. That is the real pain of this kind of fieldwork. The complete, utter, maddening, realization that there's not a fucking thing that you can do.

Another scholar reflected similarly on the never-ending, exhausting, and frustrating nature of fieldwork under Israeli military occupation:

I feel tethered to Facebook, both because I don't want to miss anything that comes up for fieldwork, and because I'm worried about my friends being shot or arrested. There were months when [I would put my child to] bed and open Facebook to watch for alerts about who might have been arrested that night, because the arrests happen in the middle of the night, early evening Eastern Standard Time.

Also, in Palestine, I find it wrenching to manage all of the extra privilege that I have, especially regarding movement. I basically do not go inside Israel except to do [occasional, necessary] fieldwork. I've been hassled at the airport, but it let up a bit when (1) I got an Israeli passport and (2) I had a child. But even with the Israeli passport, when traveling alone, I am searched heavily. It's just a matter of fact, and literally numerical evidence of their racism. They give stickers with barcodes and numbers, and if your number starts with a 1, you're usually Ashkenazi Jewish, and if you get a 6, you're the biggest threat. With my child, I'm a 3, without her, I'm a 6.

Experiences like these are par for the course for Palestine scholars, and as all MENA scholars know, they are enacted by an Israeli state fully supported by the US government. Scholars in other MENA countries also faced difficult circumstances due to wars and revolutions in which their own privilege and US complicity (or direct involvement) had to be navigated. US support for Israel and other oppressive regimes in the region generated consistent challenges, as they faced tough questions from their interlocutors about that support.

Job Market Realities

When scholars think that in order to get or keep a job, they need to avoid discussing these research challenges or calling out the US and Israeli roles in perpetrating violence in the region, they often feel disaffected towards anthropology and pessimistic about the discipline's progressive claims and academia's ostensible support for the free pursuit of research. While many of our interlocutors did not take the job market into account when they formulated topics, many did (and this is increasingly the case; as a recent graduate student said, "9/11 happened and all of sudden the Middle East was like the hottest place that you could be studying"). Going on the job market is the first moment of career vulnerability with major stakes. Missteps can mean years of graduate training down the drain. It is no surprise that people understand the politics of getting a job through the prism of the aforementioned experiences and navigate those politics using the skills of self-protection they learned during graduate training.

Despite the persistence of fears about possible political reprisals on the job market for those who either worked on Palestine-related issues or were outspoken about Palestinian rights, MENA anthropologists' actual job market experiences have varied widely. Of course, reflections upon job searches are refracted through the end results; it is difficult to pinpoint why people do not get particular jobs. For this reason, we analyze patterns in interlocutors' reflections on those experiences, rather than diagnose specific cases. It is clear that no matter whether Palestine scholars had extreme difficulty getting jobs (prior to the 1990s) or less difficulty (from the late 1990s onward), for decades faculty and administrators have inserted Israel-Palestine politics into every stage of academic searches in MENA anthropology. We document a substantial pattern of outright discrimination as well as a series of microaggressions faced by MENA scholars on the job market, no matter their personal political views on the issue.

Anthropologists generally viewed the academic job market as "pretty good" prior to the 1970s, and the few concerns they described were usually related to gender, most markedly being the first woman ever hired in a particular department. The massive post-WWII increase in faculty hiring to staff colleges and universities after the G.I. Bill may explain this view; in the 1960s, the professoriate grew by 150,000 positions. But the 1970s saw cuts in state funding for education, due to a combination of the growing economic crisis spurred by then-nascent neoliberalism and the backlash against the 1960s politicization of college campuses.[26] And our interlocutors looking for employment between 1970 and 2001 generally viewed it as a struggle, which continued as faculty lines decreased in the Reagan-Bush and Clinton eras.

Until 9/11, this situation was exacerbated for MENA anthropologists because the region was not viewed as central to cultural anthropology—both for the reasons cited earlier (the purview of archaeology, not theoretically interesting, too violent) and also because other world regions had become iconic in the discipline and were thus prioritized in hiring (e.g., Native North America, Africa, and Latin America). People often spent years as adjuncts, postdocs, or even working outside academia before finding a tenure-track position. In this sense, the warnings received by scholars trained before the 1990s about choosing MENA were confirmed, revalidating the advice they then gave to their students. Little did they know that job opportunities would change, both because they were creating a structure for a field of "Middle East anthropology" and because the region would soon be in the crosshairs of the US military machine.

Many scholars also told us that this general "sour market" trend combined with politicized pushback in search committees and departments to prohibit hiring scholars who worked with Palestinians. This was part of a larger trend of compulsory Zionism that has become the norm in colleges and universities since at least the 1970s. Some of our interlocutors suggested that this pushback extended to those who worked anywhere in MENA and/or were region-related anthropologists, because they were assumed to have pro-Palestinian political views. As one anthropologist explained, "The Arab-Israeli conflict played a role in the lack of jobs. Most Middle East specialists were going to come with an opinion even if they didn't do research on it and for many departments it was easy to not deal with it by not making it a very high priority." While it is often impossible to know why search committees make specific decisions, the key point is that MENA anthropologists often believed that anthropologists and administrators would rather not hire someone who worked in the region, in an effort to avoid having to deal with a colleague who might have views favorable to the Palestinians or to evade a hot-button political issue entirely. Many also believed that explicitly Zionist anthropologists and/or administrators have prevented the hiring of MENA scholars, especially those whose research is related to Palestine.

Our interlocutors often based these views on their experiences as search committee members. As one faculty member who has served on a plethora of searches explained, "In any faculty search, it might be only one or two people who don't want to hire a particular candidate. Since many departments prefer to hire by consensus, the one or two can eliminate a good candidate. In the case of a person associated with Palestine, you might think the one or two derailed the search because of Zionism, but you can never know." Another scholar described the job market as involving "this little ritual called 'asking around.' So you've made the short list, or they want to put you on the short list. I've heard that people would ask around. So [they ask], 'What are his politics?' You know, that kind of thing. And I did see people being discriminated against, I think, for their politics, in my department in job searches. There was a candidate in one job search who had very strong pro-Palestinian politics. . . . And I think this person's politics doomed him." And sometimes there is no "need" to ask around, when blatant racism will suffice. Another interlocutor told us about a colleague who, in the 2000s, had systematically opposed all Arab American or Middle Eastern job candidates because, in the colleague's view, "they'll have an agenda."

An important narrative among anthropologists who were on the job market in the late twentieth century demonstrates the politicization of the hiring process, even in the absence of direct discrimination. These scholars told us many stories of being warned about a Zionist search committee member or department chair, about being hired only after certain faculty members who were believed to be Zionists had left a department, and about experiencing Zionist questioning during campus visits. Many were directly questioned about their personal political views on Israel-Palestine. One was told by a professor in the late 1980s that he had "heard through the grapevine" from a search committee member at another institution that even suggesting to short-list a person who worked with Palestinians was impossible. This person also thought that Palestine-related research was a greater hindrance early in the search process: "It was more of an obstacle getting into the pool. Once you were in, you were already in . . . so the Palestine thing wasn't what sunk you. . . . I just think you couldn't get as many interviews." Others shared stories of learning about "being sunk" after a campus visit; in one case a scholar was told by a search committee member, "It's not going to happen. It's just not gonna happen. They are not gonna let you have this job . . . given what you do." She told us, "So that was that."

Campus visits also involved hostile lecture audiences and questions irrelevant to the research. Julie Peteet told us how her job talks were followed by questions and arguments like, "They don't love their children, they send them out to kill Israelis and blah blah blah" or "Israel doesn't engage in any human rights violations" or "bizarre questions, like 'What do you think of Yasser Arafat?' Or 'When are the Arabs gonna come around?'" She was also asked questions like, "Do you think if we hire you, we'll have troubles here?" which she noted "are unacceptable professionally as questions," concluding, "Well, of course you're not gonna get a job when people are asking you, 'Are we gonna have trouble if we hire you?!'"[27]

Eventually, most of the scholars who shared such stories with us landed tenure-track jobs, though we were told about others who left academia because they could not. And sometimes, after being hired, people heard the backstories about those searches from colleagues. In one case an anthropologist learned that a Zionist nonanthropology faculty member had circulated a memo arguing against her hire to the anthropology department as well as the dean, provost, and president of the institution and had included with the memo a Jewish community newsletter article describing the occupation as "benign" and "benevolent." The anthropology department ignored the memo, and her source told her, "We didn't take this seriously; this is lunacy." Not all departments or administrations dealt as well with such pressures.

In response to this sort of job market experience, some scholars began to self-censor, altering how they presented themselves or their work. A person trained in the 1960s who worked in a border region emphasized the Turkish aspects of her work over the Arab ones for a campus visit, and one trained in the 1980s told us, "The fact that I was not getting anywhere in terms of jobs made me stop working on Palestine and start looking at other things. I mean that's part of it. . . . I didn't want to look like I was single-mindedly focused on Palestine/Israel." This person recalled the precise job interview when they stopped presenting their Palestine research, opting for a differently edgy project instead, saying, "So I could talk about pussies, and that was safe, but Palestine I wasn't sure about [laughs]. . . . I would say there was a bit of self-censorship. Or just . . . thinking that maybe it was possibly judicious to try and do something somewhat different."

The critical mass of MENA anthropologists that obtained their degrees around the turn of the twenty-first century marked a transitional generation that described their job market experiences as simultaneously hindered and facilitated by global politics. On the one hand, Israel-Palestine politics negatively infused both ideas about the job market and actual campus visit experiences. On the other hand, these scholars sometimes said that they experienced unprecedented professional opportunities because of where they worked. Some noted that they owed these opportunities to the hard work of prior generations of MENA anthropologists who had paved the way for them, especially those who had struggled to work on Palestine. For others, this sense of opportunity reflected ideas about the greater availability of jobs focused on MENA and especially Islam after 9/11. As one described it, jobs opened because of a need to "know more about who you want to rule."

Job search outcomes during this time do not necessarily mirror either the discourse of apprehension or that of opportunity. We have no direct evidence that any of our interlocutors entering the market in the twenty-first century was denied a job because of their political views or because they work with Palestinians. But Israel-Palestine continued to haunt job market experiences, including for those whose research was wholly unrelated to it. Many anthropologists of this cohort who work elsewhere in MENA had interviewing faculty try to—as one said—"suss out their Palestine politics" during campus visits, sometimes via point-blank questions.[28] This investigating occurred in both formal and informal contexts (meals, car rides, side conversations). One scholar was asked on campus visits to two separate institutions to articulate a solution to the conflict. On one of these occasions, the questioner then revealed himself to be pro-Israel and attempted to engage the job candidate in conversation about her views of Israel's politics vis-à-vis the Palestinians in the car on the way to the airport. Another anthropologist whose research is quite far—both geographically and topically—from Israel-Palestine recounted a campus visit where he was asked to teach a class on that topic. While giving his carefully constructed lecture that explicitly presented various points "from the Israeli perspective" and "from the Palestinian perspective," he realized that students had sat through this class multiple times; all the candidates had been given the same assignment. Our interlocutor interpreted the exercise as being as much a direct way to assess one's politics as a demonstration of teaching style.

Such experiences were even more common for Palestine scholars. One person described how she was asked directly by search committee members multiple times whether she encountered problems around Israel-Palestine politics. In her words, "It's not what I said, it's the subject I work on. . . . People don't want to open themselves up to controversy. . . . Once the word Palestine is there, people go 'why do we want to make everyone upset?'" When the Palestine scholar is Jewish, attempts to figure out their political views took on different meaning, especially for those who wanted to distance themselves from Zionism. As one such scholar explained, "being Jewish and working in Israel-Palestine, you're forced to have certain kinds of positionality, and I mean it, you're forced [to be either pro or anti]."

Alongside this persistent and intense surveillance of scholars' political views, we see a pattern of continual self-protection and self-censorship in response to both fears of and actual Zionist pushback. Several scholars trained in the 1990s said that they would steer conversations away from the topic while on campus visits. One shared that they avoided going public with their position in favor of the academic boycott of Israeli institutions, a common practice among nontenured scholars. And a third emphasized that in all matters he "always stuck to the issues instead of my opinion."

Sexism and racism also affected job market experiences, especially for female region-related scholars. In the core of the discipline whose practitioners imagine themselves as committed to deconstructing stereotypes, assumptions about the oppression of Muslim women abound. One region-related anthropologist told us that she was often asked in job interviews, "How was it to be a woman working in this field?" She continued, "I was like, 'Noooo, I don't talk about that [i.e., gender in my research]. Haven't you noticed?' Like, I don't talk about that." Another noted, "You'd get these really odd questions that I felt prompted you to pick your allegiance." Others described faculty members trying to assess their "sympathies" for their Muslim interlocutors. And one person even turned down a job offer because she felt "Orientalized" during a campus visit.

Nonwhite anthropologists of any background that might be read as "Muslim" recounted job interviews where "inappropriate questions" were posed. Attiya Ahmad told us about situations "where someone is trying to acknowledge that I'm, quote, 'different,' but it comes out in inappropriate ways, in particular . . . because I am of diasporic South Asian background. . . . Somehow I can be conflated with my research subjects" (who were South Asian domestic workers in the Gulf). All these experiences must be understood as part of the larger gender and race politics of anthropology and academia, as Ahmad and her colleagues discuss in a 2013 article. In that piece, Ahmad describes a job interview at the American Anthropological Association conference that began with the interviewer commenting on her clothing: "Traded a scarf for a suit, eh? I bet you don't have to wear a suit in the Middle East."[29] Regardless of gender, when scholars' ethnicity was not immediately legible to interviewers, they were often questioned about their background in ways that—had an adverse hiring decision been made—could have been unlawful.[30] One person described this as "the question that you're not supposed to ask but you're still asking—From, 'oh [yours] is an interesting name' to 'you speak Arabic . . . how, why?' You know, just sort of hinting." While such experiences represent a shift from earlier forms of overt prejudice, they remain discriminatory nonetheless.

For these anthropologists on the market in the twenty-first century, approximately half viewed their MENA focus as an asset rather than a liability. Many even argued that a MENA focus was beneficial if one worked on certain topics, as long as one did not approach Palestine. "A Middle East anthropologist," one interlocutor explained, should in the view of search committees look like "somebody who works on Islam; like somebody who works on gender if it's a woman." There were multiple responses to search committees' seeming fixation on gender and Islam. Some reflected the deep hesitations felt keenly by region-related female scholars around assumptions that they somehow represented "Muslim women"—whether or not gender was part of their research agendas. As one such person put it:

> There wasn't a small liberal arts college . . . that didn't want me to teach something on gender, though I never, ever wrote anywhere that I worked on gender specifically. And that was to me outrageous that that was one of the things that they wanted me to do. . . . And I would say, "Well, I'm sure I could come up with a syllabus over time. It's not my area of focus, but . . . " like, where did it say on my cover letter that that's what I was doing?. . . . Where did they get the idea that I would be able to just pick up . . . and teach a class on sexuality and gender in the Middle East, for example?

Having to speak to US obsessions even if they are outside the realm of one's expertise was common; based on our continued conversations with colleagues, it shows no sign of abating. Another scholar told us in 2014, "I had a job interview via Skype last week . . . I was asked about ISIS and mass rapes of women, and to compare this to the treatment of women in Israel. I said that I'm not an expert on ISIS."[31]

Some of our interlocutors argued that such questioning demonstrated the lingering dominance in some departments of "second-wave feminist perspectives" which treated Muslim women (and their veils) as prime examples of gender oppression and that this translated into hiring decisions via ideas about how one should approach gender and sexuality in the region in teaching and scholarship. Others noted that anthropology departments where more current views prevailed nonetheless pigeonholed them, and were looking for scholars who treated Muslim women as a privileged other who can teach "us" the limitations of our own feminism. Anthropologists who could be read as Muslim (usually region-related or South Asian scholars) faced additional pressure to address religion whether or not it was their research focus; if it was, they often were forced to explain whether or not they agreed or sympathized with their subjects. One person who was consistently asked about her relationship to her informants described the experience as "such a peculiar question. If somebody was working on a different kind of social movement, say the Sandinistas in Nicaragua or the Hindutva in India, the assumption would be quite different even if you were from the country. The assumption with Muslim scholars is that you are 'one of them.' Even when I was interviewing for jobs, I was often asked if I was a 'believer.' I thought it was remarkable that people felt at liberty to ask such a question." Another interlocutor was also asked this question during a campus visit (in that case, it was whether or not she was Jewish). This is the sort of question that search committees are taught to avoid, both because it is discriminatory and because if the answer were to affect their decision, the institution would be violating hiring laws. Other scholars reported questions about Islam during campus visits even if it was not the topic of their research. As one interlocutor said, "I don't think Bruno Latour gets asked about Catholicism, right? So, um, so why do I have to talk about Islam when I'm talking about, you know, I'm talking about ports, I'm talking about ships." And several people responded to this job market environment by reframing themselves to intentionally highlight "the Islam side" of their work, to varying degrees of success.

The post-9/11 jump in employment opportunities, during which Islam or the region appeared on the radar of far more institutions as areas of interest for hiring, proved temporary when the 2008 economic crisis precipitated a decline in the entire academic job market. Our interlocutors who had looked for jobs in its wake were even more hesitant than their predecessors to voice unpopular perspectives and expressed a heightened sense of the risks campus visits might entail. One recent PhD explained that in presenting their scholarship for the market, they have conducted "a lot of self-censorship. There are a lot of things

I have not said." When pressed for an example, they responded, "There is nothing about Israel in my project. I mean, I don't even think I used the word." They instead finagled indirect ways to discuss issues relevant to their project that were related to Israeli military incursions.

There were also more MENA anthropologists on the job market than ever before, a trend that continues as we write. Those who were graduate students, postdocs, or actively on the job market as junior scholars when we interviewed them in 2012 and 2013 often articulated a tension between regional specialization as an asset and the dismal possibilities for academic jobs overall. Some of them were responding to grim job prospects by what they called "diversifying"—showing that they were able to research and teach anything. Here they drew on the corporate language that institutions themselves are highlighting in this economic moment. Indeed, in an ever-shrinking job market, scholarship may respond by conforming to market demands.

And the market loves Hollywood tropes. Into the 2000s, US military involvement in the region has triggered a resurgence of the "Indiana Jones" trope about anthropology in relation to MENA. One recent PhD described a pattern of response to her work during campus visits:

> 'Oh bravo, you've gone there' . . . I don't know if somehow there's this idea that it's the trenches, so there's this sort of like 'Oh, good for her'. . . . I have benefitted because I'm imagined to be someone who works in a place that's difficult . . . either difficult to be a woman or it's difficult because there's war, or that it's challenging. You're rewarded for that in some sense and at the same time I think that it's tricky . . . in the competitive market, I want that edge and yet I don't want to exploit, you know, experiences of living here and experiences of peoples' suffering and tragedy. . . . And one of the reasons they're interested in you is because yeah, it's a journalistic sense of like you were in the trenches and you've been on the battlefield and now you're going to come back and tell war stories.

Since so many non-MENA academics see the region as especially dangerous, fieldwork there has begun to carry the sort of cachet that working in nonurban small-scale communities used to hold for the discipline. Geopolitical shifts have brought MENA from anachronistic irrelevance to center stage within anthropology. It remains to be seen what kinds of effects changing US policies, as well as the recent uprisings in the region, will have—especially as the wave of scholars studying those uprisings hits the market.

Another, no less consequential, shift is occurring as well. While many graduate students and postdocs continue to self-censor their views on Israel-Palestine, some have begun to express the sense that "there's just much more leeway to talk about issues pertinent to Palestinians without anybody jumping on you" than there was in the past. This new discourse of possibility speaks to the changing tenor of Israel-Palestine politics on campuses across the United States. It is possible to read the extremely vehement and organized attacks we turn to in the next chapter as a panicked response to the fact that there *is* more space to talk about Palestinian rights in the academy than previously. That political opening does not necessarily translate into different job market experiences and may have come too late for Palestine scholars in terms of career opportunities— because in economic climates where there are fewer tenure-line jobs, institutions and search committees tend to hire "safely."[32] For this reason, a faculty member trained in the 1990s who teaches graduate students today suggested that beginning to work on Israel-Palestine in 2012 was "career suicide." In other words, this professor suggested that during the better financial moment before 2008, "there was an out" from Zionist pushback, but that the financial collapse of universities is leading to "a more conservative moment" that will negatively impact hiring in the field. It remains to be seen whether or not this will be the case.

· · ·

For many of our interlocutors, all of these early career experiences contributed to their socialization into the highly and multiply politicized worlds of Middle East Studies and anthropology. One of the key lessons people learned in graduate school and on the job market about how to handle these political aspects of working in the discipline and region was to put extra effort into protecting themselves. One recent PhD explained that they tend to "self-censor and regulate obsessively," and that this is "something that I have to spend twenty-five hours a day thinking or worrying about in almost all of my interactions." Another noted that people who don't research Israel-Palestine "don't dare mention it because it is a bomb" and "as academics . . . you will be tied up and held and crucified if you say the wrong thing." And a third explained that the intense practices of self-monitoring to manage these politics from graduate school onward take a toll on scholars themselves, who learn how "to walk around the issue and . . . to negotiate and maneuver so that it almost becomes second nature. So then it can appear like all is fine, but you have that tension or anxiety inside when you're dealing with these issues. . . . It's tough to realize, because it's an internal feeling, but it really is about self-censorship."

Yet in spite of the fears and discriminations faced in graduate school and on the job market, as well their self-censoring effects, our interlocutors chose to remain in academia. They did so out of a desire to learn more and educate others about MENA: a region whose peoples are demonized in US public discourse and who have suffered enormous costs to life and well-being, partly due to US actions. Indeed, one could read academics' persistence, despite the obstacles documented here, as a sign of commitment to being ethical citizens of the United States and the world.

3 Navigating Conflicts on the Job

Imagine starting a new career as an assistant professor of the contemporary Middle East and North Africa when public opinion is increasingly anti–Middle Eastern, anti-Arab, and anti-Muslim. When US military, political, and economic interventions, including support for Israel and certain authoritarian regimes, has devastating consequences for your research interlocutors. When those interventions kill hundreds of thousands of people in the region, as well as more and more Americans. When Israeli military attacks occur with an overwhelming regularity. When tragic consequences of once euphoric uprisings weigh heavily on one's heart. When criticism of the roles of the United States and especially Israel in perpetrating violence is not nearly as publicly acceptable as criticism of other regimes in the region. And when public empathy for Israeli or American victims vastly eclipses compassion for other Middle Eastern victims, despite the latter's staggeringly greater numbers. Imagine facing your students, colleagues, and public audiences at this time, when gross misinformation and stereotyping about a region where you have developed thick academic, social, and emotional ties dominate the media and infuse public discourse.

It is no surprise that in this climate, anthropologists have felt that they hold what one of our interlocutors called a "poison chalice"—knowledge and perspectives that one should share about the region's peoples and the interconnections of local and global power hierarchies, alongside the awareness that doing so without job security poses serious risks that must be constantly navigated to avoid negative repercussions. Imagine doing so as a person with family ties to MENA and doing so in the heart of empire: in a country that consistently refuses to hold Israel accountable in the United Nations and that increasingly subjects you to racialized policing, security, and border control processes. Or imagine doing so as a woman, knowing full well that the academy maintains gender hierarchies that favor your male colleagues—hierarchies that appear in how students treat you, in expectations for research, publishing, and service, in compensation, in public engagements, and in everyday interactions. For all scholars, but especially for women and minorities, it is challenging to start that first job knowing about cases of public attacks, tenure battles, and unhiring of MENA scholars and hearing echoes of incessant warnings from graduate school. It is challenging at a time like the 1950s to 1980s, when there are few disciplinary colleagues working in MENA to lean on for support. And it is challenging when, by the time there is a critical mass of such colleagues, the region has been positioned as the primary enemy of the United States and attacks on scholars escalate. Imagine holding that chalice as ever more students and members of the public are hungry for knowledge about the region, knowledge you can provide. This is what it has been like to be an anthropologist of the Middle East and North Africa.

Shifting Sexisms and Racisms

Gender, race, ethnicity, and generation shape how anthropologists have engaged their various publics—students, colleagues, and broader audiences—as well as the consequences they have faced for violating dominant narratives and expectations in these different venues. Some aspects of being a female and/or nonwhite anthropology professor grew easier following demographic shifts toward inclusivity in academe; some aspects of focusing on MENA in the United States grew easier as the subfield expanded. But racism and sexism persisted, albeit of a less flagrant variety.

Perhaps the biggest improvement is in terms of sexism. Women who began their careers in the 1960s and 1970s told stories about being one of a few (or sometimes the only) female scholars in their departments. Almost every female interlocutor who entered the academy prior to 1980, and quite a few who did between 1980 and 1990, described confronting sexism as junior faculty, even though this was not a specific question we posed. They recalled problems ranging from the absence of women's bathrooms in department buildings, to a lack of maternity leave policies, to harassment for being pregnant or nursing in the workplace. "I didn't know at the time that it was sinful, but I was pregnant," explained an anthropologist whose chair advised her to hide her pregnancy and who then had to take her newborn to class because there was no maternity leave. Colleagues of many of these women told them that they had to "publish twice as much as the guys" to get tenure, and one recalled learning from graduate students in the department that she was making half the salary of her male "age mates," a situation that was only partly ameliorated by the institution after it became a public scandal. Pay discrepancies continue among some scholars trained after 1990 as well.

Sexist challenges to women's legitimacy as scholars have hardly abated with new restrooms, the passing of Title IX, and struggles for pay equality. Women must still do extra work to prove the quality of their scholarship,[1] and their publications are sometimes overlooked by male scholars who do not cite them. Interlocutors across generations told us about colleagues who suggested that studies by or about women lack theory. As Catherine Lutz has written, such delegitimization has long existed in anthropology.[2] And indeed, we heard a complaint about the "feminization of anthropology" from an older-generation male scholar, who also suggested that studying women was "the path of least resistance" and a response to the "fashion" of feminism in academe. Female scholars of color, including region-related ones, face additional challenges in this regard. They described confronting colleagues' assumptions that they were somehow simultaneously an anthropologist and a native informant representing Muslim women (especially after 9/11).

What seems to have changed over time is the degree to which biases were explicitly stated. A scholar hired in the 1960s told us: "A colleague was going around [the room] saying rude things to women, and so he comes over to me and he says, 'What's your ethnicity?' And I said, 'You're a smart social scientist, why don't you guess?' He said, 'Are you Greek?' I said, 'No.' 'Are you Italian?' 'No.' 'Are you French?' 'No.' 'My, you must be one of those goddamn syphilitic Arabs!'" That's pretty explicit. Moving forward in time, a scholar hired in the 1980s expressed feeling "othered" and "diminished and pigeonholed" when a mentor who she presumed appreciated her anthropological scholarship dismissed her as one of a group of "Muslim feminist scholars." She felt she had been put in a religious category that she never claimed. And an anthropologist hired in the early 2000s shared a story of being interrogated by a colleague who the department chair had described as "very Zionist;" over lunch this colleague tried to pin down her religious identity and refused to accept that she was an atheist.[3]

As more and more region-related scholars of all genders were hired into tenure-track jobs, they often occupied an ambiguous racial space in their departments and institutions while experiencing increasing discrimination as Middle Easterners were racialized in the United States. Although shocking incidents of racism persist across the decades (especially in the xenophobic window immediately after 9/11), most have taken the form of microaggressions:

small comments here and there, notable silences or exclusions, and assumptions about a person based on their background.[4] Several people explained that they were sometimes seen as white in their departments and sometimes not, depending on the issue at hand; such experiences highlighted for them their always "not-quite-white" or "other" status. One scholar described a negative experience in a faculty collective in the 1980s as "feeling something that made me call up memories of being in fourth grade;" this person retrospectively understood their sense of exclusion as anti-Arab racism.

The intensified stereotyping of MENA after 9/11 in US public discourse provoked numerous racist incidents that infuriated all MENA scholars, but had a magnified impact on region-related scholars. One of them shared their dismay when a colleague expressed concern that a post-9/11 MENA lecture they had organized did not include "enough of a security presence" and said, "I get really nervous when I see these Middle Eastern men walking in with their computers." This scholar exclaimed indignantly in our interview, "She was literally afraid of a dark guy with his computer!" Another, trained in the 2000s, elaborated on the impact of such encounters:

> The reality is that if my name was Matt Smith and I was from California, then my actions would be very, very, very, very different. So when my name is very clearly [xxx] and people are trying to pronounce it, and then it's all of a sudden, "Where are you from?" you're immediately an "other." That's just very clear from the beginning. I've had every single type of response and reaction you can envision. And there is a kind of sense of entitlement people feel, which is to vocalize whatever comes to mind at that moment. So you just have to have thick skin, and you just have to be a good sport, and you just have to give people the benefit of the doubt and just remember that most people are good people, they mean well. I think the real challenge is that people also feel as if it's okay for them to ask deeply personal questions and also political questions. ... There's a kind of entitlement to kind of have those discussions, even when they're actually not that relevant, or even when there are other things that are at stake at that moment. Especially in professional contexts. So that's a real challenge. You have to, you just get used to your personal life and your political persuasions being scrutinized.

White anthropologists were not immune to these interactions, especially just after 9/11. A colleague remarked to one of our white interlocutors that she "must know all those terrorists." And after emailing colleagues Mark Twain's "War Prayer," a white male anthropologist trained at the turn of the 1980s received the response: "I've given your name to the FBI, because you work in the region so you obviously know some of these people." However, white scholars were sometimes able to avoid these encounters if they so chose. As one person said, "It's just a waste of my time to even engage with some of this seriously anti-Muslim rhetoric. . . . When you're just a new faculty member, you get sort of really upset and then you respond to it. . . . But nobody really engages with it because it's a waste of your time with people absolutely convinced that Muslims are such vicious people."

Skirting the matter was not as easy an option for region-related scholars, who often felt isolated or burdened with representing MENA or Islam. One told us that she regularly refused speaking invitations that began, "We're looking for a Muslim woman to speak on . . ." rather than "We're looking for a scholar to address such-and-such issues" because they conflated her work and identity. Another described feeling "like I really have to act as an apologist, or as an explainer to a group of people who are members of a society that whether they like it or not are part of a colonial world order, an imperial world order, and here I am kind of the native apologist . . . trying to explain why . . . [Muslims] are not extremists, stuff like that, that I don't feel like I should be apologizing for." And a third such scholar explained that attending the discipline's professional conference left her feeling "utter alienation" because the AAA maintains "a dominant ethos and discourse in which I certainly do not recognize myself and . . . I think that there's a racial politics to that, and that has to do more with being a post-colonial sort of non-white, non-American subject."

Feeling isolated sometimes intersected with campus politics. A scholar who is the only Arab American faculty member at their institution was serving on a committee that was discussing a student situation related to a Palestine activism event. This scholar was clearly expected to represent the Palestinian student's perspective and explain the event's context. When a colleague presented a Zionist argument against both the event and student, there was a resounding silence in the room until the scholar spoke up, even though several other committee members held similar (anti-Zionist) views about both the specific situation and Palestine politics. In this scholar's words, "during the meeting, one of my colleagues suggested that an Israeli professor calling a Palestinian student vermin was not a problem, and no one except me spoke up to disagree. This wasn't just irresponsible, this was putting the only Arab faculty member on campus on the spot." In politically inflected situations on campus, region-related scholars were often singled out to represent MENA or faced overt or microaggressive attack even if other faculty made stronger statements on the same matter. In other words, *who* is speaking matters a great deal in these contexts, and the resulting dynamics are often quite stressful for scholars.

Over time, these shifting racisms and sexisms, directed both at scholars and at the Middle Eastern and North African people with whom we work, exacted a toll. This toll is not quantifiable, but it certainly affected well-being in the workplace for all MENA scholars, modulated through their positionality. The emotional energies scholars must expend to deal with such ignorance and discrimination are most pronounced during tenure review. In that critical moment, Israel-Palestine politics becomes paramount, as does the degree to which a scholar has successfully self-censored up until that point.

The Politics of Tenure and Promotion

It is arguably tenure-track assistant professors who are the most cautious and likely to self-censor in relation to their various publics. Fears that Zionist colleagues or external organizations will instigate a successful attack against one's tenure are intense. However, we do not know of a single case of an actual tenure denial in anthropology that was clearly linked to a scholar's critical view of Israeli state policies and practices toward Palestinians. This suggests that these fears exceed the dangers and reveal the subtly menacing ways that trepidation intrinsically affects teaching, scholarship, and well-being. At the same time, perhaps there have been no such tenure denials because potentially controversial scholars do not get hired in the first place or because self-preservation efforts, including self-censorship, have successfully protected people through tenure.

In anthropology, two cases in particular have contributed to a climate of fear for pre-tenure faculty: one was a job loss and the other a very public battle (ultimately successful) for tenure. In a third case, an anthropologist was denied an administrative promotion most likely for political reasons. Our interviews revealed additional examples, in every decade, of anthropologists who encountered less severe but nonetheless disturbing problems during tenure review that the scholars in question attributed to Zionist political obstruction. Collectively, these situations demonstrate the impact that Zionist professors, alumni, and extracampus organizations can have on administrations, especially but not only when donor-based funding is at stake.

There is one (known) instance of dismissal of an assistant professor on the tenure track related to Israel-Palestine politics: the denial of Thomas Abowd's contract renewal at Wayne State University in 2008. This surprise decision came at the end of the academic year, just after Abowd received the university's President's Award for Excellence in Teaching and a significant merit raise. Not a single one of the complaints lodged against him was from his students. Instead, pressures came from Zionists in the local community as well as a few undergraduates he had never taught, including a white supremacist student. Their complaints were primarily related to a speech Abowd made at a political protest on campus organized by an activist student group and included allegations of "anti-white racism" and "anti-Semitism." In the end, the university admitted the charges were fraudulent, and Abowd agreed to resign with a settlement, "because I didn't really want to be there anymore . . . and I thought, my god, I don't know if I want to come up for tenure here, I hate it here. I just found the administration hostile." He has since detailed the experience in an essay on the violation of his academic freedom, aptly included in an edited volume that links the repression of academic dissent to American empire.[5]

This case joins that of anthropologist Nadia Abu El-Haj, whose tenure review at Barnard College made national news. In August 2007, a Barnard alumna began circulating an online petition called "Deny Nadia Abu El-Haj Tenure." The petition attacked Abu El-Haj and her award-winning 2001 monograph *Facts on the Ground: Archaeological Practice and Territorial Self-Fashioning in Israeli Society*, which was published by the University of Chicago Press. The attacks accused her of fabricating information, not having language skills, and being fundamentally hostile to Israel for political reasons. In a thorough *New Yorker* article on the case,[6] Jane Kramer revealed that the alumna lived in an Israeli settlement in the Palestinian West Bank, "which, to [the alumna's] mind, was not occupied territory but 'Israel for forty years.'" The alumna told Kramer "by the end of a few pages of *Facts on the Ground*," she "knew that Abu El-Haj was 'dangerous' and 'wrong.'" Her petition had been based on second-hand information about the book from "the militant Zionist blogs and web sites that had been tracking Abu El-Haj's career since her book appeared."[7] Despite the fact that several Jewish media sources exposed the petition as inaccurate and misleading, according to Kramer, the alumna continued to gather signatures and to threaten the university that it would lose its donor base if it granted Abu El-Haj tenure. At the same time, in a blatant violation of normal tenure procedures, a Zionist professor at Barnard began speaking against Abu El-Haj publicly on campus and in the media, and accusing the institution of bias in the review process. Other faculty put forward petitions supporting the tenure process and defending the institution against these (mostly external) attacks. The American Anthropological Association also weighed in by affirming its "commitment to rejecting public petitions as a means for influencing tenure evaluations" in a press release.[8] In the end, Abu El-Haj received tenure, and by all accounts Barnard handled the process professionally, despite what she called the "colossally public" nature of the case and the attacks against her.

Abowd and Abu El-Haj were attacked while in vulnerable pre-tenure positions. Accusations of anti-Semitism or bias can also thwart reviews for promotion to full professor or attempts to move to a new position. In 1984, when Carolyn Fluehr-Lobban sought to leave her tenured position at Rhode Island College to become the associate vice president of human resources at the University of Vermont, she faced such accusations from a very vocal faculty member—in this case a non-MENA anthropologist. During her campus visit, a search committee member told her about "rumors" circulating about her supposed anti-Semitism. Fluehr-Lobban emailed the committee chair about these rumors, saying that she would answer any questions about her "personal and professional commitment to a non-racialist view of society," as she had done considerable antiracist work during her career, including establishing committees for women's rights and affirmative action at her college. After being informed that she did not get the position, she requested and received the letter that the chair of the anthropology department, Stephen Pastner, had written to the search committee and other college officials a week before her interview. It alleged that she was anti-Semitic. Pastner's "evidence" was two passages from a 1980 edited volume chapter in which Fluehr-Lobban discussed Palestinian women's role in the growing resistance movement against "Zionist occupation" and the "settler colonial state" of Israel. Criticism of Israel and of Zionism here is erroneously equated with anti-Jewish sentiment; thus an attack based on that slippage between Judaism and Zionism may have cost a scholar employment.[9]

These three cases—along with similar ones in other disciplines[10]—highlight three critical factors relevant to the experiences of most of our interlocutors: while such problems are not new, extracampus groups and alumni have grown more influential in academic politics; a scholar's racial, ethnic and/or religious identity shapes attacks on them; and the demographics of a campus and surrounding area matter. During Wayne State's investigation of Abowd, the university lawyer asked him three times (in front of his union representative): "Are you a Muslim?" This question illustrates the persistence and intensification of discriminatory treatment of region-related, especially Arab, scholars. As Abowd told us, "I can't imagine if I were just a mainstream white guy or a Jewish professor that they would have had the nerve to ask me what my religion was or treat me like this." Similarly, a series of attacks at Columbia, including that on Abu El-Haj, have targeted Palestinian academics. Most often they are men, painted as "angry" and "violent," in keeping with the gendered stereotypes of Arabs and Palestinians in the United States.

Wayne State University is a campus located in an area which until recently was home to a large Jewish community dominated by older generation pro-Israel perspectives. Increasing numbers of Arab students and other students of color now place its alumni donor base at odds with its current student population. And as Jane Kramer noted, "As many as a third of Barnard's students and a quarter of Columbia's undergraduate students are Jewish" and "for the more sheltered of those students it may also be their first experience of a community where Israel's policies are discussed and challenged, rather than endorsed de facto; where Muslim students share their classrooms and Muslim professors, or professors they assume are Muslim, teach them. They are often alarmed by the shock of free speech that is not their own."[11]

Columbia (and its affiliate, Barnard) have also been a focus for attack because it was the academic home of Edward Said—a prominent Palestinian professor of English (and author of *Orientalism*) known for his advocacy of Palestinian rights—until his death in 2003. As Abu El-Haj told us, "It wasn't about me. . . . They had set their sights on Columbia . . . and it's New York City politics." Here she was referring to the especially strong influence of right-wing Zionist organizations and alumni in New York City, who have monitored and regularly targeted local colleges and universities (not without protest from anti-Zionist Jews or those committed to academic freedom).[12] Additionally, professors working in institutions with evangelical or millennial Christian populations (which often support Israel as part of their views on biblical prophecy)[13] are sometimes attacked for presenting critical views of Israeli state policies.

MENA anthropologists know that all of these factors matter. As one Palestine scholar told us, her promotion to tenure was relatively easy because "I'm in a place where they don't have a well-organized [pro-Israel] lobby. I mean, there is one here, but they're not very effective, and luckily we have an administration that, when they have come around to complain, they just say, we have free speech here and they move on." Our research suggests that the majority of administrators have shepherded junior scholars' careers such that the tenure review process is protected from external influence.

The cases of Abowd, Abu El-Haj, and Fluehr-Lobban represent extreme versions of more common experiences of politicized obstruction to academic practice. Nearly every MENA anthropologist has had to deal with some aspect of this problem, often filtered through their background, institutional location, and whether or not they work on or teach about Islam, US empire, and, most critically, Israel-Palestine. Dealing with obstructionism is particularly trying in the classroom, where one tries to open critical analytic vistas only to find some students seeking to block discussion. Most disturbingly, such students are increasingly enabled by outside groups.

Classroom Conflicts

Student surveillance of MENA professors' teaching and other campus activities, as well as complaints from students and parents about these professors, dates back to at least the 1970s, riding on the heels of similar tactics from the McCarthy and Vietnam eras. A confidential 1969 memorandum circulated by the American Jewish Committee (AJC) alleged an Arab propaganda campaign against Israel on US campuses and launched a decades-long offensive to fight, through monitoring and surveillance, the inclusion of Arab and Arab American faculty on campuses, as well as Arab (especially pro-Palestinian) perspectives in curricula. In the 1970s and 1980s, organizations such as the AJC, the American Israel Public Affairs Committee, and the Anti-Defamation League (ADL) published numerous tracts and held conferences to promote this strategy and train sympathetic students and faculty.[14] Some of our interlocutors noted that the period immediately following the 1990 Gulf War grew especially difficult for MENA professors, with an increase in both FBI and student surveillance.

Since then, campus surveillance and intimidation have increased in intensity and scope, fueled by War on Terror rhetoric, media technologies, and additional right-wing and Zionist organizations providing further training and material support to student monitors. Over the decades, student and external organization tactics have included recording classes without permission, walking out of class, sending threatening emails to professors, making phone complaints to faculty and administrators, threatening to give negative evaluations or outright lying on evaluation forms, interrupting the professor or other students during class in a hostile manner, and, on occasion, making threats to professors' physical safety. In 2014, there's even an app for that, called CombatHateU, which encourages students to "See it. Report it." immediately using their smartphones. This mobile phone application asks students to report anti-Semitism, but discussions on its associated Twitter feed indicate that this includes anything and everything perceived to be critical of Zionism or Israel.[15]

Over half of our interlocutors across all generations experienced some form of classroom intimidation and heightened tension. Some felt that being a young professor put one at risk because students did not trust their expertise. It is particularly striking that the scholars who students accused of being "anti-

Semitic" or of treating Jewish students unfairly or "hating" them were—in almost every case—people who were either region-related and/or assumed to be Muslim. And at all career stages, female scholars were more likely to describe political attacks on their teaching than were male scholars. This difference may be due to some students' lack of respect for female authority. It may also relate to the greater tendency among male scholars, especially though not exclusively white men trained prior to the mid-1990s, to explain their success in avoiding attacks by pointing to their "objective" or "balanced" modes of presentation.[16] It is also quite likely that white men experience fewer attacks when they speak, take attacks less seriously, and/or act as though they do not take them seriously—because they occupy a position of privilege as authoritative voices in the academy and public sphere.[17] The extent to which one feared reprisals also depended on citizenship; a scholar who does not hold US citizenship reminded us why they are especially cautious about being too vocal on political matters: "You [e.g., other MENA anthropologists] think about issues like tenure, but you don't think of larger issues, like, what if I get deported?"[18]

The lesser number of our interlocutors who have not faced major classroom problems attributed this either to their reticence to address certain issues or to their institution's demographics and location. Our quantitative analysis of patterns of classroom problems concurs with their notion that the quantity of those problems was directly proportionate to the degree to which students, alumni, administrations, boards of trustees, and communities surrounding campuses expressed Zionist views or were home to active Zionist organizations. This fact sometimes led scholars to assume that the reason they did *not* face classroom conflicts was the lower proportion of Jewish students on their campus—a problematic assumption that collapses Judaism with Zionism and sidesteps the structural and political causes of attacks on scholars. Anthropologists' observations in a few cases that Jewish Israeli students were "better" in the classroom than Americans underscore the importance of avoiding this assumption. Those interlocutors noted that Israeli students often understood more about Israel-Palestine and sometimes presented perspectives that challenged those of American Jewish Zionist students. Scholars who taught on campuses that they described as "progressive" or "social justice–oriented" often had no problems at all. And everyone who had taught in both the United States and United Kingdom noted the vast difference in those experiences, where people in the United Kingdom "are relatively totally free to say things about the Arab-Israeli conflict that you can't say openly in the U.S."—namely, to be critical of *all* parties to the conflict, but especially those that hold more power (e.g., Israel and the United States).[19]

Such national differences in classroom politics brought into sharp relief the fact that in the center of empire it was dangerous to criticize that empire or its allies, especially Israel. An anthropologist who has been teaching for decades told us that "the pressure never stopped" in her classes; she was monitored by students and the FBI when she did teach-ins on Vietnam and again more recently by students who sent recordings of her classes on Israel-Palestine to outside organizations. Another said that Zionist student activists would take her classes pass/no pass and then walk out en masse during lectures or write terrible evaluations. With us and in print, senior anthropologist Laura Nader reflected on teaching Julie Peteet's first book on women in the Palestinian resistance movement, *Gender in Crisis* (published by Columbia University Press), in a large introduction to anthropology course in the early 1990s at Berkeley. She wrote, "A lobby of parents came asking why Palestinians were being humanized when they were terrorists, while insinuating that, as a result, the class had an anti-Semitic outlook."[20] Especially common were student complaints that a class or syllabus was not "balanced"—which typically meant that the course included academic materials that either analyzed Palestinian perspectives and experiences or critiqued Israeli or US state policies and actions. Some department chairs or colleagues warned anthropologists not to teach about Israel-Palestine at all. A scholar who teaches at an institution where Zionist perspectives dominate was advised (sympathetically) by his chair that he "might want to avoid the Palestinian issue on your syllabus" for a MENA anthropology course, because "you don't want to have your ass being the first one hung out the window."

This is exactly what happened to anthropologist Smadar Lavie when she taught a class called Ethnographies of Palestine and Israel at the University of California at Davis in 1993, just before she submitted her tenure file.[21] Although she had taught the class before (and after) without incident, that year a group of students, encouraged by the Hillel rabbi, organized a series of personalized attacks on her and her teaching. Written testimony of a teaching assistant from the course states, "There has been a deliberate attempt to undermine Professor Lavie's professorial authority in the class. . . . Talking with students after their first review session revealed that several individuals connected with the Hillel House approached students after class, denouncing it as anti-Semitic." These attempts to undermine the course included, as recorded in the testimony of an enrolled student, disrupting Lavie's lectures and arguing with her "destructively" by "distorting" her arguments. The testimony noted that students had organized a phone tree to coordinate actions against Lavie and frequently met after class to discuss how "'she had a chip on her shoulder because she was Mizrahi,' and therefore wanted to make Israel look bad; how she was a self-hating Jew." It also stated that its author overheard another student say, "I will see to it that she gets fired; I have my connections," and that "he also later said that he was going to have her face smashed into the ground." According to multiple reports, the Hillel rabbi told people not to participate in Lavie's assignment to interview an Israeli and a Palestinian; this made it difficult for students to complete coursework. However, the rabbi himself granted interviews to certain students; graders reported that some papers quoted him accusing Lavie of being "near-psychotic" and a "self-hating Jew."[22] Students also disparaged one of the teaching assistants, who they claimed was incapable of grading fairly due to having Middle Eastern background. In response to this constellation of problems, UC Davis decided to offer another class on the "Arab-Israeli conflict," to be taught at Hillel House the following term and for which students could reuse papers from Lavie's class for credit. Numerous faculty wrote to the administration on Lavie's behalf, expressing consternation that student complaints were allowed to derail a course in this manner and suggesting that Lavie was, as stated in one letter, "clearly" the target of a campaign to discredit and punish her.

Many of our interlocutors believed that classroom conflicts increased in number and intensity following 9/11, a sense borne out by our data. Navigating the post-9/11 teaching minefields provoked anxiety for everyone, but especially for those who received PhDs right around that time. We were part of a cohort of MENA scholars, mostly anthropologists, who responded to this stress by creating "Academic Freedom and Professional Responsibility after 9/11: A Handbook for Scholars and Teachers." This handbook detailed strategies for fostering productive classroom discussion in the tense environment of the time; it also contained advice and resources for how to avoid problems and deal with them should they arise. It achieved wide circulation and received many requests for library acquisition, so we decided to make it freely available online.[23] In a sign that minefields persisted, in 2012 a group of younger anthropologists updated and recirculated the handbook. Continued inquiries from around the country suggest that we were responding to a distinct need not just in MENA anthropology, but also among scholars in a variety of disciplines and regions.

This need is reflected in many of our interlocutors' accounts, as they described how the teaching climate worsened appreciably in the first few years of the second intifada and after 9/11. This was especially the case for region-related professors and graduate student instructors. A student informed one graduate instructor, on the first day of class, that she had "looked [her] up." Our interlocutor continued, "And she made sure I knew that . . . and said to me,

'I know you signed the [institution's] divestment [from Israel] thing.'" During that same class, a parent called this anthropologist and "said she was really worried when she found out it was me who would be teaching her daughter." Another graduate instructor had students record his lectures without permission; other students wrote an article in the campus newspaper linking him to Hamas on the flimsy basis of his Arab ethnicity.

A region-related faculty member teaching in New York at the time had a group of Hillel students gather "50 signatures from rabbis and people that I don't know" on a petition that said "that since I got hired there was an anti-Semitic sentiment on campus." When she complained to the administration, she learned that one of her colleagues was "running around saying that [she was] anti-Semitic." A student in one of this same anthropologist's classes asked her baiting questions unrelated to the topic at hand, like "What do you think of the Jews in Iraq?" After the professor responded that this was not the topic under discussion, the student spread the rumor that she had instead claimed that Jews never existed in Iraq. Administrators called the professor in to discuss the matter but took no action. Several years later, a student activist with the Zionist group StandWithUs posted a video on YouTube (that has since been removed) attacking the professor, reiterating the allegations, and falsely claiming that the professor had been reprimanded and denied the right to teach about the Middle East for the rest of the semester.

Indeed, specious accusations of anti-Semitism abounded. Another region-related scholar reported that twice parents had accused her of not grading fairly because she "must hate Jews." And yet another was accused of teaching anti-Semitic material (Joe Sacco's work of graphic journalism) when a student who was struggling emotionally with the book's criticisms of Israel shared those struggles with the Hillel rabbi on campus. The rabbi wrote a letter to the president, dean, and provost accusing the professor of anti-Semitism without referencing the student or the situation. As in the vast majority of cases reported to us, the professor's department was supportive, but, she said, "It was stupid and it was exhausting . . . and unpleasant to deal with." The dean was less supportive and essentially asked the professor to explain "how I wasn't teaching anti-Semitism and what exactly I was up to." This sort of questioning left her doubting the level of support she would have received from senior administrators "if push came to shove, like if the university came under a lot of pressure." It also left her feeling, because she was a relatively new faculty member, that she "had to do image and damage control, like meet a lot of people and tell them how I'm a nice person and that I wasn't a raging anti-Semite." She told us that "the worst experience of the whole thing" was when a student later approached her and said, "I heard that you hate Jewish students, and I just wanted to make sure . . . that [you wouldn't] fail me if I take your class." The specific book that triggered this entire episode—Sacco's *Palestine*—is ultimately irrelevant. The larger implication here is that students think that they shouldn't have to read anything that makes them uncomfortable, and that they can enlist others who are not professors to support them. According to this logic, students would never be exposed to books that challenge them or make them confront painful or difficult histories, like Dee Brown's *Bury My Heart at Wounded Knee*, Harper Lee's *To Kill a Mockingbird*, Toni Morrison's *Beloved*, or Elie Wiesel's *Night*.

Alongside heightened surveillance, complaints, and attacks on professors, 9/11 reinforced the pressures that anthropologists felt to use teaching to counter intensified media stereotyping of Islam and the region. While MENA scholars had been doing that since the 1960s, many described a new urgency, responsibility, and burden in the wake of 9/11. Scholars sought to dispel students' preconceptions about Muslims, and many described "constantly battling gender stereotypes." Several noted that students were primed to see Muslim women as oppressed or came into class thinking that they were going to learn "how to save" them from supposedly violent Muslim men. This pedagogical mission became, unsurprisingly, quite racialized. A region-related scholar echoed others in her recollections of her gender and Islam courses:

> There is a certain hostility towards it, or reticence, or polite forms of racism. There are all sorts of issues at play and [these are] absolutely animated as well by the fact that . . . most of them keyed in pretty quickly that I'm of Muslim background, so that created problematic dynamics. . . . I had a student come up to me who said, "I'm reluctant to address this question with you, my mom told me not to, because you're a woman of color who is Muslim." . . . Like it was a weird way of trying to acknowledge positionality and racialized and gendered discourses, but . . . making it such that all my answers can only ever be understood in those ways. [It was also] a way of disempowering me.

Institutional specificity—especially location and student demographics—shaped scholars' approaches to fighting stereotypes. A longtime professor at a small-town state school explained that because her campus was "out of the way," with "no Arabs and few Jewish students," much of her teaching was about "just having to try to explain that these aren't people wandering around with camels where all the women are veiled and they're not just all backward, unsophisticated. . . . The Middle East is complex!" Overall, faculty who taught in larger institutions in rural areas or the central states were more likely to report that their students knew very little about the region beyond Orientalist stereotypes or that they faced "basic apathy" most of the time, while several who worked in New England noted that rather than exoticized images, they had to confront assumptions that "Arabs and Muslims are enraged zealots coming to kill us." As one of them explained, "A big part of my job ends up being, 'Muslims are not psychopathic lunatics,' you know, 'Muslims are human.'" Those who taught in or near New York City described having to contend with how to address the 9/11 attacks in a way that responsibly contextualized their underlying causes while remaining mindful of their students' personal reactions. And a few who taught at institutions with many Muslim students or very active Muslim Student Associations noted the challenge of teaching practicing Muslims who "think they know more than I know" about Islam. Faculty at institutions with large ROTC programs or in regions where students were likely to have a relationship to the military, as well as those with veterans of the Afghanistan and Iraq wars in their classrooms, had to navigate slightly different terrain. A few reported evaluations that accused them of being "unpatriotic," or told us that Iraq, not Palestine, was the most challenging topic to teach. One observed that veterans were far more "open to seeing the Middle East in very different ways" than ROTC students.

The chalice thus sometimes contained poison, but many of our interlocutors appreciated it nonetheless. They highlighted the sense of possibility created by new student interest in the region after 9/11 and again after the uprisings that began in 2011. In one region-related anthropologist's words,

> The task of a teacher on the Middle East . . . can be a delicate task in the sense that most of the students . . . are raised post-9/11, and so this is the new normal for them in some ways. And the new normal includes Islamophobia, includes the War on Terror, etc., etc. So there's a sort of a historically specific challenge, but it also means that there's a historically specific opportunity . . . that the stakes are greater for these students. . . . Let's say for the sort of average American student . . . there are all of these preconceptions, but there is also a real curiosity and a desire to learn and unlearn. And then for students who are either international students or sort of new first-generation immigrants, there is a different relationship to these kinds of issues, which can make for really fascinating possibilities in the classroom. . . . It makes the task of teaching this stuff a very arduous one, but it also is a really exciting opportunity, because you can literally see those flashbulb moments, and the unthinking and rethinking, and that's quite extraordinary.

Arduous possibility. Our interlocutors of younger generations expressed this sentiment more than those who had been teaching for decades; the latter often sounded resigned or simply exhausted by years of dealing with stereotypes, attacks, and the politics of the classroom. No matter the generation, however, these experiences—whether firsthand or not—motivated scholars to develop and implement strategies to protect themselves in the classroom, in order to reduce the damage these confrontations could inflict on their professional and personal lives.

Vigilance in the Classroom and in Curricular Programming

MENA anthropologists developed a variety of pedagogical techniques to avoid the aforementioned conflicts, including cultivating a nonconfrontational teaching style, ensuring that all students had an opportunity to speak in class, adding protective addenda to their syllabi, and avoiding certain topics. Junior scholars expressed feeling especially vulnerable because they lacked the protection of tenure and did not yet feel skilled at dealing with classroom conflict. They often took great care to avoid being targeted by student spies.[24] Many added language to their syllabi forbidding unauthorized recording of class lectures; others included sections detailing guidelines for class discussions involving different political perspectives or emphasizing the importance of referring to course readings in those discussions. A few reported actively watching for moles in their classes, and most vigilantly refrained from expressing their personal political views in class, while allowing students to do so. As one explained, "I learned very early on that if I took a strong political stance on anything, the students would turn me off. They will simply bracket you and say 'Oh well, he's a liberal.' . . . So I have spent a lot of time developing strategies for making them come around to the questions I wanted to scream at them." Most distressingly, several scholars said they felt intense disincentives to teach about MENA at all because of the labor required to create a smooth classroom experience.

Disincentives and cautious pedagogical strategies were especially pertinent when it came to Israel-Palestine; scholars were far more wary of teaching it than topics like Islam or the Iraq war. Many who had not conducted fieldwork in Israel or the occupied Palestinian territories, but who had expertise in the relevant anthropological scholarship, expressed extreme reluctance to teach it. Junior scholars were especially scared; several said that they would "never" teach about Israel-Palestine, even if they felt knowledgeable about the subject matter. One declared, "I simply will not teach a class about Israel and Palestine, even though that's a country that I have considerable knowledge in and expertise on. I just won't do it. It's not worth the trouble." A tenured scholar who regularly teaches about Iraq and Afghanistan said that she has "a clear sense that when it comes to Israel-Palestine, you watch out, you make sure you don't say things that will get you into trouble. . . . With the exception of the Israeli-Palestinian conflict, I never monitor myself in class. I only monitor myself in that one issue, which I think everybody has to do." In all, over ten anthropologists trained in the 1990s and several others trained in the 2000s said that they steered clear of teaching about Israel-Palestine in any of their courses, some even after gaining tenure.

Faculty who did venture to teach about Palestine-Israel carefully honed additional strategies to avoid problems. These included addressing issues in historical rather than contemporary terms as much as possible, presenting quantitative data (like numbers of deaths on each side) and allowing students to notice differences themselves, focusing on facts or theory, or only teaching the subject in seminars with large workloads to encourage students who were registering solely as monitors to drop the class. They also perfected a nonconfrontational classroom style, consistently saying things like "it's a major tragedy for both peoples" or starting semesters by deconstructing concepts like "balance" and "objectivity" to preempt criticism. One person who used to avoid teaching about Israel-Palestine—because he feared public attacks and websites like Campus Watch—decided that his position was "untenable" after attending a teaching workshop on MENA at the American Anthropological Association meetings.[25] But he still only included it alongside other material rather than explicitly, allowing it to "seep in around the edges." Another scholar, who was not reluctant to teach about Israel-Palestine, said that he nevertheless "felt sort of paralyzed by the breadth of knowledge that seemed required to really create a defense against attacks or create [what students would see as] a legitimate argument." He described the experience as "treading on eggshells." This anthropologist, like a few others whose fieldwork was not in Israel or the occupied Palestinian territories, sometimes refused to teach about it because it required amassing reams of extra data beyond course materials, a reluctance that did not prevent them from teaching about other countries and regions where they had not conducted research.

While most of our interlocutors focused on the classroom as the site of actual and potential confrontations with students, several also highlighted curricular program development as an arena that compelled self-protection. As late as 2000, many institutions—especially small liberal arts colleges, community colleges, and branch campuses of state schools—were not offering MENA-related courses. After 9/11, many of these institutions called on existing faculty (or made hires) to build Middle East Studies, Arabic, or Islamic Studies programs, often in response to student demand. But administrators did not always understand that MENA program building is when, as one anthropologist said, "all the knives come out." They sometimes questioned faculty decisions in stereotypical ways (like "Can you in good conscience encourage female students to go to Egypt and Jordan [for study abroad]?") or refused faculty suggestions to improve the aforementioned classroom dynamics. In one case, an untenured professor went to his program director and asked him in vain to facilitate a discussion of "polarity in our classes" so that junior faculty could learn from senior faculty how to handle it. Faculty at small institutions frequently felt that their efforts to meet student demands for more MENA curricular offerings were wholly unsupported by their administrations. There were, of course, exceptions, and a few anthropologists expressed gratitude that their institutions had thus far been proactively supportive, in one case regularly checking in with a faculty member to nip any problems in the bud before they grew.

One example in particular highlights the ways that administrators frequently put scholars in catch-22 situations—a practice that contributed to our interlocutors' general sentiment that they would receive no administrative support if push came to shove, so they needed to protect themselves preemptively. An anthropologist was tasked with bringing Arabic language courses to campus and establishing a Middle East Studies program, in what became an arduous process. Administrators stipulated that in order to hire an Arabic instructor, the institution simultaneously had to hire a Hebrew instructor. They also questioned the search committee's judgments about native Arabic speakers, asking whether they would be able to teach the language and conveying (in the strong impression of our interlocutor) "the hidden [negative] message that they might be Muslims." As this untenured anthropologist worked to develop Middle East Studies, the Judaic Studies program chair warned them, in an effort to be helpful, to "not pursue this too much because you will be challenged." The dean later suggested that alumni would discontinue their donations if they thought Middle East Studies was "a gateway to Islamic Studies." The anthropologist eventually postponed the project until after tenure because it was "such a hot potato for us and became so toxic." Another of our interlocutors faced similar accusations that the Middle East Studies program she was building for her institution was an Islamic Studies program in sheep's clothing. Such misrepresentations occur with alarming ease. It is also disconcerting that the scholarly discipline of Islamic Studies—well established at many institutions—is presumed to be less academic than say, Jewish Studies or Catholic Studies.

In many cases related to curricular program building, administrators and other faculty members cautioned MENA anthropologists against angering alumni donors or boards of trustees. One professor was called upon to defend the Model United Nations program to a trustee who "wanted to know why the hell we were funding a Model Arab League." The defense worked, but the incident demonstrated for him that "on the one hand, everyone believes that Arabic should be taught and that we should have a strong Middle Eastern program. But at the same time, there's some worry that it shouldn't be something that's going to cause us any grief." An administrator at another institution told an anthropologist that Arabic was "a touchy topic" and that because the institution's donors were mostly from the Jewish community, this faculty member needed to locate Arab donors to support the Arabic program. The presumption that all Jewish alumni, trustees, or donors will oppose Arabic or Middle East Studies programs again problematically collapses Judaism with an assumed (Zionist and obstructionist) political position. Similarly, the assumption that Arab donors must support Arabic language instruction conflates identity with development interests. Encounters with academic institutions related to alumni, donors, and boards of trustees extended much further than the curriculum, of course, and often came to a head around cocurricular programming, which similarly prompted feelings of trepidation and exhaustion as well as strategies of self-preservation for MENA anthropologists.

Pressures Faced in Engaging Broader Publics

Academic life is not just about teaching and research. It also involves sharing that research with broader publics in conferences, student-organized campus events, and lectures. While MENA anthropologists have always done public outreach, after 9/11 this work took on new urgency. Many found themselves called upon to educate campus communities about Islam or the region—especially if they were one of the only (or the only) faculty member with such expertise at their institution. Some had to counteract the effects of Islamophobic events; one new faculty member described feeling pressured to hold teach-ins to "undo the work that Islamophobic speaker Ayaan Hirsi Ali had done on campus." Others had to teach well-intentioned colleagues the basics about Islam.[26] And media outlets reached out to MENA scholars, sometimes in coordination with their institutions' PR offices. While some anthropologists were happy to engage these various publics,[27] others hesitated because they feared negative reprisals.

Those fears stemmed from the fact that organizations external to colleges and universities have targeted MENA scholars' broader activities in ways similar to their interference in the classroom. These groups have rallied community members to be disruptive or ask hostile (often irrelevant) questions at public events, created blacklists of faculty, and even mounted campaigns to fire faculty—all under broader threats of public shaming and ceasing donor support.[28] Such external pressures—along with frequent hostility from individual audience members—have affected many anthropologists, but female, younger, and region-related scholars, as well as those without US citizenship, described them more intensely. At the same time, while attacks on scholars for their public lectures and personal political views cut across cohorts, it was primarily those with tenure who bore the brunt of pressure on public programming—for the basic structural reason that they were in positions of leadership (directing a center or program, for example) and therefore in the spotlight.

With very few exceptions, MENA anthropologists thought that external intervention—while neither new nor unprecedented—was both more frequent and more intense in the twenty-first century, following what appeared to be a brief respite in the 1990s.[29] One region-related scholar compared these eras, describing the 1990s as the "halcyon days" when "it seemed that in a theoretically sophisticated postcolonial world in which you were able to sort of have a disciplinary grounding and orientation, that you weren't necessarily going to be bullied out of the field just because you were Palestinian or just because of a certain set of political associations and things like that. . . . And then, of course, 9/11 happened and we were all swept into a newly politicized environment, at which point everything became acute again and the threats were real again." Along with the War on Terror, the new century brought the beginning of the second intifada and widespread use of new media technologies. Additionally, it seems that Zionist organizations felt threatened by the newly open discussions of the Israeli state and its policies on campuses that marked the 1990s and 2000s.[30] We heard about the especially toxic atmosphere of the early 2000s from many interlocutors, including those who had weathered storms in the 1970s and 1980s. An anthropologist trained at the turn of the 1990s told us, "Let me tell you, my first drop-down whatever fight with a colleague . . . where he was out of control, was after the second intifada had started. . . . And absolutely, after the second intifada started, if I gave talks, it got more hostile. . . . Suddenly, the stakes were different. . . . It was unbelievable, the shift." Even in earlier decades, however, the attacks did not feel any easier. Colleagues recalled external aggressions related to their labor activism or their critical perspectives on the war in Vietnam or apartheid in South Africa. But they mostly said that Zionist attacks were, as one person put it, "the worst of it."

Sometimes, audience members were hostile to lectures on Islam in general, asking belligerent questions that ignored the scholar's research and drew instead on stereotypes about Muslims, what one interlocutor described as "Orientalist nonsense." Other anthropologists dealt with aggressive questions when they criticized US foreign policy in the region.[31] Several received comments from audience members such as, "It's people like you that caused 9/11 to happen." However, the vast majority of confrontations with antagonistic audiences followed lectures that included criticism of Israeli state policies and actions; sometimes just describing Israeli military attacks or presenting research on Palestinians that treated them like human beings was enough to provoke accusations of bias.

These public lectures frequently led to extensive and hostile questioning, as well as audience disruptions, sometimes organized by external pressure groups. As one person put it, "All of us have the experience of dealing with aggressive audiences, aggressive questioning from audiences—questions that are off topic, like where Palestinians should be relocated—when I'm trying to make a point about Foucault!" Another noted that she had "been yelled at [in public lectures] on a regular basis," especially after the second intifada began. When Lara was scheduled to lecture about the Lebanese political party Hizbullah at Rice University in a series organized by a Middle East historian, her host alerted her to a newspaper article published prior to her visit that called for "at least 101 individuals who are concerned about Israel" to attend and "ask the pertinent questions" during the Q&A.[32] Many members of the packed audience held pieces of paper to which they referred while asking questions, which suggests that a list had been produced before she spoke, presuming to know precisely what she would say. The effect was to stack the Q&A with accusatory questions about terrorism, anti-Semitism, and why "they teach their children to hate," interspersed with occasional outbursts directed either at the speaker or other audience members. Lara, as well as a number of other scholars who have faced such hostility, also reported receiving nasty or threatening emails afterwards.

A few of our interlocutors described situations where hostility escalated beyond verbal interactions. During a lecture at a liberal arts college, an audience member wearing a Christian Zionist T-shirt was caught secretly filming the speaker. When asked to stop, he made a scene and had to be escorted off campus by security. On another occasion, an anthropologist was accosted after a lecture by a group of angry audience members, one of whom grabbed her arm, shouting that she should rescind her US citizenship. Again, security guards had to intervene. And although many of our interlocutors accepted verbally aggressive audiences as "par for the course," a few noted that they—often to their own dismay—had decided to either give fewer lectures overall or avoid speaking about politicized issues as a result. Many also steel themselves before lecturing, preparing answers to typical hostile questions, even if those questions are unrelated to the research being presented. They sometimes ask their hosts to set rules for the Q&A or remind them to insist that audience members ask a question rather than simply rant.

Even anthropologists whose lectures had *nothing* to do with Israel-Palestine sometimes encountered hostility from audience members who saw any discussion about Arabs as inherently problematic. A scholar who gave an academic lecture that dealt theoretically with ideas about resistance described an audience member who asked repeated questions like, "'By resistance, do you mean throwing hand grenades at playgrounds in Tel Aviv?' And I was like, 'No, that's not the topic of my talk.'" An Egypt scholar explained this dynamic, saying "Palestine . . . is the flash point. . . . It's the slope that you're fighting uphill against. The frame is that Arabs are terrorist, barbaric, and uncivilized, and the [Israeli-Palestinian] conflict has a lot to do with the production of that discourse. And we have to already know that our audience is already inundated with that. And so we have to talk uphill against it. . . . Even if you're talking about [unrelated topic] in Egypt."

Public events organized by students—especially groups like Students for Justice in Palestine (SJP)—were no exception. Students frequently ask faculty to provide an academic perspective on discussion topics or film screenings. We found that junior faculty were especially cautious about accepting these invitations because, in the words of one pre-tenure anthropologist:

It's one of those dicey things where I can't have too close of a relationship with the SJP, obviously. And the SJP students here also don't have a good sense of where our boundaries are. You know, sometimes they do and they definitely have the general sense that I'm pre-tenure and can't do everything that I want to. But sometimes they don't fully get what that means, like they ask me, "Who are the professors who would be sympathetic to x, y, z; give me their names." And I'm like, "I'm not gonna give you the names of my colleagues."

Similarly, when Palestinian students asked a junior faculty member of color to speak at an event honoring Edward Said after his death, the staff person coordinating event logistics informed the professor that Hillel students had asked to record him "because he is anti-American and anti-Israel." The professor asked for this information in writing and forwarded it to his dean, who told him that he was protected for "whatever views you have." Not all administrators have been as supportive.

In fact, administrators may find that there is very little they can do to protect faculty whose names are being circulated on the internet as part of public shaming campaigns—an insidious tactic. External organizations have created lists of professors who they deem threaten their interests, claiming that those professors are biased, dangerous, un-American, or anti-Israel (often conflated with anti-Semitic). Of course, this tactic dates at least to the McCarthy era, during which blacklists definitively excluded individuals from working in some industries. These lists of faculty do not exclude them from the profession, but they do act as blacklists by casting aspersion and disapproval on scholars in an effort to tarnish their professional reputations. At the very least, these lists provide direction for student and other campaigns to monitor or harass faculty. At worst, they can foment massive public pressures on institutions, calling on them to rein in or even fire particular scholars.

For at least thirty years before the internet permeated academic and public life in the United States, there have been photocopied "black books" listing scholars critical of Israeli state actions toward Palestinians. In 1983 the New England Regional Office of the Anti-Defamation League (ADL) produced a sixteen-page single-spaced blacklist of scholars and Middle East academic organizations across the United States, with a special focus on those in Northern California.[33] They distributed it as part of a confidential booklet to campus leaders in an attempt to acquire ADL liaisons to monitor those professors. The booklet claimed that the scholars' work on "the Arab world is a thinly veiled disguise for their deeply felt anti-Semitism." Twenty percent of those listed were MENA anthropologists. The scholars went to the Middle East Studies Association (MESA) claiming defamation. MESA passed a resolution against the blacklist in 1984, decrying "false, vague, or unsubstantiated accusations which amount to no more than drawing conclusions based on the circumstantial evidence of religion, race, ethnicity, association."[34]

The convergence of 9/11, the second intifada, and the internet ramped up the intimidation. An organization called the American Council of Trustees and Alumni (ACTA)—which has the power to threaten donor bases for universities and colleges[35]—released a report titled "Defending Civilization: How Our Universities Are Failing America and What Can Be Done about It," which lists 117 academics who supposedly threatened national security. Six were anthropologists, including prominent scholars Jean Jackson and Catherine Lutz, senior anthropologist of Iran and prolific op-ed writer William Beeman, and then–graduate student of Palestine Lori Allen. The very first name on the list was anthropologist Hugh Gusterson, because he had spoken at a rally at MIT against the US invasion of Afghanistan.

Websites like Campus Watch also started targeting faculty, including anthropologists, deemed to be unpatriotic and complicit with terrorism. In 2002, Campus Watch published "dossiers" on individual academics. Many anthropologists and other scholars who were not included demanded to be added to the list in solidarity with their colleagues and to show how ludicrous the list was. One of our interlocutors recalled, "And we got a response back, mine was something like, 'Well, [name], we're really sorry to see that you are in support of terrorism,' or something like that." In 2006, David Horowitz—whose "Freedom Center" serves as the umbrella site for *FrontPage Magazine*, Discover the Networks, and other watchdog sites—published *The Professors: 101 Most Dangerous Academics in America*, which included several anthropologists, not all of whom work in MENA. Scholars viewed the book (which was neither subjected to academic peer review nor published by a university press) as evidence of a new McCarthyism; Horowitz indeed defended Senator McCarthy in it.[36]

Many times it was personal political expression, such as signing a petition or being involved in activism, that landed people on blacklists. Other times it was teaching Arab perspectives. Apparently it could even be one's dress: one MENA anthropologist told us he "got on one of the hate lists because . . . [as quoted on its website] 'he also wore a kufiyyeh as his winter scarf (a kufiyyeh is sometimes worn as a sign of solidarity with the Palestinian struggle).'" Laughing, he told us, "Well that's enough to get you on the hate list." So was being a "militant lesbian feminist," a "dyed-red laborista radical," or a "self-hating Jew," according to the 2005 "Dirty Thirty" website claiming to expose "UCLA's radical professors." Four of the scholars listed in this blacklist's top ten positions were attacked partly for their criticisms of Israeli state policies. One was MENA anthropologist Sondra Hale; anthropologist Karen Brodkin also made the list. The website purported to be a project of the "Bruin Alumni Association" and offered to pay students for recordings of these professors' lectures. It was soon revealed to be the brainchild of a right-wing alumnus and was thus easily discredited.[37]

However, it continued to impact faculty negatively, serving as a catalyst for continued harassment in subsequent years and a situation described by a prominent anthropologist who teaches on the East Coast as "harrowing." Tensions at UCLA escalated when award-winning anthropologist and daughter of Holocaust survivors Susan Slyomovics began her term as director of the UCLA Center for Near Eastern Studies in 2007. Things came to a head when the center held a panel, which Slyomovics organized and moderated, about human rights in Gaza in 2009, in the wake of Israel's Operation Cast Lead military assault.[38] The panel prompted outcry from the local Zionist community, pro-Israel faculty and students, and the Hillel rabbi, as well as a letter from the Zionist Organization of America.[39] Participating faculty received abundant hate mail, anonymous hate phone calls, and threats of violence, including threats attached to one professor's office door. When a group of faculty went to discuss the matter with the university chancellor, he sent other administrators to the meeting instead and issued a statement calling on the community to "engage in civil discourse," characterized by one of our interlocutors as "a milquetoast statement like 'Can't we all just get along?'" Meanwhile, an anthropologist colleague of the targeted scholars accused them of being anti-Semitic on a website associated with the Zionist organization Scholars for Peace in the Middle East. Only after they reported him to their department chair and dean did these administrators intervene; he then removed the accusations from the website.[40] Yet there is little recourse for those subjected to smear campaigns outside their institution, such as the fake academic boycott of Israel website which presents a racist, sexist, and homophobic profile of anthropologist Smadar Lavie, accusing her of "whining" about sexism and racism in Israel.[41]

Blacklists' effects reverberate in damaged reputations, hate mail, physical threats, assaults on programming, and calls for dismissal. Outside demands that institutions fire faculty are another tactic external organizations use to pressure academics and administrators. A white anthropologist faced what she described as "a relatively weak attempt to get me fired," which included hate mail, anonymous letters asking her "extremely politely" to resign, and a "whole stack of documentation about, you know, I was a terrorist and terrorist supporter, and all the standard things" that was sent to her provost. This "documentation" also falsely accused her husband of being a Hamas member on the sole basis of his Arab background. None of the material referred to her teaching or research, and she is not very vocal politically on campus. Instead, the attack focused on her organization of cultural activities related to MENA and Arabic language (such as feature film screenings), as well as on her spouse's ethnicity. Several anthropologists described how, after they spoke at a campus event, someone (often a Hillel advisor or rabbi) called their dean or other administrators and claimed that they had said "nasty things about Israel" or were "inciting students." In one case the university chancellor took up this claim, though in the end another administrator who was present at the event in question provided convincing factual evidence in defense of the faculty member. One of these scholars related that as far back as the 1980s local rabbis would call her department chair and ask him directly to fire her. He defended her, consistently asking them to bring in evidence of anything she said that was inaccurate. No one did.

Calls for dismissal were also aimed at non-MENA scholars if an external organization viewed them as supporting Palestinian rights. When Daniel Segal, an anthropology professor whose focus is not MENA, served as an advocate for a Palestinian student after the student was verbally assaulted by an Israeli professor during an SJP political event, the Zionist Organization of America (ZOA) wrote a letter to Segal's college president demanding, among other things, that he be fired. Ellen Schrecker, a history professor at Yeshiva University, notes that despite being tenured, she "steer[s] away from Israel and the Middle East in [her] teaching, research, and off-campus political activities" and that the only time she signed a petition with "Jews Against the Occupation"—a relatively mild public action—"there was an immediate response on campus, with letters to the school paper headlined 'Terminate Schrecker.'"[42]

In these attacks, the type and location of an academic institution matter. Historically, large research universities such as Columbia, UC Berkeley, and UCLA have been in the crosshairs. As was the situation at Columbia, Zionist donors have threatened to withdraw financial support from UCLA, which is home to a donor-driven Israel Studies center that, in one of our interlocutor's views, is "so far right-wing that a number of faculty won't have anything to do with it." As a public institution, UCLA is increasingly dependent on donor money; this case serves as a bellwether for the potential academic consequences of the privatization of public institutions in the United States. At the same time, the attentions of external organizations may be shifting. The incident prompting the ZOA to call for Segal's dismissal occurred at a small liberal arts college. According to the executive director of The David Project, the organization's focus as of 2012 is specifically on "small liberal arts schools" across the country.[43]

In circumstances like these, it is no surprise that many MENA anthropologists prefer to avoid teaching about hot-button issues and/or shy away from public engagement in many forms, choosing instead to focus on their research and publishing. Some explained that publishing was a better use of their time because it is an area of their careers that is more valued by their institutions and where they are less likely to run into political minefields.

The Politics of Publishing

Overall, publishing was the area of least conflict in anthropologists' careers, perhaps an indication of the seriousness with which most scholars and editors take the peer review process. However, there was one major exception:

Israel-Palestine.[44] In 1982, anthropologist Elizabeth ("BJ") Fernea made an ethnographic film about women in a Palestinian refugee camp *(Women Under Siege)* with a grant from the National Endowment for the Humanities (NEH). After the national director of the ADL complained to NEH that the film was "unabashed propaganda" for the PLO, the NEH chairman retracted the Endowment's official support—even though only one of the women portrayed in the film was in the PLO and there was a scholarly purpose to profiling her.[45] Several Palestine scholars reported that journal editors (including at some selective anthropology journals) tend to solicit more reviews for their articles than for those written by peers working on other topics or that the review process often takes longer than usual.

One such article went through eight peer reviewers before it was accepted, and then just before publication the editors rewrote a footnote without the author's permission, altering the author's interpretation of an episode of Israeli state violence. When she told them to revert to her original language, the editors refused. She accepted the change because "you know, you pick and choose your battles, and it was a footnote.... It wasn't worth withdrawing an article." Another anthropologist submitted an article that discussed Palestinians' explanations for a bombing, and, as he explained to us, in the community where he conducted research, "the talk was that it was Israeli agents who set it off, or collaborators of Israeli agents. So I wrote about this [narrative]." A reviewer asked, "Well, how do you know it was the Israelis? Do you have proof of that?" and refused to accept the author's explanation that he was "reporting a story that was circulating" and analyzing that circulation. A scholar of Israel was asked to replace a reference to "Palestinian citizens of Israel" with "Arab citizens of Israel"—a common tactic Zionists use to deny Palestinians their own identity. An academic press pressured another anthropologist to add material about suicide bombing to her manuscript. When she refused because it was unrelated to her research, the press dropped their request. Others described receiving the occasional peer review comment that was "completely not talking about the substance of the article, and more about how it wasn't politically palatable to the person."

For the most part, such issues did not prevent the ultimate publication of pieces, or in Fernea's case the distribution of her film, though sometimes authors had to switch journals or presses. One scholar moved to a new press after receiving what she called "extremely positive" peer reviews, because when the editors took the project to the faculty committee that generally "rubber-stamped" their recommendations, a math professor accused the book of being "overly nationalistic" in how it referred to Palestinians. When the author was asked to write an explanation of how she used various terms, she instead decided to move to another academic press because she thought it was a bad sign that she had to "tiptoe and compromise from the very get-go." In another case, a scholar told us that a press rejected their manuscript because "no one wants to have another Norman Finkelstein affair."[46]

Another anthropologist had difficulty publishing her piece in an edited collection that resulted from a United Nations conference where a range of scholars had discussed various refugee situations. As she explained it, participants were "advocating certain kinds of solutions. This is an applied field as well as a theoretical one, and it's a humanitarian issue that requires responses." In her paper, she "simply said, you know, that the solution is a Palestinian state," and the paper "was well-received." Then, she told us, one of the non-MENA anthropologists who had invited her to participate took her aside at the end of the conference, and, she continued, "He said, 'I'm sorry to tell you, but we can't have your paper in our book.' I said, 'Why? Is something wrong with it?' He said, 'No, no, but,' he said, 'you advocate for a Palestinian state.' And then, and this is a quote, he said, 'I'm not going to let the Zionists fuck my book.' Okay? This is what he said to me!" The piece was included in the book because another organizer intervened, but the lesson this anthropologist learned was that "they didn't want this chapter in their book cause they thought they were gonna get flack."

Several of our interlocutors told us about a journal editor who had experienced pushback. In January 2005, *Anthropology News (AN)* published a piece by Smadar Lavie that castigated Israeli anthropology departments for their dismal record of hiring and tenuring Palestinian citizens of Israel and Mizrahi Israelis. Then coeditor of *American Anthropologist* Susan Lees wrote a letter published in *AN* in May 2005 charging Lavie with "vitriolic invective" and "verbal abuse" for her description of Israeli academic anthropology as an apartheid system and criticizing *AN* for publishing the piece in the first place. Stacy Lathrop, then *AN* editor, justified her decision to publish the article and wrote that she was afraid she was "being made the target of someone's anger for providing a forum for expressing different opinions on a complex issue." Multiple MENA anthropologists suggested that Lathrop was subsequently pushed out of the AAA as a result of both this incident and politicized criticisms of a series of *AN* articles about the Middle East co-curated by Susan Slyomovics and Kamran Ali. We have been unable to independently verify this disturbing claim. Regardless, examples like these show that, for a minority of anthropologists, even academic publishing is not protected from political interference.

Additional Labor, Stress, Emotional Tolls

Working in this politically charged climate—whether one must negotiate discrimination and microaggressions in the workplace or develop strategies to protect oneself when sharing knowledge with a range of audiences—has significant consequences for MENA anthropologists. These experiences, combined with ongoing human tragedies in the region of the world where they work, can lead to high levels of stress and exhaustion. Many of our interlocutors referred to what one termed "emotional exhaustion" and another "personal stress and angst."

What set working in this region apart from other areas for many of these scholars was not necessarily the intensity of crisis, but rather the explicit involvement of the United States in those crises. One senior colleague, who was trained in the 1970s, spoke of

> An emotional exhaustion with the crisis after crisis. . . . Your informants and friends, their lives getting worse, not better. . . . It saddened me and made me at one point want to give up and refashion myself as a Europeanist . . . and of course I didn't. Maybe when you work in Latin America [with] all the civil wars going on . . . or if you work with the ravages of Africa, you also feel a sense of it there. But there was a way in which I felt the United States, the politics of the United States is directly to blame for this. You know, part of it is the unyielding and unwavering support of Israel, but part of it is also the Gulf Wars, the war in Afghanistan before that. So it wasn't just the existential crisis going on. It was also the political crisis that the United States was directly involved in. It's just part of the politics of our area studies.

In the initial heady days of the MENA uprisings in 2011 and 2012, it seemed that finally things would get better, for both our fieldwork interlocutors and the region's reputation in the United States. That moment of hope was short-lived, as the uprisings led to disaster and violence in many countries and the Israeli military killed thousands of Palestinians in yet another war in summer 2014. But the uprisings and wars also reinvigorated scholars' sense of ethical responsibility to share knowledge about the region, and anthropologists have embraced the so-called chalice in classrooms and the media.

As has been the case for over forty years, sharing this knowledge is not without cost. Most concerning are the potential costs to personal safety. Across the decades there are scholars who have received personal threats to themselves and their families for taking anti-Zionist stances, threats that show just how deep the consequences can be for conducting scholarship, teaching, and public outreach on particular matters. An anthropologist who has received multiple threats since the 1980s explained: "Every single time something like this happens, my knees would buckle, and I would get scared. I absolutely cannot say that I don't get scared every single time. . . . I think it's okay to be fearful, that there's something real to fear. And when the Jewish Defense League was still in operation there was something physical to fear. And the hate mail, and the calls, and so on, are just chilling." While this level of attack is not common, it has occurred across institutions and disciplines. In just one example, an Arab faculty member in the literature department at a liberal arts college received threats of bodily harm to himself and his family, including his children, in the wake of a public attack by a right-wing Zionist undergraduate student. It remains to be seen how and if such threats will continue as the move to boycott Israeli academic institutions gains traction in anthropology. Recent incidents of intimidation (including physical) of graduate students at the AAA meetings around this issue do not bode well.

Accusations of anti-Semitism—or, as Jewish scholars were often labeled, being a "self-hating Jew"—carried particular emotional weight for some of our interlocutors. Anthropologists who had been activists against anti-Semitism during their careers pointed to the irony of those accusations, as well as to the tragedy that long histories of such activism could be so readily erased. This sort of defamation also ignored anthropology's historically ahead-of-the-times stance against anti-Semitism: one academic who was blacklisted in the early 1980s for being an "anti-Semite" told us, "as a cultural anthropologist in the tradition of Franz Boas I find anti-Semitism to be a form of prejudice that I strongly condemn." When colleagues brought charges of anti-Semitism against non-MENA anthropologist Lisa Rofel after she organized an academic conference called Rethinking Zionism, she was particularly appalled that they (as part of a national movement) tried to apply their interpretation of a revision to the Title VI Act to her case. This revision was adopted by the Office for Civil Rights in the Department of Education in 2004 (under the tenure of an Assistant Secretary of Education for Civil Rights). It did not prohibit discrimination on the basis of religion, but did so when discrimination was based on ethnic characteristics or shared ancestry (whether actual or perceived). The colleagues spearheading the attack interpreted this revision as both adding Jews to the previously protected categories of race, color, or national origin and defining anti-Semitism to include anti-Israel or anti-Zionist activities.[47] Rofel told us, "[It] upset me on so many levels, but one level is, and this I even learned from my mother who is not radical on these issues, but because of the Holocaust, my mother and others of her generation are adamant that Judaism is not a race! So to inscribe that into civil rights legislation is really disturbing."

Exhaustion, for some of our interlocutors, was a quite literal response to such politics on the job. Those who accepted invitations to speak to media and public audiences about the event du jour paid a price in hours that could have instead been spent doing work that is valued for promotion in an academic career, like publishing. One person described this toll, saying,

> The challenge is that, you know, when bad things happen, media start calling, and they usually have dumb questions, and you spend a lot of time talking to them sometimes, and there's hardly any reward. . . . Here's the difference between us and Melanesianists. Melanesianists publish their butts off because nobody bothers them. Right, they're constantly publishing books and articles and really great, wonderful stuff. And we're always expected to keep up with the news and we're expected to know about this whole big damn region and we're expected to be able to say reasonable things about it.

Others pointed out that attacks and harassment essentially created a vortex that sucked up their time and energy. Even when attacks are minor, scholars must dedicate time to explaining them to administrators and helping those unfamiliar with the region's politics to craft their own responses. In other words, pushback—especially when instigated by well-connected external organizations—produces more administrative labor for faculty, adding to an already oversaturated workload in the neoliberal university. In this way, attacks on scholars proved successful as a tactic of distraction. As one anthropologist told us, "They get to you by a war of attrition, by exhausting you."

While some people brushed off these stresses, others chose to step back from the spotlight, essentially relearning the lesson of self-censorship—whether this meant rejecting speaking invitations or forgoing leadership opportunities related to MENA programming at their institutions. In one extreme and high-profile case, anthropologist Nicholas Dirks not only recanted his anti-Zionist position but also attacked his former colleagues in order, it seems, to be hired as chancellor of the University of California at Berkeley. This case epitomizes the intensity of Zionist pressures on careers and the betrayal felt by colleagues when such pressures are successful. Dirks, along with many other faculty members, had signed a petition in 2002 calling on Columbia University to divest from companies that manufacture or sell "arms or other military hardware" to Israel.[48] When approached by UC Berkeley, he not only denied signing it, suggesting that his name had appeared on the petition and then been removed at his request, but he went a step further in an interview conducted by UC Berkeley's Office of Public Affairs. When the interviewer falsely characterized the petition as calling for divestment from "all things Israel," Dirks did not correct him. He then reiterated accusations that Columbia faculty members were anti-Semitic—accusations that were originally made by Campus Watch and The David Project, and that a university committee that he himself appointed when he was a vice president of Columbia had found baseless.[49] Thus, an anthropologist presumably aware of how racism works, who had formerly been critical of Israeli state actions, now essentially endorsed the idea that such criticism was anti-Semitic, thereby conflating Jews with the Israeli state.[50]

. . .

Despite all of these fraught workplace politics, MENA anthropologists generally shared an assumption that underlies much of anthropology: that we have an ethical obligation to communicate the perspectives of people in places where we conduct research and, relatedly, to advocate for social justice and a more egalitarian world. For them, engaging with various publics through teaching, programming, lectures, and publishing provides an opportunity for ethical scholarly practice that can lead to better-informed publics. One anthropologist viewed this as a responsibility to "balance" discussions about MENA in the United States by providing perspectives rarely heard in mainstream media. To explain, he told us about an audience member who asked him, after a talk at a local church, why he presented Palestinian rather than Israeli perspectives.[51] He replied,

> Based on what I know of survey research of American attitudes on Israel and Palestine, just about everybody in the audience is going to be feeling favorably towards Israel, because it's just terribly lopsided, right. People tend to be very negative about the Palestinians, and when they have an opinion, they tend to feel very favorably toward Israel, and I can assume that my audience already feels that way. I don't really feel the need to give the Israeli perspective, because they know the Israeli perspective, because they have the Israeli perspective, which is the American perspective in so many ways.

The politics saturating academia and public outreach sometimes close down avenues for such scholarly practice by fueling fears (justified or not) about career costs and emotional tolls. Yet there are signs that the degree of self-protection undertaken by MENA anthropologists may be changing—partly due to shifts in public discourse, including the US public turn against the wars in

Iraq and Afghanistan and a growing national conversation about US and Israeli state policies and actions that contravene international law and human rights norms. A scholar trained in the 2000s gave us a sense of how the decades-long struggle of MENA anthropologists to fight stereotyping of the region has finally begun to have an impact: "In college [after 9/11] someone found out I was Palestinian and turned to me and said, 'Oh, I never knew there was affirmative action for terrorists.' And I was silent at that moment. And have vowed that I will not be silent again." Graduate students like this one have, for the past decade, played a key role in public discussions within the American Anthropological Association about US wars in the region and US complicity in Israeli state actions against Palestinians.

Previous generations laid much of the groundwork that enabled this context in which graduate students have begun to feel more comfortable speaking out. They worked hard to cultivate a voice for MENA anthropology over the decades through institution building. We now turn to excavate important histories of how MENA anthropology was built through early networks and research groups and, later, through the Middle East Section of the American Anthropological Association. These histories show the hidden labor, often done by women and junior scholars, in developing academic institutions. They also reveal how the shifting nature of US empire changes the ways the region is configured in relationship to disciplinary conventions, norms, and institutions. Long-standing tensions are reproduced over time, yet how they are expressed, and the stakes embedded in them, transform with new generations.

4 Building Disciplinary Institutions

Should anthropologists work with the US government, including the CIA or Department of Defense? Should they assist for-profit corporations of any kind? Can they engage in secret research? And what constitutes "secret"? Should they take collective positions against war, violence, and human rights abuses? Do they have an obligation to advocate for social justice, especially for their interlocutors? Such questions may not be the most pressing for other disciplines. But for anthropology, they have produced major, often heated, disagreements for over a century. These debates have been especially prominent in the discipline because many anthropologists have focused on trying to make sense of the lives of marginalized peoples—a practice that has increasingly involved trenchant critique of power structures, including those abetted by US global economic, political, and military dominance.

Such disagreements appear most clearly in the activities of academic associations—the vehicles through which scholars develop standards, ethics, regulations, and public representation. Examining this process for MENA, as the region became a focus of US imperial endeavor, reveals core tensions at the heart of anthropology as a discipline. These tensions include whether and how anthropologists should provide knowledge to institutions that can use it in instrumentalist ways that might cause harm; who is permitted to speak for the discipline and for different regions; whether and how anthropologists should advocate for the well-being of their interlocutors; and, relatedly, what kinds of political positions fall within anthropology's purview. Demographic and theoretical shifts in the discipline shape the various positions people have taken on these matters.

To navigate disciplinary frictions, scholars interact with a variety of academic institutions outside their colleges and universities. Anthropologists have engaged with institutions in order to argue that certain regions and issues deserve disciplinary attention and to articulate views about the limits of anthropology's application—views that often translated into progressive or more conservative political positions. MENA anthropologists have been part of this process since at least World War II (WWII), as the region was a key theater of that war. They began to participate in institutions more concertedly in the 1970s, as more MENA cultural anthropologists entered the field and the region gained prominence in US foreign interests. Scholars, often female and/or junior, either built new institutions or worked within existing ones to both forge a presence for regional specialists within the discipline and enact their (various) understandings of the correct relationship between ethics and politics for US academic engagement with MENA. The lesson MENA anthropologists learned, as US and Israeli power in the region consolidated, was that Muslims, Middle Easterners, and especially Palestinians often constituted an exception to that dominant anthropological trend of trying to understand marginalized peoples on their own terms and criticizing the structures of power that oppress them.

Anthropology, MENA, and the World Wars

In what is perhaps the earliest expression of US anthropological dissent to the idea that anthropologists should contribute to various government intelligence and military efforts, Franz Boas wrote a letter in 1919 to *The Nation* publicizing and criticizing the "wartime activities" of four anthropologists. He wrote that these unnamed archaeologists who worked in Central America had "prostituted science by using it as a cover for their activities as spies."[1] The American Anthropological Association (AAA) censored Boas, reprimanding him and expelling him from the Council—the voting membership of the AAA—for this action.[2] David Price argues that with this response, "American anthropology avoided facing the ethical questions Boas raised about anthropologists' using their work as a cover for spying. And it has refused to face them ever since."[3] Furthermore, Price suggests that censoring Boas sent the message that using scholarship in the service of the state, whether clandestinely or not, was acceptable, setting the stage for later decades' disciplinary entanglements with government projects as well as many anthropologists' protests against them. Indeed, the Boas moment continues to haunt US anthropological engagements with MENA, beginning with anthropologists' contributions to the war effort in that region.

During WWII, approximately 50 percent of anthropologists "contributed to the war effort" in various (typically nonclandestine) ways ranging from training army officers to working directly for a variety of war agencies.[4] Unlike during both Vietnam and the War on Terror, when junior scholars were (and are) more likely to argue against anthropological contributions to the wars, during WWII, younger scholars called upon the AAA to more actively support the war effort.[5] From the perspective of some, the war created new opportunities for anthropologists, many of whom enlisted, volunteered, or did intelligence work.[6] Others, including Margaret Mead, viewed WWII as an opportunity for anthropologists to prove their importance to international relations and foreign policy in a globalizing world.[7]

There were several wartime projects specific to MENA, in addition to a plethora of activities elsewhere, including Latin America and Asia and the Pacific (most famously Mead's multiple "national character" studies and Ruth Benedict's "culture and personality" work on Japan).[8] Anthropologists wrote cultural studies to help the military navigate the North African front, including "Pocket Guide" booklets on Egypt and North Africa. They participated in the Smithsonian's Ethnogeographic Board, which developed rosters of experts for various world regions, including North Africa.[9] And they served in MENA (Morocco, Algiers, Beirut, Cairo) via the Office of Strategic Services (OSS), the precursor to the CIA.[10] Most notoriously, Carleton Coon—a Harvard PhD who by some accounts is the first American cultural anthropologist of MENA[11]—ran secret missions for the OSS in North Africa that included managing a ring of local informers, training local populations in sabotage and attacks on railroads, creating and spreading propaganda in support of a US invasion (by disseminating to mosques a translation, into classical Arabic, of one of Roosevelt's speeches), operating a covert radio station, using kidnapping to extort intelligence from locals, and planning an invasion of Albania from Cairo.[12]

Anthropologists were also involved with what was perhaps the most fateful result of WWII for MENA: a series of studies and proposals for the postwar resettlement of Jewish refugees from Europe (i.e., where to establish the state of Israel), known as the M Project. The project began when a representative of President Roosevelt contacted Henry Field, assistant curator of anthropology at Chicago's Field Museum, and asked him to estimate how many postwar refugees Iraq could support. It soon developed into a major initiative run through the museum with significant anthropological support and focused primarily on European refugees.[13] The M Project reports suggested Jewish refugee resettlement in places ranging from Australia to Nigeria and Brazil to Palestine. Several of these reports, often penned by anthropologists, framed Palestine as "an underused and empty land awaiting the arrival of industrious newcomers" and drew on "erroneous claims that the Muslims, Jews, and Christians of Palestine had left vast tracts of arable land unfarmed."[14] While the reports also treated other places as "empty" and generally reflected a "misreading of the world as an unclaimed or underused resource waiting for American management"—in the case of Palestine, the M Project dovetailed with Zionist political desires and justifications for establishing Israel there.[15]

These various wartime collaborations, Price argues, were problematic because "the acceptance of such practices in one circumstance opens the possibility that such practices can occur in *any* circumstance."[16] Case in point: in the 1950s, the AAA executive board secretly worked with the CIA to create a database of scholars' names, areas of expertise, and research interests—providing this information to the CIA without AAA members' knowledge.[17] In keeping with Price's assessment, Laura Nader notes that in the 1950s, during the early Cold War, "the structures of power were invisible" in relation to government and military work, as well as their ties to funding, and anthropologists were essentially "sleepwalking" through this political context.[18] Another result of wartime collaborations was that applied anthropology emerged as a strong and growing subfield; the tensions between applied and academic anthropology that began during this time would continue to impact discussions about research ethics and the relationship between the discipline and the state for decades to come.[19] MENA scholarship would also feel the impact of the development and continuation of war-era area studies programs, which had "demonstrated to federal officials and university administrators that anthropology was more than a curiosity—that it had tangible uses in a world where America was the emerging super power."[20] After the war and subsequent National Defense Education Act, US-based MENA area studies programs and departments grew massively, although MENA *anthropology* in particular would not boom until well into the 1970s.[21] Before then, a series of revelations about scholars conducting research for US government agencies without disclosure to their informants rocked the anthropological community. These revelations prompted new debates about research ethics within the discipline—debates that continue to intimately affect US anthropological engagements with MENA.

Ethics as Politics?
From Project Camelot through the Vietnam War

The Vietnam War, as well as American corporate involvement abroad, brought anthropological disagreements to a fevered pitch in the 1960s and early 1970s. Many scholars expressed concerns about engaging with government projects in particular, on the grounds that "using anthropology to alter and undermine indigenous cultural movements cut against the grain of widely shared anthropological assumptions about the rights of cultures and people to determine their own destiny."[22] This focus on rights presented a political argument for opposing research that supported counterinsurgencies, an argument that positioned anthropologists on the side of their interlocutors. However, as would happen in twenty-first-century discussions about anthropology and the War on Terror, the AAA repositioned the conversation in terms of research ethics and focused more on the dangers to anthropologists and anthropology than to the people upon whom our research depends. Also presaging twenty-first-century AAA politics, during this period disagreement emerged about what evidence "counts" as anthropological when taking political positions, symptomatic of broader tensions over whether or not the discipline should publicly adopt such positions. From this time forward, both this privileging of scholars over interlocutors *and* a more constrained purview of what counts as proper politics for the discipline are used to argue against taking public positions on MENA—positions similar to those that anthropologists and their institutional associations have frequently adopted for other world regions.

In 1964, the US Army tried to quietly initiate Project Camelot in an effort to enlist social scientists, including anthropologists, to conduct research to assist counterinsurgency operations in Latin America. Congress shut the program down in July 1965, after it was publicly exposed.[23] Camelot was only one of many US military projects that sought to apply anthropology and ideas about culture to military problems and only seems to have involved one anthropologist. But it received a great deal of press as well as attention within the discipline,[24] instigating significant discussion at the 1965 AAA business meeting about the ethics of anthropological engagement. The immediate outcomes of that meeting were the appointment of Ralph Beals as chair of the AAA Committee on Research and Ethics and a survey he conducted with then-Executive Director Stephen Boggs about Problems in International Research, including the impact of government activities and relationships on that research.[25]

MENA was a region of interest, but its scholars were no longer simply supporting state entities, as they did during WWII in North Africa. Soon after the meeting, in December 1965, MENA anthropologist Robert Fernea wrote to Boggs about this very issue. As an example of the challenges researchers confront when government and research are blended, he reported that the air attaché in the United Arab Republic (i.e., Syria and Egypt) had asked him to "keep my eyes open and report military movements in the Aswan region" in return for free use of the mail pouch. Fernea eloquently noted his worry that "fly-by-night" researchers would lead to locals assuming all foreign scholars were spies. Foreshadowing critiques of anthropology that would appear in the 1970s, he also suggested that our interlocutors are well aware of the relationship between anthropological knowledge and power, highlighted the importance of not exploiting places and people to extract knowledge, and stated his absolute political objection to working with government agencies.[26] Boggs' response noted that "a number of" anthropologists working around the world had reported being approached by their local US embassy to serve as a "stringer" and that his interviews with anthropologists thus far had "impressed [him] with regard to the difficulties which have been created for social science research in the Near East by a number of actions of our Government and other governments in the area. I am referring particularly to the Arab-Israeli conflict, the use of 'social scientists' as sources of political information and as outright intelligence agents, the Voice of America surveys, and the use of ethnologists by governments in some areas for the forcible control of certain peoples."[27]

Fernea suggested that Beals seek the opinion of Federico Vidal—a Harvard-trained anthropologist who worked for Aramco (Arabian American Oil Company) researching local Bedouin for the oil company's benefit. Here we find the first archival evidence of AAA concern with anthropology's cooperation with US business interests in MENA.[28] In his letter to Vidal, Beals wrote that some had suggested "social scientists might learn something from the activities of corporations [like Aramco] abroad," but also that "some anthropologists have indicated they looked upon working for a private corporation as some sort of a perversion of social science and Aramco has several times been mentioned as a horrible example." He added that those critical voices had compared such work to "prostituting [one's] talents" and that "the data or information being collected is being employed for unworthy or evil ends."[29] We found no record of Vidal's response.

From the results of his survey Beals published a "Statement of Problems of Anthropological Research and Ethics" in the AAA January 1967 *Fellows Newsletter*. This statement exemplified, some fifty years ago, many of anthropology's as-yet unresolved disciplinary tensions. On the one hand, he stated that government should not interfere in research, researchers should be open about project aims, funding, and other support, and anthropologists should not use research for intelligence gathering or other covert actions. On the other hand, he also suggested that social scientists make their knowledge more readily available to the executive branch of government and that anthropologists be included in policymaking.[30]

The following year, 1968, saw growing protests against the Vietnam War and an outcry in the AAA when a Department of Defense advertisement seeking a scholar of Vietnam appeared in *Anthropology Newsletter*. In 1969, a recently formed Radical Caucus of anthropologists staged a take-over of the annual meeting and passed no fewer than eighteen resolutions.[31] Two of them opposed clandestine research and using anthropology as a cover for intelligence work and pushed the association to draft a code of ethics that took those stances.[32]

The 1971 AAA business meeting was a flash point for these debates about the relationship between research and politics, triggered by what became known as the Thailand affair—a moment in institutional history that haunts ongoing discussions about anthropology's entanglements with government. Many written sources as well as several of our interlocutors described this meeting with words like "tumultuous" and "a showdown."[33] The previous year, a graduate student snuck into UCLA faculty member Michael Moerman's office and stole documents showing that he and other anthropologists had clandestinely used ethnographic research to support counterinsurgency actions in Thailand. When Eric Wolf, then chair of the Committee on Ethics, received the documents, he and fellow committee member Joseph Jorgensen issued public statements, including in the *New York Review of Books*, condemning this use of research and questioning the ethics of the anthropologists involved.[34] In response, the AAA executive board reprimanded Wolf and Jorgensen for supposedly overstepping their role on the committee and speaking in the AAA's name. We will see this exact scenario play out in the twenty-first century; in the next chapter we discuss a battle between the Committee for Human Rights and the executive board over "who speaks for anthropologists" on political issues. Ultimately, Wolf and Jorgensen resigned, and Margaret Mead was appointed chair of an ad hoc committee to investigate the situation. At that "turbulent" 1971 meeting, the Mead Commission presented a report exonerating Moerman and the other scholars and reprimanding the ethics committee members who had spoken out.[35] The Radical Caucus took over the meeting, and ethics committee members read from the documents in question.[36] In what might be interpreted as a clash at the intersection of generation and politics,[37] a motion was made to reject the Mead Report, and in the ensuing vote, the AAA membership, including some MENA anthropologists, did so.[38]

Our interlocutors who recalled these events had differing perspectives on them. Some held that institutionalization prevented progressive politics. One anthropologist who shared this perspective thought that radical opposition to anthropologists working for the military was dominant "outside the AAA establishment forces" but that "the AAA administration" was "part of the problem." Others thought that personal politics have no place in the institution. An anthropologist of this perspective was upset at the time, because he thought resolutions should only be passed when they were "based in our knowledge as anthropologists." Another elaborated on this view:

> We need to address issues like creationism; there we know what we're talking about. But when we pass motions about the politics of XYZ, as anthropologists, we don't have something special to say. . . . It would be one thing to say we would not do secret research. That I understand. But it was also resolutions against the United States being at war. Wait a minute, I'm against the war but not because of any special knowledge I have as an anthropologist. I don't have anything as an anthropologist to bring to that discussion and if you think that I'm to be the voice of the voiceless or always on the side of hope, that's my politics, it's not my anthropology.

For that period as now, we found that those most likely to claim such a separation between anthropology and personal politics were white male scholars trained prior to the 1990s. Female and some male MENA scholars were largely united in their view that being an anthropologist required opposing the Vietnam War (and subsequent ones). For them, the separation of anthropology from personal politics instead circumscribed what counted as relevant in and to the discipline.

At that same meeting, the membership voted to adopt the Principles of Professional Responsibility (PPR), essentially an ethics code, which stated AAA members can do "no secret research, no secret reports or debriefings of any kind should be agreed to or given," and scholars should reveal funding sources and research uses.[39] It also asserted that an anthropologist's primary commitment is first and foremost to do "no damage" to the people they study.[40] This PPR can be read as building on Beals's 1967 statement, as it embodied the same tensions. Hancock suggests that Beals's proposals were "designed to protect government-sponsored research from criticism on ethical grounds" and that they justified "anthropological engagement with, and its potential supporting role in, the ongoing American colonial project" by setting rules and boundaries for that participation, namely, that it take place openly and not "in a clandestine fashion."[41] In other words, by establishing rules against secret research and reports, one left the door to *nonsecret* work with government, military, and intelligence agencies wide open, an interpretation borne out by the fact that the 1971 PPR did not explicitly forbid such work.[42] Price concurs with Hancock's assessment, but notes more broadly that by focusing on defining ethical rules for research, "The AAA avoided addressing the political meaning of using anthropology in military contexts that include the occupation and conquest of the peoples anthropologists work with and study."[43] Such implications cast a shadow on anthropology through the following decades, when first Latin America and then the Middle East overtook Southeast Asia as the primary site for US military intervention and counterinsurgency.

Scholars concerned about the ethics code suggest that it served primarily to protect anthropology and anthropologists, not our interlocutors.[44] This prioritization, along with the general framing of the Vietnam-era crises in terms of ethics, as Price argues, allowed the AAA to skirt the political issues at stake.[45] They also set the stage for continued resistance "to confronting the ways that disciplinary ethics are linked to the political context in which anthropology is practiced."[46] Despite the association's political positions on matters of social equality and resolutions against certain wars, it "remains skittish" about taking positions on whether anthropology should be used in imperialistic and nondefensive wars.[47] Such politics would create a wedge between official AAA concerns and those of many MENA anthropologist members.

In addition to the Vietnam War, anthropological drama around counterinsurgency work, and the new ethics code, two other events in the 1960s shaped MENA anthropology: the establishment of MENA-related academic institutions and the 1967 Arab-Israeli war (which led to Israel's occupation of Gaza, the West Bank, and the Golan Heights).[48] Different stances on Israel-Palestine, as well as MENA's still miniscule presence in cultural anthropology, led many scholars to shift associational allegiances or build altogether new ones.

In 1966, the Middle East Studies Association was founded, in keeping with the Cold War trend toward the formation of area studies. An anthropologist who attended its first meeting told us:

MESA was begun as a kind of counter to the *Middle East Journal* and the Washington crowd that were heavily into the Arab-Israeli dispute. It was meant to be an intellectual forum, and how would we handle the Arab-Israeli thing? Well, someone decided we will have a Jewish president one year, and we will have one who isn't the next year. In those days it was called the Lebanese solution. Yeah, when Lebanon actually worked that way.[49] And the rule, not formal, but everybody understood it, was you don't really talk about the Arab-Israeli dispute except once a year, the president gets to do so at his or her final speech at the banquet.

Another scholar explained this "informal system" in terms of political stances on Zionism rather than presuming that ethnic or religious identity implied a particular stance. He noted that at least two older MESA members had told him MESA used to "alternate between presidents of the organization who were perceived as pro-Palestinian and presidents of the organization who were perceived as pro-Zionist." Whether or not MESA operated this way, the fact that people think it did tells us something about their understandings of its initial political bargains. The majority of our interlocutors who were in academia at that time told us that they did not feel at home within MESA in the 1960s and 1970s because the organization was run by what one called "Orientalists and State Department people" and was hostile to Palestinian perspectives.

Indeed, many of our more politically activist interlocutors from that time quickly grew disillusioned with MESA's neutral stance on Palestine-Israel and preferred to attend AAA meetings instead (AAA and MESA have for decades typically been scheduled around the same time, forcing scholars to choose between them). Yet some of these same anthropologists also did not feel at home in their disciplinary association, due to its focus on MENA primarily as a site for archaeology, and a sense that discussions about Palestinians had no place at the AAA. The 1967 war brought academics together in shared concern for people in the region and with shared purpose of wanting to provide Arab perspectives to counter the rising tide of US public opinion against them. One female scholar explained that after the 1967 war, papers related to Palestine were "unwelcome" at the AAA, due to what she perceived as its resistance to progressive politics despite discussions of Vietnam, and also unwelcome at MESA, due to its Orientalist inclination. The perception that there was no space for scholarship about Palestinians at either organization inspired her to work to expand MENA's presence in the AAA.

Some MENA anthropologists ended up joining the new organizations that were formed in reaction to MESA's politics, sometimes finding better homes there than the AAA. Scholars fondly remember collegial discussions at the Association of Arab American University Graduates (AAUG), established in 1967. One recalled that she and several colleagues joined AAUG seeking a space to present research related to Palestine.[50] Many anthropologists also mentioned the Middle East Research and Information Project (MERIP) as critical to their scholarly formation. An activist collective dedicated to publishing material on the region to counter mainstream media portrayals, MERIP also serves as a network for scholars who share leftist perspectives.[51]

The 1967 war was especially prominent in the narratives of female scholars from earlier generations, who tended to be more interested than their male colleagues in linking scholarship with progressive politics. This in part led to the creation of new feminist, antiwar networks—which for one scholar evoked an expression of gratitude in our interview to the "absolutely pioneering" female scholars ahead of her for being sources of support, "especially after 1967." Many female, and some male, scholars repeatedly lauded Lucie Wood Saunders, then a professor at Lehman College of the City University of New York, as the key figure bringing MENA anthropologists together, first locally and then more broadly. As one person said,

> She kept Middle East anthropology alive in New York, at a time when no one was doing Middle East anthropology. She'd have gatherings in her house . . . and she had one person after another after another. . . . As everyone passed through town, they'd end up at Lucie's one way or another and she'd have a dinner and invite all these young scholars and have them together at her house, especially women who were doing Middle East Studies.

Our interlocutors also honored Elizabeth (BJ) Fernea as an important senior figure in these feminist (and often Marxist) networks, for mentoring junior scholars who were, as one person said, "trying to figure out how to break through the wall of AAA and MESA." Eventually, MENA anthropologists decided to form their own formal institution—a place where they could navigate and forge the relationship between politics, ethics, region, and discipline on their own terms.

Building a New Network of MENA Anthropologists: MERGA

By the early 1970s, Saunders was anchoring a reading group that, in 1975, submitted a panel on rethinking Orientalism for the AAAs. When the panel was rejected, the AAA program chair suggested forming an affiliate organization to hold it anyway. This inspired the group to establish the first organization dedicated specifically to MENA *anthropology* and the precursor to today's Middle East Section of the AAA: the Middle East Research Group in Anthropology (MERGA). Beginning in 1976, MERGA met in conjunction with the AAA Annual Meeting.[52] Its typewritten and photocopied newsletter—*MERA Forum: Forum for Middle East Research in Anthropology*—published a broad range of member-generated content including research reports, theoretical provocations, and reviews of significant new publications in the field (and the occasional rejoinder, including one by Pierre Bourdieu).[53] The *Forum* also served as a "clearinghouse"—similar to listservs today—for announcements and reports[54] and made available, in a centralized mailing, access to the kinds of contact, networking, and bibliographic information we frequently take for granted.[55] Our interlocutors agreed that MERGA's key purposes were to foster and facilitate scholarly networks and to establish visibility for the Middle East within the AAA. It was also less hierarchical and institutionalized than AAA and MESA, which was part of the appeal. As explained in an early *Forum*, "MERGA has no formal membership or officers and is open to all interested persons. Its aim is to facilitate communication among those interested in Middle East Anthropology."[56]

Analysis of MERGA activities reveals the genesis, persistence, and eventual institutionalization of anthropology's key tensions as they played out in relationship to MENA. MERGA's initial meeting included discussion about placing more MENA-related sessions on the AAA program and a workshop on Critical Anthropology of the Middle East, during which Robert Fernea called for, among other things, "an anthropology of the Arab-Israeli conflict."[57] Attendees made comments that show they were contending with tensions found in anthropological discussions dating back to Boas. They assessed how scholars' politics affect their research, debated "whether we want to get involved" with governments and government agencies, questioned how one could "safeguard ways in which our work will be used in policymaking," discussed anthropologists' involvement with development organizations, and advocated for including scholars based in the region in their networks.[58] By thinking in such critical and nuanced ways about the possible political consequences of their research, these MENA anthropologists actually prefigured broader anthropological discussions of these matters.[59]

MERA Forum shows us the work of building a subfield and laying out research agendas that address both current events and theoretical innovations in anthropology. This last point is crucial because, in the estimations of many of these same MENA anthropologists, the subfield was theoretically "behind" anthropology of other regions and deeply marginalized within the discipline. *Forum* content contradicts the first assumption;[60] the latter was likely reinforced by the region-specific venue of these discussions as well as the fact that MENA anthropologists frequently *talked about* their marginalization. They regularly bemoaned the numbers of region-related panels at AAA conferences, called for integrating MENA into anthropology by presenting papers on nonregionally organized panels, and worked to publicize MERGA.

At the same time, MENA anthropologists were concerned about anthropology's invisibility within Middle East Studies. The *Forum* shows a consistent desire to link to area studies organizations, including but not limited to MESA.[61] MERGA members were actively involved in both the Association for Middle East

Women's Studies (AMEWS) founded in 1985,[62] and the Alternative Middle East Studies Seminar (AMESS) formed by forty scholars at the 1977 MESA conference "in response to the shared dissatisfaction with dominant methodological approaches and their political implications."[63] The newsletter covered MENA anthropologists' persistent complaints about the scheduling conflicts between their disciplinary and area studies conferences. Published evidence of efforts to fix this problem, along with numerous discussions about it in our interviews, show that this historical scheduling conflict is more than an inconvenience: it has made it difficult both for MENA scholars to have a significant presence at the AAA and for anthropologists to have a significant presence at MESA. At stake is how regions and disciplines get represented (or not).

Finally, we also see in the *Forum* evidence of the progressive activist inclinations of many—though not all—MERGA members, in keeping with several of our interlocutors' recollections that a major reason for forming the group was that anti-Zionist views were unwelcome in existing organizations. Many also recalled being motivated to join due to their frustration with AAA discussions about the proper relationship between scholarship and political position. MERGA members were instrumental in prompting the AAA to pass what are—to our knowledge—its first three resolutions related to the Middle East, which the newsletter featured prominently.[64] It also reported on other organizations' political statements, including a call to end deportation and harassment of Iranians in the United States, a condemnation of Israeli government harassment of Bir Zeit University administrators, and an objection to all US military intervention and arms sales in the region.[65] The *Forum's* detailed treatment of these resolutions shows that MENA anthropologists in the 1970s were decades ahead of their time—in comparison to both anthropology and Middle East Studies—in calling for civil rights for Muslims in the United States and Palestinian academic freedom and standing against US military intervention in the region.[66]

MERGA must be credited for its major role in establishing a world region as an important area of study within a discipline. By 1980, it had grown from its approximately 50 initial members to 175 members in seventeen countries. In a sign of the shifting demographics of anthropology more generally, it included slightly more female than male scholars and a mix of white and region-related scholars in the United States, as well as scholars based in the region, including Israel.[67] This institution building required significant amounts of volunteer labor, which—like much academic service work—was marked significantly by age and gender. The *Forum* shows that early on, women were more likely to organize panels and events, while men were more likely to participate as speakers and chairs, in authoritative or knowledge-providing roles. Some of this discrepancy is no doubt related to the academy's gender hierarchy prevalent in the late 1970s and early 1980s, such that senior faculty were more often male.[68] Our interviews, along with correspondence and documents shared with us by MERGA members, also show that female faculty or junior scholars of both genders did much of the behind-the-scenes nitty-gritty work.[69] Three male graduate students or recent PhDs held the time-intensive, publicly recognized, and critical role of managing the money, mailing lists, annual meeting, newsletter editors, and AAA relations.[70]

In the 1980s, as the AAA embarked on a restructuring plan, MERGA began to debate the potential costs of seeking greater visibility through more formal institutionalization and bureaucratization.[71] Their discussion eerily foresaw the consequences of such changes for progressive politics in the subfield in later years. The collective rejected formal affiliation with the AAA several times during this decade on the grounds that it would limit the group's independence while increasing its administrative work. MERGA remained independent until the 1990s. Eventually, as a critical mass of MENA anthropologists emerged, and alongside the larger push in academia towards bureaucratization,[72] MERGA decided to convert into a formal AAA section, a process that once again depended heavily on the labor of female anthropologists.[73]

Middle East Politics Hits the AAA

Until the 1980s, the contemporary Middle East and North Africa was an exception to geographic "coverage" in anthropology; it was simply not on the AAA's radar. All of that changed in 1979, when supporters of the Islamic Revolution took fifty-two Americans hostage in the US embassy in Tehran. From that point onward, MENA became an exception in anthropology in another sense—an exception to what had become, since World War II, the dominant trend of speaking out against state violence and in support of marginalized peoples.[74] In 1978, the AAA reported that over 50 percent of its political statements in the prior two decades "demonstrated the membership's overwhelming concern with human rights issues."[75] Would Middle Eastern human rights get the same support?

This anthropological advocacy against oppression (military, political, and economic) seems to have been focused mainly on Latin and South America and on indigenous peoples in the Americas. In April 1973, the executive board unanimously passed a statement "on the events at Wounded Knee" and one opposing a House bill proposing to relocate eight thousand Navajos from territory granted to the Hopi in a land claim judgment on the grounds of "self-determination for peoples of varying cultural traditions within the United States."[76] Later that year, the board heard a report that "Mapuche Indians were being killed as result of the new political situation" in Chile, which led to an "ad-hoc investigative commission"[77] and unanimous adoption of a motion regarding Puerto Rican independence. In 1977 there were several discussions about the situation of anthropologists in Central and South America,[78] and 1978 saw motions adopted in "support of the rights of homosexuals," on "the protection of Indian peoples and cultures of Brazil," and on "use of coca in the Andes"—the latter passing despite its reliance on a "fact unknown to the board."[79]

Given this pattern, it is no surprise that MENA anthropologists in the 1960s and 1970s detected exceptionalism. Many thought the AAA ignored the region, either because its people were viewed as less important or because the association and its executive board defined indigeneity so narrowly that the hundreds of thousands of Palestinians forcibly removed from their homes and/or living under military occupation did not count as a crisis of indigenous peoples.[80] Some of our interlocutors suggested that anthropologists either shared broader US unconditional support for Israeli actions or did not yet understand that one could simultaneously oppose anti-Semitism and be critical of Israeli state actions and policies. And several people with AAA experience explained MENA's relative invisibility as due to the greater numbers and louder voices of Americanist anthropologists historically in the association and on its board. To our knowledge, there were no MENA anthropologists on the executive board during the 1970s and 1980s, but Americanist anthropologists filled multiple positions. The above issues in Native North and Central/South America, as targets of US imperialism, certainly warranted anthropological attention. But MENA anthropologists were tracking, with unease, increasing US interest in MENA. In their fieldsites and stateside jobs, they saw the effects of US involvement in the 1967 and 1973 wars, US support for Israel, rising oil consumption, the 1978 Camp David Accords, and mounting arms sales to several MENA countries.

Records suggest that the hostage crisis in Iran was the first time the AAA membership writ large took significant political notice of the Middle East. The process by which this transpired reveals schisms that would persist and multiply in future association engagements with MENA.[81] At the 1979 annual meeting, three anthropologists introduced a motion about "the American-Iranian crisis," calling for "moderation and restraint on both sides" and the ending of discrimination toward Iranians and Muslims in the United States and more broadly.[82] The motion originated in a post-panel discussion that continued late into the night[83] and was then, according to some of our interlocutors, "changed slightly" by someone in "the AAA office" in ways that its original authors felt diluted its power. At the MERGA meeting that preceded the AAA business meeting, one of its authors "conceded that the resolution is inadequate, but the best that we could hope for the AAA to support." Attendees also predicted the tenor of the impending AAA-wide discussion, with one person suggesting that "the resolution is a very mild one that no-one was likely to have objection to," while others anticipated "a free-for-all and venting of spleen" because "not all the group of Middle East specialists agreed on the issues in the crisis, and many within the AAA may see Islam as [the] anti-Christ."[84] All twenty-eight MERGA members in attendance voted aye in a straw poll on the motion. It was later adopted by voting members of the AAA during the business meeting, with one amendment—the telling addition of the phrase "and that the Association express the hope that comparable aims [e.g., towards peace] will be pursued by the Iranian people" at the end of the text.[85]

This statement foreshadows two patterns we will see in later debates over whether and how anthropologists should take collective stances on MENA issues, especially as the AAA becomes increasingly bureaucratized. First, one of the motion's three authors was not a MENA scholar. Later resolutions have been more likely (though not guaranteed) to succeed if they were similarly authored by a coalition of MENA and non-MENA scholars and were most successful when authored solely by the latter. The voices of MENA anthropologists on their own were not strong enough to produce AAA political statements in the way that Americanist scholars' voices could.

Second, the AAA leadership raised concerns about the resolution's language, and in the end a notion of "balance" was added. Non-MENA colleagues would in future discussions frequently assert that MENA-related resolutions needed to be "balanced" even when those statements addressed situations of significant structural inequality. This would *always* happen with Israel-Palestine; those seeking to defeat or ignore potential resolutions regularly invoked balance.[86] Such a discourse inevitably dilutes anthropological support for Palestinian rights, because it overlooks the structural inequalities between a fully fledged sovereign state with a massive military and a stateless people who lack sovereignty over their affairs and land.[87]

At the same time, the language of the 1979 motion is far more radical than that of statements after 1990. The MERGA discussion called out potential

Islamophobia in the AAA, *among colleagues*. And the motion used the phrase "the cause of justice and peace"—broad social justice language that is less prevalent in more recent AAA statements on MENA. In 1982, similarly radical statements were proposed and eventually passed. Yet most of the later statements on MENA did not, even if they were written in significantly more liberal or centrist language and even if they dutifully invoked "balance"—a clear sign that anthropology's politics, at least regarding MENA, were shifting rightward.

Despite their success, because the 1982 statements concerned Israel and Palestinians, the AAA's double standards on questions of human rights and indigeneity, sensed by many MENA anthropologists since the 1960s, came out into the open and onto the record. The construction of these motions, as well as reactions against them, also reveals some of anthropology's core tensions. That year, the executive board, acting on the membership's behalf, officially reaffirmed AAA concern for the protection of Native Americans' human rights and took action against politicized demotion of anthropologists in the Soviet Union. But when members brought forward concerns about Arab human rights and Palestinian academic freedom, a major uproar ensued. At the AAA business meeting, anthropologists presented two statements condemning Israeli state and military actions.[88] For the first time, explicit criticism of the Israeli state was in the foreground at the AAA. And as a result, for the first time the AAA was a forum for Zionist attacks on the statements and the scholars who supported them.

The first was a resolution addressing the 1982 Israeli invasion of Lebanon and Israel's role in aiding and abetting the massacres of between 800 and 3,500 Palestinians at the Sabra and Shatila Palestinian refugee camps there that autumn.[89] It was submitted by a coalition of MENA and non-MENA anthropologists, including at least one Israeli. The proposed statement condemned the "systematic and deliberate destruction of the Lebanese and Palestinian peoples and cultures" and called for an end to US military aid to Israel and Lebanon and for the United States to facilitate the withdrawal of foreign military forces from Lebanon.[90] By the time it came up on the agenda, it was very late at night, by most accounts around midnight. One person recalled that many Americanist anthropologists were at the meeting to support another statement and were about to leave after that vote, "and we said wait, wait, stay for our motion. . . . And a lot of the votes that we had came from good leftist Central Americanists who voted for our resolution."

Julie Peteet, who had recently returned from doctoral fieldwork in Beirut, took the lead in presenting the resolution at the meeting. She described the Israeli invasion of Lebanon, its impact, and the massacres from the perspective of an anthropologist who had been conducting research in those very refugee camps, stating:

> The war the Israelis unleashed on the Palestinian people can be characterized as nothing less than genocide. What anthropologists quaintly used to refer to as "my village" or "my people" has, in my case, been deliberately obliterated by Israel and its allies, the Phalangists and the Lebanese army. Israel's stated aim in invading Lebanon was to destroy PLO military and political capacities. I feel that an unstated but equally pursued aim was to destroy Palestinian society and culture (and as many of the people as possible), which justifies condemning their policies and actions as genocide.[91]

She then detailed the US-supplied weaponry used in the invasion, listed the camps and facilities that had been destroyed, described the rounding up of "all men between the ages of 14-60" by the Israeli army and their subsequent labeling by nationality and religion, detailed the Israeli siege and "indiscriminate bombings" of West Beirut, and provided survivors' accounts of the Sabra and Shatila massacres. And she did this as a graduate student, something that the vast majority of our interlocutors would characterize as extraordinarily brave, given the potential career consequences of such an action.

In the ensuing discussion, AAA members who opposed the resolution used strategies to suppress criticism of the Israeli state that continue to appear in association discussions to this day, including accusing supporters of anti-Semitism, stating that Israel acted in self-defense, and using procedure to thwart votes. One MENA anthropologist who was at the 1982 meeting called this "the usual Zionist shtick," while another characterized it as "shenanigans," explaining that a group of people "tried to prevent it from even coming to a vote by suggesting the absence of a quorum. And then they all got up . . . and they walked just outside the doorway and stood there with their arms folded and watched while somebody went around and counted hands." When a quorum was declared, "there was pandemonium among these people, and then they all rushed back in to vote against the motion, but it passed."[92] This was a major coup and, in subsequent years, one that would be difficult to imagine reoccurring.

The meeting then grew even more exciting when someone introduced a new motion from the floor in support of Palestinian academic freedom in the Israeli-occupied West Bank. This statement condemned a number of Israeli actions against West Bank universities and their professors and students and was again signed by a diverse coalition of scholars.[93] An anthropologist who was present recalled that the AAA president, M. Margaret Clark, said the statement was out of order because it had not been submitted as a resolution prior to the meeting and placed on the agenda. The person who made the motion asked for an exception because it addressed very recent events. Clark said no, the person appealed, and the parliamentarian ruled that there should be a vote on the appeal. A majority voted to allow the motion, which meant that the statement could be discussed. Then, in the words of an attendee, "We debated [the statement] and then we voted on it and then it passed. There was absolute pandemonium."

Both statements begin by asserting that the AAA has historically supported political statements based on broad values of protecting cultural heritage, human life and rights, and/or academic freedom.[94] They claim that it is appropriate for the AAA to make these particular statements based on that history and that MENA anthropologists possess the expertise to both analyze and represent the region on these issues. The second statement also draws on the association's long-standing concern with academic freedom. But in neither case do we see a focus on "anthropological relevance"—that criterion that some earlier scholars had emphasized. And crucially, neither statement waters down its language or constructs a false sense of "balance." A massacre is called a massacre, and the suppression of academic freedom is named as such. Their final calls are broad and sweeping, suggesting a sense that it was fully appropriate for the AAA to call upon both the United States and foreign governments in relation to political, military, and rights concerns.

After the meeting, the incoming AAA president informed the listed government authorities about the statements. The December 21, 1982, letter to President Reagan focused mainly on a resolution about nuclear disarmament that was also adopted at that lively business meeting and then noted that four other statements, including the Lebanon one, were enclosed.[95] AAA records contain a three-page response to the MENA statements on Israeli Embassy letterhead, signed by the minister of information. The response denied Israeli state suppressions of academic freedom and involvement in Lebanon (the latter claim was later reversed by the Israeli government). It also described Israel's military administration in "Judea, Samaria, and the Gaza district" as "among the most liberal and benevolent." Judea and Samaria are the terms Zionists use to assert biblical historical claims, suggest that the territories belong solely to Israel, and, sometimes, convey support for further Israeli expansion. To our knowledge, there was no further communication from either party.[96] That, however, was not the end for these statements; they revealed, once again, disciplinary frictions that have yet to be resolved.

Heated debates (primarily over the Lebanon resolution) persisted in the AAA for around two years, as *Anthropology Newsletter (AN)* printed at least nineteen letters to the editor both supporting and opposing the statement. Some of these letters show the common oppositional tactic of doubting procedure, including questioning the voting credentials of AAA members present at the meeting.[97] Other letters, including one from then-president of the Israeli Anthropological Association, Shlomo Deshen,[98] paralleled the Israeli government response and focused on denying the resolution's claims. However, the vast majority of oppositional letters drew upon ideological arguments or accusations of bias or imbalance, and many singled out specific statement supporters for personal attack. An anthropologist from the University of Haifa called the resolution a "one-sided, biased polemic initiated by some individuals who succeeded in using the *AN* for political ends and giving vent to their hatred of Israel" and then specifically called out its Israeli cosponsor as one such individual.[99] Most troubling were accusations, like those by Jacques Soustelle and Ernst Wrechner, respectively, that the resolution demonstrated "a systematic anti-Israeli bias" or was somehow anti-Semitic.[100] Stephen Pastner went so far as to suggest that it "bolsters the futile fantasies of those who deny the right of Israel to exist," and "nourishes the rapidly spreading climate of anti-Semitism in Europe."[101] In a second letter published eighteen months later, Pastner also suggested that Palestinians were acting "out of cultural values that make them collaborators in the perpetuation, even the genesis, of their own misery."[102]

Supporters of the resolutions also wrote letters. Laurence Michalak responded to the accusation of "one-sidedness" by noting that the resolution called for *all* foreign military forces to withdraw and criticized both the Israeli and Lebanese governments.[103] Barbara Aswad and Louise Sweet underscored the importance of listening to anthropologists who had conducted fieldwork in the area—a sign of the relatively recent establishment of MENA cultural anthropology as a subfield.[104] Others, like Roselle Tekiner, sought to establish the facts of the Israeli invasion, using international commission reports to correct misinformation[105] or, like Frederick Huxley, emphasized that the "war" had been "largely 'one-sided'. . . . Israelis did most of the fighting. Lebanese and Palestinians most of the dying."[106] The Israeli cosponsor of the resolution, Henry Rosenfeld, responded directly to his attackers and suggested that he would have made its language *stronger* because he thought the phrase "destruction of peoples and cultures" was "too anthropologically euphemistic for straight military brutality, the death and pain of thousands, and the attempt to destroy a (Palestinian) national movement."[107] Rohn Eloul supported the resolution by pointing out that it was no more prejudiced than a previous one condemning the US invasion of Grenada.[108] Supporting letters also emphasized that criticism of Israel was not anti-Semitic,[109] with one calling out opponents who had used "the all-too-familiar tactic of leveling accusations of prejudice and hate [e.g., anti-Semitism] against those who dare to criticize Israel."[110] And Michalak likewise reiterated that the resolution was directed toward particular state policies, which were also opposed by many Israeli Jews: "The motion was neither anti-Semitic nor anti-Israeli. The motion condemned specific policies of specific governments. If to oppose the Israeli intervention in Lebanon is anti-Israel then, by analogy, was it anti-American to opposed American intervention in Viet Nam? Were the other AAA motions anti-Guatemalan and anti-Brazilian (and anti-Latin American)? And were the 400,000 Israeli protesters who protested the invasion, and the Israeli commission which condemned the government's role in the massacres also guilty of 'nourishing a climate of anti-Semitism'"?[111] Even one of the statements' opponents, Moshe Shokeid, stated in his letter that there was nothing anti-Semitic about criticizing Israel.[112]

This debate continued for over two years, until *AN*, according to one of our interlocutors, "announced a moratorium on letters about the topic." Yet the 1982 statements and their aftermath would continue to reverberate in two significant, though seemingly contradictory, ways. On the one hand, these statements broke the AAA's silence around MENA politics. "The AAA has passed resolutions concerning other regions. The Middle East has remained tabu," wrote Suad Joseph in *AN*, continuing, "The sustained, and occasionally shrill, debate reflects both differences in views and relief and fear resulting from silence shattering."[113] On the other hand, the opposition's attacks—and the fact that they took place in a climate of compulsory Zionism and organized campaigns against those who criticized Israel—reinforced and augmented existing silencing mechanisms. Some of our interlocutors described feeling very "burned" by both their disciplinary colleagues and the AAA as a result of experiencing this backlash against speaking out in support of Palestinians. As one senior scholar explained, after 1982, AAA discussions of Israel "would become so incredibly charged and the words flung out with hatefulness instead of thoughtfulness . . . people were shouting at each other. . . . It was kind of a breaking point for me. I was just so disheartened, so disillusioned." These responses prompted some MENA anthropologists to shift their attentions away from the AAA.

Some scholars went back to MESA, which had grown less Orientalist and more welcoming to Palestinian perspectives.[114] But for many of the female scholars who had felt burned by anthropology, MESA was not feminist enough. Legend has it that in the mid-1980s, feminist scholars walked out of a MESA business meeting that included a belly dancer and vowed to create their own organization. They had already begun to organize to ensure that the conference program included more panels about women and gender. In 1984, in a "standing-room only" meeting, feminist scholars debated whether to create a separate association or work to mainstream gender into Middle East Studies more broadly. The former view won (though the latter was a welcome consequence). The following year, they established the Association for Middle East Women's Studies (AMEWS)—a new academic home for feminist MENA scholars, including those critical of Israeli state actions.[115] Almost every female MENA anthropologist trained before the late 1990s mentioned it as a formative network that linked her back to MESA. In a sign of change, one of AMEWS's founders, anthropologist Barbara Aswad, was elected MESA president in 1992; another AMEWS founder, region-related anthropologist Suad Joseph, served in that position in the 2000s. Anthropologists also continued fostering area studies networks via MERIP. One female scholar trained in the 1980s described these two groups as "the comfort places" in comparison to the AAA. At AMEWS and MERIP,

> You could say whatever you wanted to say. You didn't have to censor yourself. There was that sense of being with likeminded people. They knew what you were talking about. And you were all, I don't want to say we were all on the same page, but we were in a conversation that didn't involve a lot of censorship or a lot of sort of people saying, "Huh? You work on Palestine? Where's that?" And I remember once at an AAA [conference], someone said, "Why would you want to work on Palestinians?"

Moving into the 1990s, we begin to see renewed engagement with disciplinary institutions among some of our interlocutors. The subfield's growth was one impetus, as more MENA anthropologists attended the AAA meetings for career purposes or because anthropology was becoming theoretically more exciting to them. MENA anthropology's increasing institutionalization also attracted some of our interlocutors (and alienated others), as MERGA become the Middle East Section of the AAA.

The Separation of Ethics and Politics?
1990s Institutionalization and Regulation

In 1995—on the tail end of an AAA restructuring process that centralized affiliated groups as "sections" of the association—MERGA and MENA anthropology were institutionalized into the AAA as the Middle East Section (MES).

This enhanced the region's visibility within anthropology. The new section's mission and goals statement emphasized outreach to other anthropologists and to broader publics, echoing earlier concerns with making MENA anthropology relevant in both the discipline and broader discussions about the region.[116]

But that visibility came at a cost, as earlier discussions in MERGA had foreseen. The collectivist sensibility and progressive political ethos of the 1970s gradually gave way to a bureaucracy that emphasized order, process, and, in many cases, a narrower range of what could be considered anthropologically relevant political stances.[117] MENA anthropology's relative loss of autonomy meant that political advocacy was subject to greater regulation, as well as centralized decision making. It also embroiled MENA anthropology in long-standing AAA debates about the discipline's proper relationship to governments and the people with whom we conduct research, just as the region was taking center stage in post–Cold War US foreign policy.

Institutionalizing required a great deal of time and labor, often done by women like Saunders and Aswad.[118] A male then-graduate student noted, "It wasn't the high profile Middle East anthropologists who were doing that work, because I guess the Dale Eickelmans and the Paul Rabinows were too important to run just a low league little section so they left it to the women."[119] In an indication of the sudden increase in bureaucratization to which MENA anthropology was subjected, the labor to create MES included drafting bylaws, collecting dues, corresponding with the AAA on multiple rules, and, most crucially, recruiting enough members to meet AAA minimum requirements for a section. It was indeed an achievement, but no one could have predicted its consequences for the relationship among discipline, region, and politics.

Around this time, the AAA implemented two important changes that would affect the discipline's later engagements with the War on Terror. In 1995, the executive board established the Committee for Human Rights (CfHR). While this committee initially focused mainly on the Americas, especially indigenous peoples, it eventually played a role in shaping the AAA's MENA politics in the 2000s, often in alliance with MENA anthropologists. The creation of the CfHR not only signaled the explicit centrality of human rights to AAA activities, but also institutionalized such concerns into the association's structure. In addition, the AAA spent much of the 1990s developing a new ethics code. This code, approved in 1998, was very clear on the relationship between anthropology, ethics, and politics: "Anthropologists may choose to move beyond disseminating research results to a position of advocacy. This is an individual decision, not an ethical responsibility."[120] While some MENA anthropologists agreed with this statement, many others (especially women, junior scholars, and region-related scholars) instead understood advocacy, especially speaking out against injustice, to be an ethical responsibility they held *as anthropologists.*

On another perennially fractious matter: the new code did not outright condemn secret research. Instead it stated that anthropologists "must be open about the purpose(s), potential impacts, and source(s) of support for research projects with funders, colleagues, persons studied or providing information, and with relevant parties affected by the research," that research should be made "appropriately available to sponsors, students, decision makers, and other nonanthropologists," and that "persons studied" should be informed of the "purpose(s), potential impacts, and source(s) of support for the work." This language is ambiguous enough to not require that anthropological work be made "public" in the broadest sense of the term. It also indicates that research fulfilling these requirements (and others listed, including to do no harm to subjects) is "ethical, regardless of the source of funding . . . or purpose." Yet there are a great many anthropologists who think that certain sources of funding are deeply ethically compromising, and that research supported by such funding cannot guarantee the pledge to do no harm.[121] Furthermore, despite the seemingly regulatory thrust of having an ethics code, this particular version of it represented the culmination of a long process of deregulating collective responsibility for anthropologists' ethical violations (what Gerald Berreman called "Reaganethics"), by placing much of the determination of responsible ethical practice into the hands of individuals, rather than the association.[122] In the absence of an explicit condemnation of secret research or problematic sources of funding, and without official AAA ramifications for violations of the code, anthropology's core tensions remained unresolved. Accordingly, the ethics debates would grow even more heated during the War on Terror.

The 1990s also saw the widening of geographic and topical foci for AAA political statements alongside the narrowing of what constituted a legitimately *anthropological* political concern.[123] In an early assertion that contributions to public discourse should be specifically anthropological, an executive board resolution opposing California's Proposition 187 stated that the AAA should seek to inform people about immigration issues "based on sound anthropological research." For well over a year, the board discussed boycotting Chicago as a meeting site until the University of Illinois abandoned its offensive Native American mascot.[124] And at the decade's end, in November 2000, the board established a task force to address the El Dorado controversy over allegedly unethical practice by anthropologists in the Amazon; it also established guidelines to protect native populations in South America.[125] In general, most of the issues addressed by 1990s AAA statements represented a narrow range of anthropological possibility: anthropologists in the field, where they hold their meetings, where the objects they study might be illegally sold, and what constitutes ethical anthropological research.

This narrowing of purview, along with increasing bureaucratization and longstanding divisions within the discipline, shaped the fate of the three MENA-related statements brought to the association in the 1990s. Non-MENA anthropologist Carol McClain (who trained in the late 1960s to early 1970s) presented a motion on "the Persian Gulf crisis" at the 1990 business meeting.[126] The motion opposed the (then potential) US invasion on the grounds that it would cause the deaths of American soldiers, Iraqi troops, and civilians and foreign nationals in Kuwait and Iraq, as well as "widespread devastation and unforeseeable threats to peace and stability" in the Gulf. It used the broad language of international citizenship to frame the issues[127] and then called upon President Bush and Congress to seek only nonmilitary solutions to the crisis and to work toward arms reduction in the Middle East.[128] It passed by a majority oral vote at the business meeting, but because there was no quorum, became "advisory" to the executive board.

Executive board documents show that significant changes were made to the motion's original text, and McClain was only informed after the fact. A copy of the motion from the board meeting at which it was discussed includes the handwritten phrase "contentious point" in the margin next to the item: "Be it resolved that the [AAA] call upon President Bush . . . to: Pledge not to order a U.S. military offensive first strike in Kuwait or Iraq." This suggests that, as in the Vietnam period, anthropologists debated whether or not to support a United States–led war. The board then asked William Beeman, an anthropologist of Iran trained in the late 1960s to early 1970s, and Ronald Cohen, an anthropologist of Nigeria trained in the 1950s, to rework the motion.[129] The two faxed the AAA office a text with an entirely rewritten "be it resolved" section. This new version was adopted and then-AAA president Jane Buikstra sent it verbatim to President Bush, Vice President Quayle, and Speaker of the House Foley in January 1991.[130]

Several telling revisions to this motion hearken back to anthropology's other history—one of disciplinary support for enhancing US global influence, including through engagement with the US state and military. The new text allowed for the possibility of a military solution if economic sanctions and diplomacy failed. Rather than decreasing US presence in the region, as McClain had advocated, it suggested that the United States "increase contributions of other than US armed forces in the multinational military resources deployed." The revised statement also privileged US State Department solutions by emphasizing diplomacy and "formal peace negotiations."[131]

In contrast, the other MENA-related motions of the 1990s demonstrated efforts to continue MERGA's activist legacy through MES, while establishing the section as the region's voice in the AAA. Like the original Persian Gulf crisis motion, these were spearheaded by women trained in the 1960s and 1970s. At the 1997 annual meeting, two different statements condemning US sanctions against Iraq were passed. MENA anthropologist Soheir Morsy brought one motion to the AAA business meeting, where, after a brief procedural hitch,[132] it was passed in a nonquorum vote of 24 to 3. The full AAA membership then adopted it in a spring ballot.[133] That same year, MENA anthropologists Aswad and Ann Bragdon brought another motion about the sanctions to the MES membership, which adopted it in a unanimous vote.[134]

Unlike the motions of the 1980s, neither of these statements based their claims on long-standing histories of the AAA taking ethical political stances, but unlike the revised Persian Gulf motion, they unequivocally advocated decreasing US presence in the region. In parallel with the recent formation of the CfHR, the AAA statement highlighted international law and human rights and called simply for an end to the sanctions.[135] The broader MES statement added a call for humanitarian assistance to rebuild Iraq.[136] Both thus drew on the burgeoning trend to make legitimizing claims through human rights principles. The most striking difference between them is that the MES statement explicitly draws on the *Section* as well as anthropologists as repositories of knowledge, highlighting the desire to establish the visibility and expertise of MENA anthropology both in the AAA and more broadly.[137] Indeed, following the meetings, MES President Barbara Larson asked the AAA executive director to add "our specialized voice to that of the AAA membership in general" and disseminate the MES statement alongside the AAA one. The AAA did so prominently in the next issue of its newsletter.[138] At last, it seemed, the expertise of scholars who focus on the region, especially women, was being recognized and granted a voice in the larger anthropological community.

· · ·

But these would be the last statements brought forward by MENA anthropologists that would pass smoothly. The events of September 11, 2001, and the subsequent War on Terror were on the horizon. From that point forward, MENA became not just one, but *the* primary lens through which anthropology's tensions were reproduced, navigated, and debated. As many MENA anthropologists sought to make the AAA speak out against US-supported state violence targeting Middle Easterners and Muslims at home and abroad (and the potential complicity of anthropology in that violence), they faced roadblock after roadblock. Their expertise was willfully or unintentionally ignored or minimally represented in discussions. And they confronted ignorance of and double standards toward MENA on the part of some anthropologists who specialize in other regions.

While institutions provide opportunities for building subfields, alignments, and relationships, they also constrict such opportunities or narrow their possibilities. Over time, we see how anthropology's main disciplinary association became especially limiting for scholars who have asked it to take stances supporting MENA peoples and opposing US involvement in the region and support for the Israeli state. In the words of a former AAA officer, "Often well-meaning left-leaning people, like myself, and others, people who strive to be inclusive and collaborative . . . the institutions and associations have repressive structures that do have constraining effects on us." Indeed, since the late 1970s, many MENA anthropologists have viewed the AAA as thwarting their efforts to actualize what they understood as an ethical responsibility to their research interlocutors— a responsibility they think anthropologists of other world regions are more easily able to fulfill. For them, bureaucratization has had a depoliticizing effect on their disciplinary practice.[139] Whereas MENA was once an exception in terms of disciplinary coverage, it soon became an exception in terms of whose expertise was recognized. It also became even more of an exception in terms of how political and ethical principles were applied. This was true for MENA anthropologists on all sides of the looming War on Terror debates.

5 Dis/Engaging the War on Terror

In March 2003, the United States spearheaded a massive military invasion of Iraq based on lies that then-President Saddam Hussein had weapons of mass destruction (WMDs) and was linked to al-Qaeda. Most Middle East experts immediately knew that the latter claim was preposterous, and within a couple of months we learned that the WMD intelligence was faulty as well. What was the cost of this invasion and consequent war and occupation built entirely on lies? Nearly *half a million* dead Iraqis. The virtual destruction of Iraqi society, including historical sites and material culture.[1] Almost five thousand dead US and allied soldiers. And thousands in Iraq and the United States living with permanent mental and physical injuries. One might expect that anthropologists, given their oft-stated commitment to support human cultural diversity and their robust critiques of colonialism and imperialism, would have been opposed to—if not outraged by—this war from its beginning. Many were. But in spring 2004, the leadership of their representative institution, the American Anthropological Association (AAA), explicitly refused to issue a public statement condemning the war.

Over the next few years both the AAA and its Middle East Section were slow to respond to the War on Terror and the shifting US political climate it fomented. Indeed, at the very moment when many MENA anthropologists' fieldsites were being pulled into a politicized spotlight and our research interlocutors deemed "the enemy" by the US government, the section representing these anthropologists in the AAA took an explicit step *away* from political advocacy. And AAA attentions more broadly were turned *everywhere but* toward the war in its national midst.

How did this happen? How did the discipline that often prides itself on caring for human society and speaking truth to power *not* respond quickly and forcefully to condemn US empire and its vast destruction of human life? Much of the answer lies in the historical tensions at the discipline's core: tensions over taking collective and public political positions, defining anthropological relevance and expertise, working (secretly or not) for the government's defense and intelligence agencies, and prioritizing protecting anthropologists over their research interlocutors. It also lies in processes of institutionalization; persistent hierarchies of gender, race, and generation; and the historical treatment of MENA as an exception in anthropology—especially through the lens of compulsory Zionism.

All these factors shaped disciplinary engagements with the War on Terror and Israel-Palestine politics in the twenty-first century. The AAA struggled to steer a course for anthropology as the war spread, overtly and covertly, across the globe and within the United States, resulting in skyrocketing deaths, detentions, imprisonments, incidents of torture, and oppressive surveillance and securitization. The association refused to act in response to complaints that most Middle Eastern and/or Muslim noncitizen adult males in the United States were subjected to special registration and profiled in extra security measures on the streets and at airports. Debates raged over whether and how anthropologists should participate in the war effort, especially as they were increasingly sought out by the US government, including the military and the CIA. Battles erupted over whether anthropologists should condemn the main recipient of US foreign aid—Israel—for its rapidly intensified colonization of Palestinian territory and its brazen attacks on Palestinian life.

Eventually, the AAA denounced the US occupation of Iraq. Nonetheless, frictions around government engagement simmered, as did the historic disregard for Middle Eastern peoples and the discipline's inability to develop a clear approach to Israel-Palestine. As the international movement to bring an end to Israel's oppressions of Palestinians grew exponentially in the twenty-first century, Israel-Palestine politics continued to haunt anthropology—the discipline with a long (if checkered) track record of speaking out against human rights violations[2] and a large proportion of practitioners who consider it the champion of all oppressed peoples—except one.

Initial Institutional Responses (or Lack Thereof) to 9/11

Just two months after 9/11, with a war underway in Afghanistan and a spate of vigilante attacks against Arabs, Muslims, and Sikhs in the United States, the Middle East Section (MES) of the AAA decided to move away from public political advocacy on behalf of Middle Eastern peoples. The November 2001 minutes from the MES board meeting, presided over by MES President Jon Anderson, state: "Past President [Fadwa El-Guindi] stressed activism and now [there will be] a shift towards Expressive Cultures." While political *context* appeared in the 2001 MES business meeting's panel that provided information about 9/11's impact on the Arab American community, an overall shift away from activist *engagement* came in the form of reluctance toward political statement making. The first several MES presidents of this century—mostly white male scholars trained before the 1990s—focused mainly on institution building (including outreach and internet presence) and further integrating the section into AAA bureaucracy.[3]

Meanwhile, AAA leadership focused its attention elsewhere, once again on indigenous peoples in the Americas. The executive board devoted most of its November 2001 meeting to the El Dorado situation: the aftermath of Patrick Tierney's bombshell of a book accusing anthropologist Napoleon Chagnon of ethical breaches in his work with indigenous groups in the Amazon.[4] Clearly this situation was crucial to the discipline; it was an issue of anthropological negligence, and anthropologists were rightly concerned about those indigenous communities. At the same time, the AAA's intensive multiyear focus on the El Dorado affair during the expanding War on Terror also suggests a narrowed purview of anthropological relevance. It deemed certain situations (e.g., those directly involving anthropologists or violations of the ethics code), topics (e.g., "kinship"), and peoples (e.g., those who fit a dominant understanding of "indigenous") as appropriate for association attention. As MENA anthropologists would soon learn, rural Afghans killed by US bombs and hate crimes in the United States against anyone assumed to be Muslim apparently did not seem anthropologically relevant or deserving of association comment.

Neither did Palestinians, who by that point were nearly a year into their second intifada against Israeli occupation, having lost hundreds of lives and faced, according to the Israeli military, over one million bullets in the uprising's first two months alone.[5] The 2001 MES board's institution-building focus was especially striking because it did not reopen discussion of a resolution about the second intifada that the previous MES board had passed and submitted to the AAA business meeting in 2000. That resolution named Israel's occupation as the root cause of the Palestinian uprising and condemned the Israeli military's excessive use of force against Palestinians. It emphasized biased US media portrayals and the failings of US policy on Israel-Palestine. And it called on the AAA to "speak out in defense of the Palestinian people's humanity and against the excessive use of force against them, to recognize their legitimate grievances, and to support their right to international protection."[6] The resolution's text recalled earlier eras of politically engaged MENA anthropology. In contrast, its trajectory represented an era of AAA bureaucracy and MES eschewal of political advocacy. As there was no quorum at the AAA business meeting, the resolution landed on the agenda for the February 2001 executive board meeting. The board sent it to the Committee for Human Rights for "guidance"—a relatively uncommon move. In May 2001, after obtaining CfHR opinion, the board sent it "back to the MES to revise and rephrase"—again treating Israel with kid gloves not typically worn when the AAA criticized other states.[7] This record suggests that the resolution would have been on the agenda for that November 2001 MES board meeting, but it does not appear in the minutes.[8] There is no way to know who bears responsibility for its disappearance, but the statement in the MES minutes about turning away from "activism" suggests that a decision to ignore it may have been made at that time.

So why were the War on Terror and the escalation of Israeli oppression off the radar of these institutional boards in 2001? It is possible anthropologists still did not grasp the extent to which US support for Israel enabled the violence that would eventually kill thousands, the vast majority of them Palestinian.[9] It is also possible that November 2001 was simply too soon for sustained discussion about the causes and ramifications of the 9/11 attacks. Perhaps everyone was simply shell-shocked and had not yet processed these events' significance for anthropological work and the peoples upon whom it depends. Indeed, over the next year, the executive board affirmed support for Earth Charter principles and free speech rights in US higher education, but made no statements addressing the situation in MENA. MES was largely muted on the consequences of the War on Terror. Its 2002 business meeting program focused on research funding, and then-MES President Anderson told us that what he "viewed as important in 2002 was finally addressing practical matters about sources of funding for graduate studies and research, which had been repeatedly raised but hadn't been previously addressed and would have been on the business meeting in 2001 had not 9/11 intervened and that session been devoted instead to Arab-American experiences in the wake of 9/11." This partially pragmatic focus may have reflected AAA institutional culture; many association activities were related to professional matters. Perhaps the particular senior scholars who occupied AAA and MES leadership positions held different views about political engagement from the majority of junior scholars; they may also have differed on how to represent the discipline and delineate its purview. As senior scholars, they might not have experienced 9/11's repercussions for teaching and research in the same way as early career anthropologists; they may also not have done fieldwork as recently with affected communities.

Some anthropologists trained in the 1990s viewed this lack of unequivocal outcry against the War on Terror, as well as Israeli state violence, as irresponsible on the parts of both MES and AAA. They also thought these institutions were unable or unwilling to support junior scholars confronting a newly politicized landscape with little guidance. In retrospect, these scholars displayed a certain naiveté and set of assumptions about anthropologists' political views and commitments, as well as about AAA politics and structures. Their naiveté was accompanied by a strong feeling that MENA anthropology should collectively speak out—in the discipline, classroom, and public sphere—in a way that they wrongly assumed had never happened before.

The situation led a group of graduate students and postdoctoral scholars (including ourselves) to begin a conversation at the November 2001 AAA meetings about the challenges of writing and teaching about MENA. At the 2002 conference, six young female anthropologists (including two Arab Americans) quietly inaugurated a collective. Their first two projects were to plan a teaching workshop about the "Middle East, North Africa, and Islam" and to ghostwrite and submit four resolutions to the AAA membership. The collective met again in 2003 and discussed a range of issues, some of which, unbeknownst to them, refracted earlier MERGA and MES conversations through a new motivation to counteract the War on Terror's effects: deghettoizing MENA anthropology and MES within the AAA, doing outreach in primary and secondary schools, collecting oral histories about MENA anthropology in different political contexts, and taking action to prevent impending changes to Title VI legislation that would link area studies funding to War on Terror directives. At the end of that meeting, the group publicly emerged as the Task Force on Middle East Anthropology.

Aspects of the Task Force's mission statement echoed those of MES and even MERGA.[10] The statement emphasized increasing MENA anthropology's public relevance, conducting outreach, and creating "anthropologically informed conference panels and reports."[11] But it diverged from MES when it came to overt political advocacy. The Task Force statement took an explicit political stance in support of the region and its peoples, one that not only reflected earlier anthropological stances against prejudice and oppression, but also opposed US wars in the region *and* the Israeli occupation of Palestine. This group of junior MENA anthropologists chose to organize within their discipline, rather than defect to MESA as earlier scholars did, reflecting their emphasis on the AAA as the space for professional development.

For the next decade, the Task Force, which grew to over twenty members, planned AAA teaching and methods workshops, published articles and letters to editors, and disseminated an alert about attempts to pass the right-wing Academic Bill of Rights on college campuses. The group also researched and wrote the internationally circulated "Academic Freedom and Professional Responsibility after 9/11: A Handbook for Scholars and Teachers."[12] But it was the group's attempts at political advocacy, alongside allied MENA anthropologists, that renewed intractable assertions about the proper definition and use of "politics" within anthropology's institutions, assertions made from the vantage point of those in positions of institutional power. Once again, it seemed, MENA—and Palestine in particular—was an exception to how the discipline approached most regions.

Renewed Political Advocacy Efforts

After the invasion of Iraq, Task Force members felt that they had to try to get the AAA to oppose the War on Terror and its negative effects through political statement-making. They were shocked and disappointed when the association—which represented a discipline they imagined as progressive—responded in (according to many of our interlocutors) bureaucratic, conservative, and depoliticizing ways. The AAA response seemed typical to those who knew about its history of support for WWII and lack of action (or profusion of controversy) when it came to MENA issues. But Task Force members and others of their generation thought it reflected a double standard, a valuing of some peoples over others. Indeed, the fate of four resolutions that they submitted to the November 2003 AAA business meeting spoke volumes about anthropology's politics.

One of the resolutions on the table was a re-revision of the statement about the second intifada that MES had apparently ignored. One of its original authors, Fadwa El Guindi, had revised and resubmitted it to the executive board in 2002. At its spring 2003 meeting, after adopting a motion to publish reports of attacks on Guatemalan scholars in *Anthropology News* and support those scholars' visits to US campuses,[13] the board rejected the revised Palestine statement. El Guindi received a letter explaining that it was rejected because it did not refer to Israeli victims of suicide bombings. She gave up and passed the letter to the Task Force. Task Force members, well aware of the dominant practice of imposing an untenable notion of "balance" on discussions about a conflict with two structurally unequal sides,[14] added language about Israeli victims and recruited senior anthropologist of Palestine Ted Swedenburg to resubmit the resolution, *now in its third version*. This phenomenon of junior scholars ghostwriting political statements (especially those critical of Israeli state policies and actions) for tenured faculty to sign suggests that despite the overt politics of the Task Force mission statement, this was a generation so scared of its own discipline that its members were actively making their labor invisible. The other three resolutions—all signed mostly by junior scholars because they did not think they would be as controversial—condemned the US invasion of Iraq; supported academic freedom during the War on Terror; and supported the civil liberties of Arab, South Asian, and Muslim Americans who were being regularly pummeled in the press and on the streets. All four were passed by a large margin in a nonquorum vote during the 2003 AAA business meeting, reflecting the fact that many anthropologists wanted their association to take a stand on that fraudulent war, its racist domestic fallout, and Palestine.

But new forms of bureaucratic proceduralism melded with renewed arguments about what counts as anthropological (e.g., relevance, expertise, findings) to direct the trajectory of these resolutions. Because there was no quorum at the business meeting, they became advisory to the board, which would discuss them at their May 2003 meeting, deciding whether to pass, reject, or send them out for a full membership vote. Two other resolutions, addressing graduate assistance at Yale and marijuana laws,[15] joined the four MENA-related ones on the agenda. According to the meeting minutes, *prior* to discussing these resolutions, the executive board adopted a new set of guidelines for evaluating political statements.[16] One stipulation was that the board take stances only on situations where an impact seemed possible, which contrasted starkly with that part of AAA history that included political statement making on broad public issues where anthropology was a bit player. The guidelines also stipulated that statements "address matters of clear common professional interest" or about which "members have special knowledge and expertise" and that they "present anthropological findings, conclusions, or recommendations." In addition to departing from aspects of AAA history, this framing cast the executive board as judge of what counts as "anthropological," arguably narrowing disciplinary purview by leaving it to the board's discretion. It also assumed the uniformity of anthropology ("clear common professional interest") and agreement on what constitutes our areas of expertise.

We do not know what prompted the board to adopt these new guidelines at that particular moment. It is possible that opposition to one or more of the MENA-related resolutions played a role. The text and timing of the guidelines suggest that they implicitly construct an opposition between expertise or professional interest and political advocacy in order to sideline thorny

MENA-related issues. It could also be argued that in their attempt to standardize what counts as anthropological findings or conclusions, the guidelines separate knowledge from specific positionalities—a separation that many anthropologists have criticized since the 1970s. Certainly, the guidelines could be interpreted to deem the issues raised by the MENA resolutions as peripheral to professional interest or to suggest that their stances do not derive from expertise. They could also be used to defeat any resolution the AAA leadership judged undesirable. In any case, we see their impact on the ensuing discussion of the resolutions under consideration.

The board first discussed and adopted the resolution Graduate Assistance at Yale, which condemned reported intimidation of graduate students seeking to unionize at that university.[17] With the possible exception of the stipulation about feasible impact, this statement did not meet the criteria of the new guidelines. While protecting graduate students is important, it is not necessarily of greater "common professional interest and concern" than the issues described in the other resolutions, nor did this statement draw specifically on anthropological expertise. The fact that the board passed it unanimously suggests either that they understood statements on the May 2003 agenda to be grandfathered from the new guidelines or that the guidelines themselves were to be selectively applied.

The latter appears to be the case, because the board rejected all of the MENA-related resolutions except the one about academic freedom.[18] The minutes note that the board "appreciated the spirit" of the Iraq resolution and that they had already dealt with "the issue of antiquities in Iraq."[19] The MENA anthropologist on the board, William Beeman, then moved not to adopt the resolution "in accordance with the adoption of the guidelines for the consideration of public statements," because "While the issue of Iraq is still important, given the passage of time and current events, the issues raised in this motion are no longer relevant."[20] The idea that "issues" related to the invasion of Iraq were outdated seems, to put it mildly, rather shortsighted, given that the US occupation there would continue for years. Rather than relying on expertise as instantiated in AAA office structures, the board might have consulted scholars who researched on Iraq or the US armed forces. The board also rejected the other two MENA-related resolutions on grounds related to the new criteria. A rejection letter (and the minutes) stated that the civil liberties resolution required revision to "narrow the focus of this motion to that of anthropological interest and expertise"—suggesting either that such an interest excluded nonanthropologists or that it was unclear what an anthropological perspective added to the defense of civil liberties. The board agreed that the AAA president would redraft it "in consultation with the Middle East Section."[21] To our knowledge, that redrafting never took place, and the Task Force remained confused as to how supporting civil liberties lay further from anthropological expertise than protecting the rights of graduate students. Finally, the minutes note "The Board expressed concern about the wording" of the Palestine-related resolution and took no action on it and that "all citizens are concerned about this, but this was not a well-crafted statement. It was suggested that the authors be asked to review the newly adopted guidelines for the consideration of AAA Business Meeting Motions."[22] This resolution was certainly no further from meeting the new guidelines than the other ones under consideration, yet it was the only one for which the response letter directly invoked those guidelines.[23] The fact that the board, during this meeting, unanimously passed two resolutions (Yale and academic freedom) that did not fully satisfy the new guidelines suggests that the guidelines themselves were selectively applied when it came to the Middle East and to Arabs and Muslims.

Disciplinary tensions, narrowed anthropological purviews, and MENA-as-exception continued through official association actions (or inactions) in 2004. That year, the board adopted two other statements, one on "ethnography and institutional review boards" and another that criticized then-President Bush's call for a constitutional amendment condemning same-sex marriage by stating that there is no proof "across cultures and time" that "viable social orders depend upon marriage as an exclusively heterosexual institution."[24] The board and MES also jointly spoke out against the revocation of Islam scholar Tariq Ramadan's visa, which prevented him from taking a position at Notre Dame. Such expressions of concern about scholars' access to jobs or their dealings with review boards, as well as public statements about kinship, showed a significantly straitened definition of "professional interest or expertise" increasingly being applied in the new procedural bureaucratic regimes.[25]

Task Force members thought that MES at that time was a depoliticized space with little room for activism beyond protecting scholars and research. The 2004 MES board meeting minutes validated their interpretation when, in addition to the usual bureaucratic work,[26]

Those present discussed under what conditions policy statements should come from the MES and how such statements would be approved. The consensus was that we should not publish, circulate, or support as an organization any statement that takes political sides (for example, Arab versus Israeli). We should speak to general principles like protecting cultural heritage or, as in a recent case of a professor denied a visa, the primacy of academic freedom and the possibility of presenting many points of view on matters that fall within our purview. These statements may fall heaviest on certain parties, but all parties involved should be referenced.

Where matters [*sic*] of obvious agreement, like urging the United States government to protect the peoples and culture of a place like Iraq, the Board could vote for the membership. In cases that might be more controversial a ballot of members would be necessary.[27]

But the more activist strand of anthropology could not be completely silenced. That same fall, the Task Force wrote a letter conveying "the concern of experts in Middle Eastern anthropology and human rights, regarding the dire humanitarian situation in Falluja, Iraq, following the US-led military offensive on that city"[28] and obtained support from the Committee for Human Rights, which would emerge as a key ally in MENA advocacy. MES eventually signed on, perhaps because this situation was so dire, it seemed to be a "matter of obvious agreement," and/or there was clearly broader institutional support for the letter.

Nonetheless, with their recorded "consensus" about political statements, the MES board solidified a policy that would remain in effect, at least informally, until 2012, when Task Force members began to be elected as officers on the board. This policy essentially prevented the section from taking stances on issues like the Israeli occupation of Palestine. While we do not know whether there was a relationship between this MES direction and the new AAA guidelines, both reflect impulses to circumscribe anthropological relevance, establish bureaucratic structures and hierarchies of expertise, and essentially prioritize scholars over their research interlocutors. Both also had the effect of stifling informed public stances against forms of oppression, most obviously in relation to Palestinian rights.

In a final effort to push forward a Palestine-related resolution, the Task Force ghostwrote a statement condemning the wall Israel was building through occupied Palestinian land[29] and asked distinguished senior anthropologists Lila Abu-Lughod, Michael Gilsenan, Catherine Lutz, and Brinkley Messick to help them submit it for consideration at the AAA business meeting. In what was now a familiar pattern, the resolution passed in a vote with no quorum and landed on the executive board agenda.[30] AAA president Elizabeth Brumfiel emailed outgoing MES president Daniel Varisco, a Committee for Human Rights member, and Paul Nuti (then-AAA Director of External, Government, and International Relations), asking for their input: "Does it accurately describe the facts concerning the construction of the wall? Does it adequately bring anthropological perspectives to bear on the construction? Is it fair to both sides of the issue? Is this a human rights issue upon which the AAA should take a stand?" The incoming MES president, Jenny White, reported that the MES board had decided to "limit ourselves to projects (and presumably pronouncements) that fit within the purview of academic freedom, etc., and that we could not be in a situation to support statements of a more general political nature." She then added,

> As president of MES, I feel very strongly about this. We must support justice and human rights, but we also have a duty to represent ALL of our members, and when it comes to politicized issues, especially in places like the Middle East, this is a hard balance to maintain. In the case of this resolution, there has been a worldwide consensus that the wall is inhumane (viz the International Court of Justice decision), BUT the wall is a response to Palestinian killings of Israeli civilians which, in turn is a response to Israeli actions. . . . The complexities and finger pointing are endless. I note with approval that the resolution also condemns Palestinian killings of Israeli civilians.[31]

With this statement, a senior anthropologist elected to lead the MENA anthropology community said that she did not think that the AAA should take political positions on behalf of Palestinians and that it was paramount to represent "ALL" MES members. However, our research shows that this position did not in fact adequately represent the views of most MENA anthropologists trained since 1990 and many trained in earlier decades. Furthermore, nearly all anthropologists who had actually conducted ethnographic research in the West Bank or in Palestinian communities thought—based on their ethnographic and anthropological expertise—that such stances were possible and often ethically crucial. In this matter, we see how institutionalization emphasizes hierarchies of authority within both the subfield and the discipline at large.

The final nail in the wall resolution's coffin seems to have been Nuti's response to Brumfiel detailing four reasons why the executive board should not adopt it.[32] In a lengthy memo, he asked why Israel should be singled out—a question that ignored the AAA history of speaking out on many other situations. He then argued that the statement was not "anthropological," giving comparative examples of issues about which the AAA had made statements: the conflict in Darfur *was* anthropological because it had "cultural and ethnic drivers." It is anthropological when "one of our own"—in that case a sociologist—is assassinated (as though Palestinian academics are neither "our own" nor facing dangers as they navigate the landscape Israel's wall created). Same-sex marriage is anthropological because it draws on an ethnographic record (as though there were no history of ethnography of Palestinian communities). And "ongoing work with endangered tribal peoples, a traditional domain for anthropological activism," is anthropological simply because it always has been. Not only did this comparative list ignore the AAA's extensive history of what by Nuti's standards would constitute "nonanthropological" political statements, but it also positioned "tribal peoples" or other (non-Palestinian) scholars as the only people worthy of anthropological defense.

Nuti's third point in the memo asserted that no stance could be taken on the "Israeli-Palestinian conflict" because, in his view, this was a moment of potential progress toward peace talks—a view history has belied in ways Palestine scholars could have easily predicted had they been consulted. Indeed, his idealization of "peace" ignored the power dynamics the regional experts who wrote and submitted the resolution described in it. Instead, Nuti argued that the resolution's "rhetorically charged language . . . has been recycled over and over since the 1970s." He gave no example of what exactly constitutes "rhetorically charged" language, nor did he justify the idea that the length of time a claim against oppression has circulated diminishes its validity. (Native Americans might be surprised to hear an AAA representative suggest this idea). Finally, Nuti asked why the United States should be singled out: "The call for modified American foreign policy on this issue is irrelevant to the rest of the resolution and, frankly, irrelevant to any anthropological contribution/insight that AAA might offer on it." Here it seems that commentary on US foreign policy was deemed outside the purview of what is, after all, the *American* Anthropological Association. His final word on the matter was to advise that "AAA let the resolution die" because "it will not enhance our credibility." Credibility to whom, one must ask. Clearly the AAA was principally concerned about self-image, especially in a War on Terror environment where Zionism was hegemonic.

And because one nail in the coffin was apparently not enough, when AAA Executive Director Bill Davis sent five statements, including this one, to the executive board for consideration at their May 2005 meeting, he only reminded them of the new guidelines in relation to the resolution about Israel's construction of the wall. He then wrote, "I agree completely with Mr. Nuti and would recommend that the Board act to defeat the Motion." Unsurprisingly, this is exactly what the AAA Board did, voting unanimously to "take no action on the motion since it does not adhere to the previously adopted guidelines for consideration of annual meeting motions."[33] The full membership never got a chance to weigh in on the issue. Many MENA anthropologists were disgusted.

Confusing "Narrow Professional Focus" for "Humanity"

In a comprehensive response in *Anthropology News*, MENA anthropologist Gregory Starrett criticized the board's refusal to pass the resolutions or submit them to the larger membership for a vote. He cogently wrote that "One communication the AAA has sent to its members is a perverse one that confuses narrow professional focus . . . for humanity."[34] He argued the rejections sent the message that anthropologists only cared about Middle Easterners when they were scholars like them and that "a picket line appears more significant than war" (referring to AAA's decision to move its annual conference due to a hotel labor strike).[35] Starrett's assessment perfectly captures one of the main sentiments expressed by our interlocutors in response to the new guidelines' emphasis on anthropological relevance.

The new guidelines were only one of multiple board efforts to control certain kinds of political statement making. Their timing and very particular invocation whenever MENA issues were discussed supported the idea many MENA scholars shared that, once again, anthropology treated their region differently from others, especially when it came to Israel-Palestine. Some anthropologists told us they thought that both the AAA and MES were either "apathetic" or deliberately apolitical or obstructionist. Their explanations for interpreting these institutions this way depended upon their personal political views, experiences, and ideas about the relationship of scholarly associations to political engagement. Many MENA anthropologists trained since 1990 felt "bitter" after the rejections of the 2003–2004 resolutions, akin to the "burn" that earlier activists had felt in the 1980s after the vitriolic responses to the 1982 resolutions condemning Israeli actions in Lebanon and the West Bank. This experience of political failure shaped these anthropologists' understandings of and relationships to their disciplinary association. Even more MENA anthropologists thought there were double standards at work in how the criterion "anthropological relevance" was applied and in whose anthropological expertise counted. As one person put it, "You can yell all you want about the Yanomami or Guatemalans but not about Palestine." Here "the Yanomami" signals the Chagnon case (and Amazonian indigenous peoples more broadly), while "Guatemalans" reflects a generalized sense that the AAA deemed issues facing Central American communities "anthropological" more frequently and consistently than those facing Middle Eastern ones.

It seems likely that AAA executive board response to such criticisms would have been an appeal to standardized criteria. From the perspective of a former board member (a non-MENA anthropologist) from this era, defining anthropological relevance made sense because it circumscribed what was actionable:

> For instance, we often got [a resolution] that the AAA should support the legalization of marijuana. . . . And one of the tests was, do we think that [it requires] anthropological knowledge or expertise, you know . . . I am for decriminalization of marijuana and maybe I could argue for that because . . . I know something about the unequal sentences between, let's say, of white high school kids and Black kids. . . . But if there was a statement about climate change, I, *as an anthropologist*, do not know that green house gases operate like little lenses and allow solar energy in as light, but then it's converted to heat . . . I believe it and I'm persuaded of it, but not *as an anthropologist*, and so one argument is that we shouldn't pass anything that we don't know as anthropologists. . . . If you want to talk about the effect of climate change on people on islands, that's different. But if you're going to say, we as anthropologists know that it's the fossil fuels that are causing it, we don't know that *as anthropologists*.

We argue that what is understood to be "known" because one is an anthropologist is contingent on the research foci, interests, and expertise of executive board members at any given time. Certainly, one of the reasons the AAA has made so many statements about the Americas is that historically more board members have worked there.[36] This logical concordance between board expertise and AAA political stances can be seen, for instance, in the rapid issuance of the aforementioned statement on marriage and family. It was initiated by an email from a board member who thought "this is where we should intervene" because "if somebody like the President of the United States is using an anthropological claim and we let it pass . . . we actually have to get in a habit of noticing when other people are speaking anthropology and speaking back to them if we think they've done it wrong."

The desire to correct misuse of anthropology relates to yet another reason for MENA's exceptional treatment in the AAA. The association often privileges its institutional stability and anthropology's reputation over making political statements that might threaten those priorities. A senior MENA anthropologist with some AAA committee experience noted that the association "of course has its own vested interests in the profession, you know, their main thing is to keep a decent public image, and even a positive public image of anthropology.

So anything that smacks of controversy . . . they really work very carefully."
This person went on to suggest that anyone who wanted to work with the association had to first learn "the terrain of AAA politics and how you play that
particular game. And I don't mean it to be too cynical, but the AAA's got this
gentle concern about the image of anthropology." To many of our MENA interlocutors, this concern with anthropology's public image felt like the AAA "is
more concerned with protectionism of the discipline," as one put it, than with
the people who live in the region where we work. Combined with the idea that
double standards were applied when defining "anthropological," this suggested
to many that political reasons led to the dismissal of MENA resolutions. Some
more explicitly stated that the problem was the Zionist leanings of other anthropologists, including executive board members. One person expressed the
views of many when she said, specifically about Israel-Palestine, "Anthropologists like to think of themselves as progressive, but they can't get on the right
side of this issue." Another scholar explained, "You get this perception that everyone is like you and they take the same positions, because you know, they're
against the occupation . . . you feel like . . . there's this critical mass here like
you. But then you get disappointed when you scratch a little bit and you realize
it's only in words and they're not willing to take that position and confront."
And a former executive board member told us, "I mean obviously there are
some members in the AAA that are, well, especially with regard to the Israeli-
Palestinian issue as you can imagine, there are some people who have very
strong opinions on either side"—but went on to note that these opinions rarely
entered into board discussions.

Many of our interlocutors, however, thought that it was precisely such opinions that dominated AAA decision making. An astonishing number of MENA
anthropologists trained since 1990 expressed "surprise" upon learning that
their disciplinary colleagues were not "progressive on Palestine"—which they
understood to mean anti-Zionist, opposed to oppressive Israeli state policies
and actions, and supportive of Palestinian rights. Their surprise reveals both a
naiveté about academia that was not shared by older-generation scholars and
an understanding of anthropology that hinges upon its identity as "progressive" relative to other disciplines, like political science. One person who had
learned this lesson noted, "As everywhere, Palestine-Israel ignites all kinds of
conflicts and otherwise good leftists or left-leaning or at least relatively progressive people, including academics, lose all sense of social justice."

While it may be unlikely that the executive board deliberately derailed
resolutions solely to defend Israel, our interviews do suggest that some board

members wanted to skirt the matter altogether in order to avoid confrontations. In other words, desires to maintain AAA unity contributed to a refusal to put Palestinian rights on the table, even for a full membership vote. A former AAA officer whose research is not in MENA told us very hesitantly that "the Middle East and politics are um, how can I say . . . you know kinda probably anthropologists, and this is just a guess, are more um, in agreement and homogeneity when it turns to Central American or you know, Asian politics than maybe Middle Eastern politics. Middle East politics are very fraught . . . there is probably less homogeneity um, than say politics and policy in say other parts of the world." Indeed, a number of former AAA officers expressed worries about the potential "divisiveness" of Israel-Palestine, with a few mentioning the Vietnam era as "something we don't want to go back to." A MENA anthropologist cogently diagnosed the impact of such worries on political statement making:

> I don't think you would find terribly many people in AAA who would say great things about Brazilian gold miners . . . going into the jungles and dispossessing people of their land . . . but there are people who would say good things about Israel. . . . In order to keep the organization from falling apart, you need to make sure that certain kinds of speech are not allowed within the organization, or that certain things don't happen. And so I think that making political statements about Honduras or about whoever is much safer than making political statements of whatever sort about the Middle East, because it's a live emotional issue among even people who don't work there, and I think that's one of the issues, right. What kind of emotional engagement do Middle East anthropologists really have with the Brazilian rainforest? Well, maybe, okay, y'know, a romantic, primitive kind of sustainability stuff.

Other former board members framed their worries as concerns about accuracy, standing up to public scrutiny, the association's financial health, and fears of liability. One explained that their board colleagues "agonized over" discussions about political stances in relation to the AAA's "credibility." Yet numerous political resolutions *were* passed over the years about other situations. And for the most part, board members made decisions about what would damage credibility based on assessments of anthropological relevance. Those assessments themselves relied on the foci and political perspectives of the scholars making them in the first place.[37]

These tensions were present even within MENA anthropology, to a certain degree and in relatively clear demographic patterns. A number of MENA anthropologists (all trained prior to the 1990s, and all white men except one white woman) viewed MES's new direction away from political advocacy positively, sometimes with a sense of relief.[38] As one scholar explained:

> We have members of our organization who are very pro-Palestinian and we have some who are less pro-Palestinian, shall we say, or maybe pro-Israeli, whatever that means. . . . And . . . certainly my understanding was that we shouldn't have a litmus test that you have to have a particular point of view. I mean, clearly it's a very tragic situation, but as anthropologists we should be interested in understanding what's going on and not casting stones and there are so many forums for the political. . . . So I think it's important for MES to have an academic approach to bring attention to issues, certainly. But not in a way that's going to draw, drive people out.

As with the narratives of former executive board members, this view links avoiding divisive issues to organizational unity, separates what is considered "academic" from the "political," and emphasizes anthropological knowledge— "understanding what's going on"—as devoid of political stance. It is reflected in senior MENA anthropologist Dale Eickelman's position that MENA Studies requires the "academic discipline to sustain a social science autonomous from . . . political advocacy."[39] Notably, none of the scholars who embraced such a view of the section's role had conducted sustained ethnographic research in Palestinian communities. Those who had (and many others) instead argued that anthropological knowledge about the Israeli occupation shows a clear direction in which to cast the stone and that research and knowledge production agendas are, as highlighted in postcolonial and poststructural theory, themselves already political. One of these anthropologists drew explicitly on ideas about ethical responsibility to our interlocutors to argue that anthropologists *in particular*, because of their research practices, have a responsibility to speak out on matters like the Israeli occupation—in effect using the same principle of "anthropological knowledge and relevance" to arrive at the opposite conclusion.

What set those who generally supported statement making apart from those who did not was, at core, a fundamentally different idea about what the AAA can and *should* do. In other words, while some viewed the AAA's primary purpose as supporting the profession, others argued that part of that purpose was to model a broader ethical imperative for the discipline that included concern for our interlocutors. As one person explained, political resolution making "*is* related to what we do [e.g., anthropologically relevant] because anytime we go to war we affect people." The MENA anthropologists who wanted the

AAA to pass such resolutions had no illusions about action in the real world or the literal utility of such statements.[40] Rather, they expressed a desire to see public statements because, in their view, they raised awareness and prompted discussion of issues that impact our research communities. They also thought that resolutions demonstrated, for the sake of the historical record, that one's profession had taken an ethical stance on matters that affect the lives of the people upon whom we build our careers. The fact that the AAA regularly made political statements about other peoples and issues drove this point home. As one noted, "It makes no impact, but there are issues of internal consistency that do bother me. . . . [So] why [do] we bother making statements about Honduras and Guatemala . . . y'know? Let's either do all of them or none of them." Soon this inconsistency, along with the sidelining of MENA issues, would become untenable.

Renewed Debates over War and Government Engagement

As public tide turned against the Iraq War and the US government explicitly recruited anthropologists to assist with the War on Terror, the AAA began to pay more attention to MENA-related matters. Even so, the issue that captured the most institutional energies—partly because it renewed long-standing disciplinary debates—was anthropologists working in various capacities for US intelligence agencies and the military, rather than the people in the region who were bearing the brunt of the war. And, in another continuity, many of these War on Terror discussions, including a (finally) successful resolution opposing the Iraq war, did not draw directly on MENA anthropological expertise.

At the 2006 AAA meetings, a rare quorum approved two resolutions. The first condemned the Iraq War and called for an end to all US military operations there. A second denounced the "use of anthropological knowledge as an element of physical and psychological torture," as well as torture more generally and extraordinary rendition. It also called for the closure of all US overseas prisons and reparations for those tortured by the United States or its proxies.[41] Both resolutions were then adopted in a full AAA membership vote in spring 2007. The following year, a resolution against "any covert or overt U.S. military action in Iran" passed during the business meeting.[42] In addition, since 2006, the executive board has issued numerous MENA-related statements, including resolutions and commissioned reports.[43] One statement criticized the Pentagon's Minerva Project, which gave Department of Defense funding to researchers doing work in line with its goals. AAA letters supported an anthropologist scheduled to present at the meetings whose visa request had been denied and, in collaboration with MESA, condemned the arrest of an Iranian anthropologist in Iran.

So what changed? Possible factors prompting this transformation include changes in AAA leadership and staff as well as in US public opinion.[44] By 2006 it was clear that the Iraq war was indeed not "outdated." It was also quite unpopular. The Abu Ghraib scandal not only brought torture to light, but also showed that the US military had been relying on a discredited anthropological work to develop its interrogation techniques.[45] The AAA press release about the 2006 resolutions noted how rare it was to achieve quorum at the business meeting; that these resolutions inspired attendance "hinted at broadening rank-and-file interest in expanding the AAA public policy role."[46] Some of the Iraq resolution sponsors became founding members of the Network of Concerned Anthropologists, initiated by (mainly) Americanist anthropologist Hugh Gusterson in 2007 in response to concerns about anthropology's growing militarization.[47]

Indeed, anthropology's new interest in the region brought issues that had long been of concern to MENA scholars into the association without involving those scholars. Perhaps that was a key to the success of these actions: they were supported by a broad group of anthropologists with long-standing connections to prestigious regional specialties and disciplinary institutional structures. The 2006 resolutions were put forward without a single MENA anthropologist's participation. As one of our interlocutors said, "They [the resolution sponsors] were Americanists and that's one of the things that pissed me off—is that when the experts, when the experts spoke, there was silence, and then when the Americanists spoke, [the response was] 'we'll do something.'" Similarly, the Network's founding members did not include anyone actively doing research in MENA. In edited volumes critiquing anthropology's militarization published during this time, few MENA anthropology voices, if any, were represented.[48]

Why were MENA anthropologists invisible in these important disciplinary conversations? One possibility is that the Network developed as many networks do—through relationships between colleagues and friends—and thus any snubbing of MENA anthropologists was unintentional. Another possibility is that the MENA anthropologists who held association leadership roles were opposed to AAA political statement making or took a minority view in relation to matters like CIA job ads. Other senior MENA scholars had long been disillusioned with AAA exceptionalism when it came to their region and had by that time turned their attentions to other institutions. When such scholars participated in the AAA, it was through committees like CfHR (Committee for Human Rights); for instance, MENA anthropologists Susan Slyomovics and Kamran Ali coedited a

CfHR series on anthropology and the Middle East for *Anthropology News*. Junior scholars may have been protecting themselves from political trouble on the job market and for tenure or remained discouraged by their failed advocacy efforts immediately after 9/11. They were perhaps less likely to be in the networks of those mostly Americanists who led these conversations. Yet MENA anthropologists *were* and *had been for some decades* at the forefront of militarized corporate and government recruitment, which sometimes verged on harassment. Despite this, between Vietnam and the War on Terror, the AAA does not seem to have discussed the discipline's relationship to intelligence and security agencies, at least not via any major commissions or reports.[49]

Indeed, our MENA interlocutors of all generations experienced CIA and other agency efforts to recruit them specifically for clandestine intelligence work over the years.[50] Everyone who reported being approached for clandestine work told us they either responded with hostility or attempted to ignore the recruitment efforts.[51] Several people were approached while on Fulbrights— in two cases, during different decades, directly by the CIA rather than a local embassy or attaché (which was more common). They all said no, more or less politely, sometimes multiple times, until the recruiter gave up. Another person "got kind of nasty" in an interview with a local FBI agent who wanted her help surveilling diaspora community networks. Sometimes scholars were not quite sure which agency was approaching them. One person turned down an offer from a consulting firm to do highly paid work because she realized "this is clearly not what it's supposed to be." A graduate student told us that they received an email from someone who would not reveal the agency she represented. When the student asked for more details, the recruiter asked for "a secure landline" and for the student to "please keep this exchange confidential." After saying no to the request, the student consulted a friend who works for the government, who told her it was probably the CIA.

More troubling were the occasions when recruitment efforts amounted to harassment of scholars. One faculty member explained that he has had to protect two region-related graduate students in recent years from harassment by intelligence contractors. And in a particularly harrowing case, the CIA telephoned an anthropologist at both office and home almost every day for three months. When the scholar asked what they wanted, they experienced "an hour and a half grilling" during which the CIA first asked for specific information about political organizing in the region and then asked the anthropologist to get it from their interlocutors. After multiple efforts to deflect them politely, the scholar lost their temper and scolded the agents about US policy in the region.

Our interlocutors generally agreed that clandestine research or government engagement of the type sought by organizations like the CIA is unethical. As one senior scholar put it, "The bottom line is . . . you don't do clandestine work, you don't use false pretenses to get information from people in any way." By the time of our interviews, this was a common precept of anthropology, although it is possible that an interlocutor could have done clandestine work without telling us. Beyond this shared view, however, there were significant generational and racial differences in scholars' willingness to engage the US state.[52] Approximately one-third of those trained prior to 1990 had done some sort of work with the US military or intelligence communities—which mainly involved participating in seminars, lectures, conferences, or meetings with audiences including the State Department, the Department of Defense, intelligence analysts, foreign service officers, military officers, US or multinational armed forces, diplomats, and students at US military colleges.[53] With very few exceptions, these were white scholars, both male and female. In stark contrast to prior generations, all but two people trained in or after the mid-1990s told us that they had *never* done any such work (one had given a few lectures and one had fact-checked a report for a government agency).

Across generations, those who engaged the government explained that they did so because they felt a sense of duty to discipline and nation and an obligation to educate: "I'm an educator and my job is to educate them," one said. Another senior scholar put it this way: "It would be, I think, a grave injustice to our society to say that no qualified academic should speak to people in government or to brief ambassadors before they go out on their mission." And an anthropologist who speaks regularly in government venues said, "If we want to complain about American foreign policy then we also have a duty to try to have an impact on policy by working together with the government and advising them." Several people emphasized that the information they presented in these seminars was basic, publicly available, and uncontroversial; one called it "political kindergarten" with "people with huge amounts of power who don't necessarily know what they're doing." Nonetheless, a number of these interlocutors drew a line between "State Department" and "military," refusing all engagement with the latter. And most were aware that their contributions could be used in ways they did not intend, but assessed this risk as minimal (because the government consults multiple experts) and worth the greater potential for educational benefit.

Yet this issue of unintended consequences is precisely what concerned almost all MENA anthropologists trained since 1990, who joined two-thirds of those trained before them (often feminist scholars) in refusing *all* government, intelligence, or military consulting or educational work. While earlier opposition to this work was frequently influenced by Marxist perspectives, the later generation's aversion reflected their training in poststructuralist, often Foucauldian, critiques of state power. Some of these more recently trained scholars expressed discomfort with how their research has been politicized or shaped by political events—discomfort that reflects both the vulnerabilities of their career stage and the ways the internet has changed the distribution of writing and lectures. Interlocutors from all generations who were wary of government work often made statements like "I would never do that." One person told us:

> I think it's really, really important we not cooperate in any of this. Not even a whiff of it. And it's pretty hard to pass up because first of all, they disguise it sometimes so you don't really know what you're stepping into. . . . I mean, the invitations I get, which you must get too, where: 'We're holding a workshop and we really want to know more about X.' . . . Okay, I could say to myself, 'Yeah, I'd like to tell those military people a thing or two.' But I think it's really important not to get sucked into it.

She articulated the views of many other MENA anthropologists when she continued, "I don't have to go to a military-sponsored workshop, you know, I'm on the radio, I get interviewed every now and then. I think that that's my contribution, and that if we all were to try to be more active as public intellectuals, that . . . would be our really major contribution. I don't think we have to give in to a framework that they set up for us."[54]

MENA anthropologists who opposed government engagement were often very aware of the potentially negative consequences of that position. As one said, "I mean, you can't simultaneously say, look our discipline is the one that's generating the most valuable . . . frameworks . . . for studying what's going on in the world, but I'm not going to tell you anything at the same time. And you know, personally that's my own reflex as well. But I can understand that people who have a lot of power and authority and money would be pretty frustrated with that. So I think we're going to have to come up with something else." This person captured a key tension that dominated high-profile AAA discussions, beginning in 2005, about anthropologists' participation in the War on Terror. Those debates reinvigorated disagreements between applied and academic anthropologists while also revealing divisions among academic anthropologists. In 2005 the AAA finally voted to "uncensure" Boas for his 1919 statement condemning anthropologists' pretending to be researchers while operating as spies.[55] That was also the year several CIA job advertisements appeared in association online and print publications, apparently submitted via an automatic, unvetted system—leading to protests from a wide variety of AAA members.[56]

In response, the executive board adopted a motion to reject all future CIA ads. Both AAA Executive Director Bill Davis and the National Association of Practicing Anthropologists (NAPA) opposed this decision on the grounds that banning the ads was unfair to practicing (i.e., applied) anthropologists.[57] A long-simmering division between academic and applied anthropologists returned to the foreground. There was also heterogeneity on either side of this rift. We cannot assume that all practicing anthropologists agreed that CIA recruitment was acceptable or that academics concurred that it was not. While the vast majority of our interlocutors thought that anthropologists should neither work for the CIA in any capacity nor do any covert intelligence work, not all of them shared this view. Indeed, then-MES president Jenny White presented the minority view *against* the decision to ban CIA ads at the 2005 section assembly meeting:

> I was one of the few who stood up and said I thought there should be discussion and that I thought we had no right to decide for students and faculty whether or not they wanted to . . . apply for jobs in the U.S. government. And I thought that, especially as concerns the Middle East, that perhaps we *needed* well-educated people in the government to advise the policy makers. It's as if I put a pile of shit in the middle of the room and everyone just looked away and they continued their conversation, you know. I mean, that was the impression I got, and I felt personally really offended. . . . I consider myself to be left and liberal, but this is the old Soviet style of leftism where we know what's good for you and if you talk to the government, then we're going to ostracize you.

White framed the issue as "a rights argument. . . . Who are we to tell anyone who is in our field what they can or cannot apply to? I think that's completely unjust. If they wish to apply to government jobs, then we should not be standing in their way." Importantly, she also noted both that she was speaking as an individual and not for the section and that MENA anthropologists were going to be significantly affected by the ban. Whatever one's position on anthropologists working with intelligence agencies, her point that MENA anthropologists should be a part of the conversation was crucial for two reasons: because clearly they were being recruited by those agencies and had been for years and because thus far the AAA had frequently overlooked their perspectives.

Following these discussions at the November 2005 AAA meeting, the executive board established the Commission on the Engagement of Anthropology with the US Security and Intelligence Communities (CEAUSSIC). The commission was convened in 2006 and charged with providing recommendations on whether and how anthropologists could engage intelligence and security agencies. Although CEAUSSIC's initial report began by acknowledging that the Iraq and Afghanistan wars framed its investigations, it only included one MENA anthropologist: Carolyn Fluehr-Lobban.[58] That report—in typical AAA fashion—took no position on anthropologists working with military, intelligence, defense, or national security organizations. It clearly stated that CEAUSSIC "recognizes both opportunities and risks to those anthropologists choosing to engage with the work of the military, security and intelligence arenas" and that it neither opposes such engagements nor endorses "positions that rule such engagements out *a priori*." In this way it mirrored WWII-era anthropology's openness to assisting the war effort. But the report also reflected Vietnam-era debates about counterinsurgency work in recommendations that anthropologists pay attention to the ethical considerations of such work and reminders about the rule to "do no harm" and the importance of transparency and communication. Indeed, it specifically recommended revising the Code of Ethics to "sharpen guidelines for informed consent and transparency" and to reinstate the more direct 1971 language opposing secrecy. The report also noted that moves to give the government "non-public reports without receiving permission from studied populations to provide such reports risk violating assumed and negotiated ethical commitments." This stipulation was in keeping with our interlocutors' views that any information provided during consultations and seminars must be publicly available. It also can be read as a suggestion that the Chatham House Rule, which governs many intelligence conferences and workshops, blurs these ethical lines because it forbids participants to reveal the identity or affiliation of any other participant, adding a layer of secrecy to the proceedings.

In 2007, as CEAUSSIC was completing its initial report, anthropology was thrust into the media spotlight when the Human Terrain Systems (HTS) program came to national attention.[59] HTS was a program implemented by the Department of Defense from 2007 to 2015 to integrate social science research into military operations and planning. As an HTS staff member explained, its goal was "to provide cultural insight to brigade command staff by interviewing local populations and utilizing social science methodologies to better enable culturally astute decision-making."[60] One aspect of this multifaceted program involved embedding social scientists with military battalions in Afghanistan and Iraq. HTS also included sections that compiled sociocultural data on different indigenous groups in these areas and that provided various forms of advice about "culture" to the military. Many MENA anthropologists reported HTS recruitment attempts, often through email; their responses ranged from "There's no way I would do such a thing" to "I shudder with horror at HTS."

Given the general anthropological aversion to HTS, it is no surprise that only a handful of the program's several hundred employees held PhDs or MAs in anthropology.[61] Yet because the program triggered broader concerns about the discipline's relationship to military and intelligence agencies and threatened to damage its national reputation, the AAA gave it immediate and significant official attention. In fall 2007, the executive board issued a statement that HTS was "an unacceptable application of anthropological expertise" and extended CEAUSSIC for two years, tasking it to further investigate the program. Again reflecting disciplinary frictions over government engagement, the statement also asserted "anthropology can and in fact is obliged to help improve US government policies through the widest possible circulation of anthropological understanding in the public sphere."[62]

The CEAUSSIC report on HTS, completed in 2009, was firmly critical of the program on a number of grounds, including its potential conflicts with the ethics code, potential to harm both researchers and interlocutors, and conflation of anthropological research with intelligence work.[63] The report also noted that ethnography determined by counterinsurgency operations and conducted in a war context with the potential for coercion "can no longer be considered a legitimate professional exercise of anthropology." The executive summary concluded, "While we stress that constructive engagement between anthropology and the military is possible, CEAUSSIC suggests that the AAA emphasize the incompatibility of HTS with disciplinary ethics and practice for job seekers."[64] That fall, the executive board adopted a motion stating its "best judgment is that the HTS program involves a mistaken form of anthropology."[65] And in keeping with AAA history, the association again revised its ethics code, this time to include stronger language about transparency in research.[66]

Reaction to this report and motion among MENA anthropologists varied. Some felt the report did not go far enough, with one of our interlocutors (of an older generation) suggesting that this was another example of an ethics statement without any teeth and that anyone who works for HTS should be kicked out of the AAA.[67] Others thought the report was "wishy-washy" and were critical of its focus on the ethical practice of anthropology rather than the ethics of the wars themselves. As during the Vietnam debates, the overall focus on ethical implications and recommendations *for anthropologists* skirted discussion of the politics of supporting US wars and counterinsurgency efforts. As Price wrote,

> There remains a great resistance to confronting the ways that disciplinary ethics are linked to the political context in which anthropology is practiced. Although the rank and file membership of the AAA have adopted resolutions condemning particular unpopular wars or military actions (the Vietnam War, the Iraq War, etc.), the Association remains skittish in adopting stances on the uses of anthropology in non-defensive wars of aggression, or wars of imperialism. Instead, professional associations like the AAA are pressured to keep the institutional focus on delineating ethical, not political, practices.[68]

A MENA anthropologist couched their agreement with this perspective like this: "[The AAA] moves to kind of water down aspects of this condemnation, making it less about . . . serving empire, more about the issue of knowledge having to be public and not serving private interest."

Not all MENA scholars held this view. One explained that while she agreed in principle with the AAA stance, anthropologists had become "the new self-appointed, self-anointed priesthood of ethics," and "it's a little bit smug" because, in her view, it would be impossible to practice ethics like this in the policy world. A few, despite being critical of HTS, expressed concerns about the process of CEAUSSIC and the AAA discussion. Two were upset that colleagues at an AAA meeting had been very rude to Montgomery McFate—the anthropological public face of HTS—when she spoke. Another, who was disappointed that CEAUSSIC had not spoken as a committee with HTS personnel,[69] averred, "We are all anthropologists and when we go into the field we want to talk to everybody who is relevant to the subject that we're studying, and to ignore, consciously and intentionally discount, a segment of this community really, it's just putting your fingers in your ears. . . . It was a sort of branding of this and that, 'Oh, we shouldn't talk to those people,' that was so unanthropological. . . . I just thought, 'This is ridiculous. How could anthropologists not be willing to talk to the people they're condemning?'" This perspective was also expressed in the 2009 MES Annual Report. Then-MES President Gregory Starrett wrote, "Given that the US Army's Human Terrain System project is probably not going away any time soon, I would like to make a personal recommendation that the AAA leadership investigate the possibility of arranging for sustained, responsible and objective ethnographic evaluation of the project in both its training and field deployment phases."

And a few of our interlocutors were critical of AAA's approach to the controversy because they thought the focus on HTS was too narrow. As they noted, HTS was a project in which very few anthropologists actually participated, and that was, by several accounts, generally ineffective. As with Project Camelot decades earlier, the combination of media and AAA attention gave HTS more importance than it warranted. CEAUSSIC chair Robert Albro acknowledged this critique, saying, "We have remained deeply preoccupied with HTS at the expense of the heavy lifting still yet to be done of thinking about the diversifying roles and applications of anthropology outside the traditional trappings of the academy."[70]

It is remarkable that the AAA spent so much time on HTS when non-HTS military actions were killing far more people and when so many MENA anthropologists were trying to share their knowledge outside the academy but faced politicized threats, obstacles, and disincentives. MENA anthropologists' absence from the HTS and CIA discussions reflected our interlocutors' notion that the AAA's overwhelming focus on these programs reinforced a narrow definition of disciplinary relevance and institutional worries about public image. As a result, most MENA anthropologists did not think that these disciplinary debates signaled either new interest in the region or a change that would affect MENA anthropology in particular. As one person opined, "I'm glad that HTS has been discussed seriously, but in general I have not felt like the AAA would support me if the shit hit the fan [meaning if she experienced politicized attacks on her teaching and research]." For her and many other MENA anthropologists, the true test of progressive political engagement was a willingness to take a stance in support of Palestinian rights. The AAA remained hesitant on that matter, but the tide appeared to be turning.

The Shifting Terrain of Israel-Palestine Politics in Anthropology

Since 2009, there have been several renewed attempts to bring discussions of Israel-Palestine into MES and the AAA more broadly. Their varying results, taken together, suggest that the second decade of the century will see the discipline break its official silence about oppressive Israeli state policies and actions and US complicity with them, although the fight is not over. In a watershed moment, the 2009 AAA annual meeting included a session about the Gaza crisis precipitated by the Israeli blockade and military attacks (including Operation Cast Lead, which killed over one thousand Palestinians). The session was cosponsored by the CfHR and, as one scholar put it, "finally organized by non-

Gaza folks." She interpreted this development as indicating not only how bad the situation had become, but also growing political agreement among non-Palestine anthropologists that Israel was violating international laws and conventions and oppressing Palestinians—political agreement also signaled, she said, by the striking lack of audience hostility at that panel. This undercurrent of change on Israel-Palestine was nourished by a critical mass of Palestine scholars who were speaking out, growing US campus activism, and changes in public discourse such that Jon Stewart was able to criticize Israel on *The Daily Show*.

But as advocacy for Palestinian rights persisted in the association, new proceduralism muddied its path. In 2008, the CfHR wrote a letter to the US secretary of state with MESA and Human Rights Watch—on AAA letterhead—condemning the Israeli government's refusal to allow Palestinian students from Gaza to leave to study abroad (including students who had received scholarships) and expressing concern about the "redirecting" of Fulbrights away from some of those students as a result.[71] A few months later, the AAA executive board adopted a new Standard Operating Procedure for the approval of AAA advocacy letters, essentially tightening the protocols for statement making and letter writing by association committees and units, and centralizing control over the AAA's voice. A former CfHR member maintained that this change was a board response to contention over a statement conveying concern to the Chinese government about conditions in Tibetan areas. Many MENA anthropologists instead thought the impetus was the letter about Gazan students.

From the perspective of several former executive board members and AAA officers, the Standard Operating Procedure was a response to concerns about who had the authority to make statements or write letters in the name of the association or on association letterhead and emerged from a protracted conflict with the CfHR over this issue. As a former officer put it, "If it's going to be on behalf of the whole Association . . . it's got to represent ways in which we think we can contribute to protecting . . . rights and resolving the situation." Another noted that the CfHR "has had a persistent behavioral pattern of trying to act autonomously and getting into conflict with the Executive Board by doing so. And it's been about all sorts of issues . . . where they have tried to send letters on AAA letterhead taking political stances on human rights issues without running it by the executive board, saying that they have the right to do that as that committee." These comments mirror earlier discussions of anthropological relevance or expertise in relation to political statements and once again reflect different understandings of the relationship of anthropology to political engagement. From several former CfHR members' perspectives, they were elected to the committee based on their human rights expertise and should be trusted to act authoritatively in that capacity. This new insistence on standardizing procedures for statement making and centralizing control over authoritative speech was the apex of procedural institutionalization and demonstrated how it could lead to diluting political statements and actions. It also showed concern with institutional preservation and with deflecting any blowback emanating from the broader context of compulsory Zionism.

A number of MENA anthropologists described the new rules as "draconian" and as evidence of Zionist panic over political statements related to Palestinian rights. This view may have been shaped by the way in which many of these anthropologists learned about the new Standard Operating Procedure. In 2009, the CfHR drafted another letter, addressed to the US and Israeli governments, as well as the European Union, condemning the Israeli attack and siege on Gaza and conveying humanitarian concern about their consequences. Some of our interlocutors recalled that when the CfHR tried to submit it as an AAA letter, they were reprimanded and sent the new procedure, in their view because of executive board opposition to it.[72]

Some former AAA officers and executive board members were aware of MENA anthropologists' perceptions and suggested to us that they were not necessarily unfounded. One of them opined, "I do have a sense that the sticking point has not been, you know, many other parts of the world. But it has often been Israel, and possibly some other parts of the Middle East. But I think maybe especially Israel." Leftist Israeli scholars and their supporters also thought the AAA would not criticize Israeli state actions: a former senior board member recalled an incident when an anthropologist tried to convince the executive board to issue a statement supporting Ben Gurion University's political science department when the Israeli government tried to shut it down due to the "too liberal, leftist, not right enough" political positions of its faculty. This person was disappointed when the board responded, "because the AAA cannot really investigate the situation and does not know the details of the situation it could not take a stand." A non-MENA anthropologist who joined the board after these events noted, "You know we all feel bad for Indians in the rainforest. We love them, we want to protect them. It's sort of a consensus position. It's not going to excite these constitutional issues, but the association is more divided on the Israel-Palestine issue. So that's when the constitutional issues get initiated."

It remains unclear whether or not Zionist opposition to the two Gaza letters influenced these institutional responses. At the very least, the timing of the new Standard Operating Procedure led many MENA anthropologists to interpret it within the long history of political invisibility and censorship when it came to Palestine advocacy. This invisibility was emphasized yet again when the November 2009 executive board actions included passing a political resolution supporting Hondurans who resisted the military coup and condemning the Honduran military and the US for financing and training it. Perhaps Palestinians failed to elicit such compassion because they are Arab; perhaps because they were not perceived as an indigenous people; or just maybe the idea of supporting Palestinian rights continued to befuddle the AAA for political reasons.

Regardless of the motivation, the new procedure was part of a broader pattern of bureaucratization and centralization that can have deeply depoliticizing effects.[73] And they did, again in relation to Israel-Palestine, just three years later. In November 2012, MES drafted and endorsed (in a full section email ballot) a statement condemning another escalated Israeli military assault on Gaza and calling on anthropologists who work in other regions to join them in their condemnation of this attack.[74] The CfHR and the Culture and Agriculture Section endorsed this statement as well. But when MES sent it to the AAA executive board, the latter declined to take any action on it. A former executive board member recalled discussions about the statement, saying:

> There were voices that were raised saying this is only part of the story, and that reflected personal as well as professional views, which is to say . . . I think that the general view was that that statement in particular should have been contextualized, at least in the view of some of the board members, in order for it to be a statement on behalf of the entire Association. So yeah, I do think it is likely that personal political positions are reflected in the discussions about whether this is something that adequately captures the sense of the whole Association.

Given the history of AAA hesitancy to criticize the Israeli state, including Israeli military actions against civilians, the board's lack of support—so freely offered in other cases around the world—for the condemnation statement came as no surprise. More surprising, perhaps, is the fact that MES initiated the statement in the first place, signaling a shift in the section's relationship to political engagement. By the second decade of the century, Task Force members and scholars who had been trained after 1990 held section leadership positions and brought their generation's more unified understanding of the role of academic associations in political statement making to the foreground.

If things are changing, they are changing slowly, and it will take more than minor statements to alter MENA anthropologists' perceptions of the AAA.

Anthropology's main institution will no longer be able to sideline discussion of Israel-Palestine or suppress members' criticisms of Israeli state actions or support for Palestinian rights. The growing boycott of Israeli academic institutions, proposed as a tactic to end the Israeli occupation, has now been adopted by several interdisciplinary academic associations. As this book goes to press, these debates are heating up in anthropology. It remains to be seen whether, finally, MENA anthropologists' expertise on the region will be heard and whether the AAA's centralized bureaucratization will result in a powerful ten thousand-member strong voice against state oppression or sidestep such a move in favor of protecting anthropologists and their academic association.

Conclusion

Undisciplining Anthropology's Politics

On a Friday evening in December 2014, throngs of anthropologists stood in a hallway trying to enter an immense, and already full, ballroom at a Marriott hotel in Washington, DC. American Anthropological Association board members and staff had to open a second ballroom to handle the well over seven hundred anthropologists who wanted to attend the association's annual business meeting, which usually attracted fewer than a hundred people. It was, in the memory of some older attendees, the most packed meeting since 1971—when they had passionately debated and eventually condemned colleagues' covert roles supporting US counterinsurgency in Thailand and an AAA attempt to exonerate them. Anticipation filled the room in 2014. Most anthropologists had never seen so many of their kind gathered in one place. The AAA even ran out of voting cards to distribute at the door. Twitter was aflutter as those in the room tweeted amazement at the crowds and implored others to come and join the meeting. When President Monica Heller rose to the podium, she quipped that she knew the membership wasn't there to hear the usual bureaucratic reports on membership and finances, but that they had to run through that part of the agenda first.

What happened next was nothing short of extraordinary, given the variety of tensions and heated Middle East politics that have shaped the discipline of anthropology from World War II through the War on Terror. The floor opened for discussion of a resolution placed by an association member on the agenda a month earlier, which called on the AAA to *oppose* the growing international boycott of Israeli academic institutions. This resolution was an attempt to stem the tide that began earlier that fall, when nearly one thousand anthropologists signed a pledge to boycott those institutions "until such time as [they] end their complicity in violating Palestinian rights as stipulated in international law, and respect the full rights of Palestinians."[1] These anthropologists joined members of three other national academic associations that had collectively endorsed versions of the academic boycott in 2013: the Association for Asian American Studies, the American Studies Association, and the Native American and Indigenous Studies Association.[2] They supported the academic boycott in response to calls from Palestinian academia and civil society.[3] Many were also motivated to sign by yet another Israeli attack on Gaza in summer 2014, during which over 2,200 people were killed (mostly Palestinian civilians). The colossal structural imbalance between the two sides was obvious as the Israeli military nearly annihilated already impoverished Gaza—which human rights organizations condemned as war crimes.[4] The attempt, on that December evening, to stem anthropology's growing support for Palestinians failed spectacularly.

Scholar after scholar came to the microphone during the meeting to speak against the resolution. Almost every speaker received a loud round of applause, sometimes cheers. Some people argued directly *for* an academic boycott, highlighting Israel's human rights abuses and US complicity in them as its main diplomatic, military, and ideological advocate. A senior white male anthropologist (and former member of the Radical Caucus) commented that the issue was a broader one of impunity, both in Israel and the United States, foreshadowing how the meeting would end. Others appealed to their colleagues not to prematurely shut down discussion of the issue. They signaled clearly that AAA members wanted the possibility of supporting Palestinian rights out in the light—not labeled as anti-Semitic or swept under the rug or archived into obscure board meeting minutes, as had happened in the past. The anthropologists who came to the mike represented different ages, genders, generations, ethnicities, and religious backgrounds and identities. Most notably, many of the speakers were MENA anthropologists; it seemed they were finally worth listening to in the larger discipline. And most surprisingly, quite a few speakers were junior scholars, including graduate students. They accepted what many knew was a major risk to their careers—including potential difficulties getting a job or tenure, among myriad other repercussions we have described—and spoke anyway. Palestinian anthropologists also took the floor, reminding the audience that the *American* Anthropological Association had a particular duty to consider this issue because the United States funded and supported Israeli state violence. Jewish anthropologists and Israeli anthropologists did the same. In a powerful moment, a graduate student declared that he supported the academic boycott because every year at Seder they say, "Our liberation will not be complete until everyone's is." The applause was deafening.

Few scholars spoke on behalf of the resolution, all likely trained in the 1950s to 1970s. Many were older Jewish and Israeli anthropologists operating under the dominant framework of the generational consciousness formed in their youth, when support for Israel, no matter what it did, seemed like the only way to end centuries of persecution of Jews. As in earlier association discussions of MENA politics, most of these speakers privileged Israelis over Palestinians and scholars over research interlocutors by arguing that a boycott would ostracize Israeli anthropologists, even though supporters iterate that it targets institutions rather than individuals. Long-standing disciplinary disregard for and racism toward Arabs was present in their neglect to mention the huge restrictions on academic freedom Palestinians face as a result of the Israeli occupation. Such a view also led one speaker (who is not an anthropologist and works for a pro-Israel advocacy organization) to patronizingly proclaim that a boycott would not help the Palestinians—even though thousands of the people on whose behalf she purported to speak have determined that the boycott is one of few remaining viable tactics. Conflating Israel with Jews, a senior Americanist declared the AAA had a "Jewish problem" because it was singling out Israel.[5] Rather than wincing at this implied accusation of anti-Semitism, the audience erupted in a chorus of boos. When a senior female anthropologist rose to "call the question" (i.e., a motion to end debate and vote) a male supporter of the resolution gesticulated widely and shouted to the president that the debate needed to continue.

Robert's Rules of Order forced a vote. And for one of the only times in AAA history, proceduralism worked to allow a large number of anthropologists to listen to the rights claims of the one oppressed group who had yet to garner widespread anthropological concern. And it worked for those MENA anthropologists—now a majority in their subfield—who think that their professional ethics mandate taking a public stand for those rights. When the president called the vote, a miniscule number stood up in support of the resolution. When it was time to defeat it, the rest of the room rose en masse. Photos of the landmark moment and victory messages quickly spread through social media and were retweeted and reposted by academics and solidarity activists around the world.

In a sign that this solidarity against state brutality was part of a groundswell movement within the discipline, nearly everyone stayed in the room to vote resoundingly to endorse another statement.[6] This motion condemned anti-Black police violence in the United States in the wake of police murders of Black men in Ferguson, Missouri; Staten Island, and elsewhere—murders for which police officers were granted impunity just like the Israeli military that had trained some of them.[7] Again, hundreds of anthropologists stood and raised their voting cards.

As people streamed out of the ballroom, the most common expression on MENA anthropologists' faces and tongues was one of exhilarated awe. Many older-generation feminists, midcareer scholars, and region-related anthropologists were saying that they never thought they would see the day when anthropologists, let alone the AAA, would give that much consideration to Palestinians and reject kneejerk support for Israel. The fact that it happened in collaboration with Black solidarity was like icing on the cake for these boycott supporters. Finally, it seemed, a broad swathe of anthropologists would begin to bring MENA politically and analytically into the fold of broader critiques of power, violence, the state, and hierarchies based on race, gender, and generation.

Whether the hope of that moment will last, and translate into greater integration of MENA into the discipline, remains an open question. As much as this episode suggests a transformation of anthropology's politics, it continues to manifest the tensions at anthropology's heart. These tensions are grounded in broader US society, dating back at least to World War II, and involve major demographic shifts and social movements as well as the expansion of US capitalism and empire. And they have, in some key ways, intensified with the seemingly never-ending War on Terror and the neoliberalization of the academy.

Contradictions between US narratives of equality on the one hand, and the US state's treatment of minorities at home and militarized interventions in MENA on the other, continue to attract people to the discipline. The presence of so many MENA graduate students and junior scholars at the 2014 business meeting is a sign that experiences of being at odds with the dominant environment, whether politically or racially, continue to draw scholars to MENA anthropology in particular. Younger anthropologists at the meeting were vociferously critical of War on Terror and Zionist rhetorics; many of them grew up as their target—either as Middle Easterners subject to racialization and state violence or as white Americans or Israelis interpellated to adopt these rhetorics. At the same time, these MENA scholars face a far less secure job market and work environment, as tenure-track lines decrease and the institution of tenure itself is at risk. Contesting these rhetorics—in teaching, research, or advocacy—is arguably no safer than it was in the past and perhaps more dangerous in the internet era. As one of the graduate students who spoke at the meeting said on the way back to their seat, "I just committed career suicide." In the second decade of the century, scholars' activities are not just monitored and attacked by domestic activist groups, but also pressured by university presidents and provosts who email faculty or alert the press to inform them of their opposition to the boycott.[8] Most disturbingly, scholars are now the targets of forces based outside the United States, including Israeli advocacy groups and the state of Israel itself.[9]

Indeed, the climate of fear and intimidation that MENA anthropologists have faced over the past sixty years was present at both the business meeting and the conference overall, despite (or maybe because of) their unprecedented discussions of Israel-Palestine: the conference included at least four sessions, and even more papers, that discussed the boycott or Palestinian rights or Israeli oppressions. Mirroring the situation in many MENA anthropologists' classrooms, public lectures, and university events, nonanthropologist Zionist activists attended panels on Israel-Palestine as well as a special AAA-organized members-only dialogue session on the conflict. In addition to asking pointed questions, some of these individuals, along with a couple of senior male Israeli anthropologists, verbally harassed several of the graduate students who publicly supported the boycott, directing groans, insults, epithets, and even threats toward them. The fact that most of these students were Jewish American and/or Israeli suggests both that they felt, as some of them expressed, an especial responsibility to speak out *as Jews or Israelis* and that other region-related junior scholars, whose numbers are rising exponentially, remained too cautious to voice their support. Even after the mass public support at the 2014 business meeting, over 150 anthropologists kept their signatures to the boycott petition anonymous out of fear of retribution and/or conflict with colleagues.[10] Clearly, the 2014 AAA annual meeting can be read simultaneously as an embodiment of long-standing generational and racial tensions within the discipline as well as the potential dissipation of those hierarchies.

Disciplinary debates around the boycott have once again highlighted disagreements over the relationship between anthropology and political advocacy. Some anthropologists, especially those who have signed a statement against the boycott, have suggested that it is inappropriate for an anthropological and academic institution to take such a stance and have done so by making claims about what constitutes anthropology in the first place.[11] By stating that political stances contradict anthropology's endeavor to listen to multiple perspectives and analyze complexity, they seek to reinscribe that line between politics and anthropology that has been drawn many times in the discipline's history. Boycott supporters draw on different moments in this history. By highlighting a definition of anthropology as critical of power and supportive of human rights, they argue that anthropology necessitates such a political stance.[12]

Many of these positions were featured in short pieces printed in *Anthropology News* or on the AAA blog. Along with the conference time allotted for discussion of Israel-Palestine, this exposure itself was a sign of change. Not only was the AAA taking MENA politics very seriously, even putting them center stage, but it was also including MENA anthropologists' voices in the debates. Nonetheless, tensions remained over who got to represent the region and whose voices were considered expert at the institutional level. That fall, the AAA executive board appointed a Task Force on AAA Engagement with Israel-Palestine "charged with helping the Executive Board consider the nature and extent to which AAA might contribute to addressing the issues that the Israel/Palestine conflict raises."[13] Its members were selected using a range of criteria, including expertise on conflict issues. Yet none of the Task Force members had significant research experience in Israel-Palestine, which was, according to former board member Daniel Segal, a major anomaly in AAA history.[14] Whatever the, no doubt complex, reasons for excluding MENA anthropologists,[15] disciplinary exceptionalism persisted. At the same time, signaling that such exceptionalism may be fading, Task Force members set about interviewing many anthropologists who work in the region, finally acknowledging their paramount expertise.

Or perhaps not; change is never so simple. The annual meeting also included an AAA-organized member's forum on Israel-Palestine, ostensibly held to "foster dialogue and information exchange among AAA members on anthropologically relevant issues related to Israel/Palestine."[16] Attendees were invited to sit randomly around tables with people they did not know and participate in a professionally facilitated conversation. Not only did nonanthropologist Zionist activists attend (reproducing a climate of fear for junior scholars), but the AAA also did not ensure that each group would include MENA scholars. One assumes that an "information exchange" would benefit from those most anthropologically knowledgeable about Israel-Palestine. Furthermore, nearly all anthropologists of Palestine, as well as many of the region—had they been consulted beforehand—would have alerted AAA leadership to the acutely problematic nature of so-called dialogue programs about such a structurally unbalanced situation.[17]

Nevertheless, for the first time within anthropology, the AAA annual meeting in 2014 witnessed a critical mass of non-MENA anthropologists listening to their MENA-specialist colleagues talk about Israel-Palestine and also speaking out themselves in support of Palestinian rights. Their heightened support and criticism attest to broader changes: cracks in compulsory Zionism widened by scholarship critical of nationalism, nation-states, and settler-colonial societies;

reiterations that criticizing the Israel state is not anti-Semitic; demographic shifts bringing minority voices into the academy, including those of indigenous peoples of the Americas who often see Palestinians' struggle as linked to their own; student movements on campuses, including Students for Justice in Palestine, Jewish Voice for Peace, and the new Open Hillel movement; egregious and ongoing human rights violations perpetrated by the Israeli state; and a critical mass of *non-MENA* Jewish academics opposing those violations. At the previous AAA meetings, in fall 2013, Lisa Rofel, an anthropologist of China, gave a paper in which she said: "As an American Jew, I also feel a special responsibility, as American Jews have been interpellated into the position of what I call 'Israel no Matter What,' that is, to support Israel no matter what it does. Israel's ongoing repression of Palestinians is done in my name. I have come on a very long journey in abandoning that position."

Of course, as we have seen, many MENA anthropologists—along with other scholars of the region, and especially Arab and Arab-American scholars[18]—have been working to bring criticism of Israeli state policies into academic and public discourse for decades. It is quite telling that only when non-MENA anthropologists, non-Arab scholars, and scholars of Jewish background began to voice those criticisms did they became more acceptable in the academy—similar to what happened when the discipline only took a stance opposing the US state's Iraq War follies years after MENA anthropologists tried to galvanize their colleagues against the war.

If, as we argue, Israel-Palestine politics can be considered a bellwether of anthropology's future, the relationship between discipline and region seems to be changing in ways that may alter the politics and frictions within academic practice more generally. Other harbingers of a potential sea change have appeared. Unrelenting domestic reverberations of the War on Terror and puzzles raised by uprisings across MENA draw more and more scholars to anthropology, pique the hiring interests of administrators, and continue to push MENA scholars center stage. Feminist and anti-racist scholarship as well as growing numbers of nonwhite scholars steadfastly chip away at sexism and racism within both the discipline and the academy. The national outcry when the University of Illinois at Urbana-Champaign unhired Steven Salaita after he tweeted explicit criticism of Israel heightened many academics' awareness of the fraught MENA politics their colleagues have confronted for decades, as well as the dangers of increasing trustee, alumni, and administrator control over academic hiring processes. And academic publishing, that apotheosis of scholarly work, remains barely subject to politicized attack as MENA publications multiply exponentially with excellent studies that further our critical analyses of power in all its forms.[19] MENA anthropology is not only at the forefront of much of this scholarship, but anthropology's disciplinary interventions have also greatly affected Middle East Studies more broadly, especially through criticisms of Orientalism and racism and analyses of the connections between knowledge and power.

As these scholarly analyses show, these forces of power are strong and will not disappear overnight. The state violence, capitalist education logics, institutional conservatism, racism, sexism, Islamophobia, and xenophobia discussed in this book are potent, interlinked, and historically dense. If anthropology's politics remain fraught, its tensions are symptomatic of larger US social frictions since World War II, marked by the intensification of capitalism, social movements, and expanding empire. These academic politics in turn have significant implications for what US citizens will come to know about the world in which their state is the hegemon and for the degree to which they will be able to think critically about history, politics, and society. If scholars continue to face pressures, silencing, and attacks from administrators, colleagues, outside groups, and even governments, then the opportunity to advance knowledge in US society will be seriously compromised. As the neoliberalization of the university challenges the protective rights of tenure and decreases tenure-track positions, this situation is exacerbated; doors are more likely to close for those who challenge the status quo. It grows riskier to present perspectives unpopular to consumers of higher education when academic institutions are increasingly beholden to bottom lines and the imperative of capitalist accumulation. Down the road, such perspectives may be even harder to come by if skyrocketing education costs and student debt reshape the academy's demographics once again.

Many academics (not just MENA anthropologists) have accepted this situation as a poison chalice, embracing ethical imperatives to share their regional and disciplinary expertise in ways that foster knowledge and critical thinking skills *despite* the possibility that they will be targeted for doing so. For many anthropologists, this ethical imperative has included representing, as faithfully as possible, our interlocutors' perspectives and advocating for a more just world for our interlocutors as well as our own communities. Scholars have navigated this environment of opportunity and threat using careful strategies for preserving one's career, energy, and sanity, including self-censorship. We should be alarmed at the possibility that this situation may continue to impede scholarship and teaching. Fear of career-damaging repercussions inhibits academic practice at precisely the moment when it could be at its most visionary. But we must also ask whether the discipline and the academy could handle it if

MENA anthropologists, MENA scholars, and academics more generally abandoned this strategy of self-preservation. Surely the beneficiaries would include research, students, and the broader public. Indeed, those of us with the privilege of tenure have a responsibility to be on the forefront of this change.

While this book has demonstrated that scholarship and teaching are shot through with tense politics of various kinds, they are also shot through with hope. Our historical analysis shows regular ebbs and flows in the capacity of scholars to remain true to their commitments and in the possibilities for expressing and hearing alternative perspectives. The growth of the subfield of MENA anthropology parallels anthropology's expansion as a whole; the discipline includes over ten thousand AAA members in 2015. This dynamic growth means that anthropological perspectives are being shared in multiple ways with a variety of audiences, both within and outside the academy. Thousands of college students take anthropology classes each year, and even if some professors self-censor in their teaching, these courses encourage students to learn about other peoples and places and to reflect on their own. The critical thinking skills and empathy that accompany this process are tenacious. And they may well change the shape of future conversations about the Middle East—in anthropology, in the academy, and in the United States.

Appendix A

Methods

This book is based on data from ethnographic interviews, participant-observation, archival and media research, and feedback from colleagues throughout the research process. We base a portion of our analysis on our collective participant-observation in the fields of anthropology, gender studies, and Middle East Studies since beginning graduate school in 1996 (Deeb) and 1993 (Winegar). This period includes experiences of being trained into the profession via different graduate programs; going on the job market; publishing, teaching, and lecturing; holding postdoctoral positions at four different institutions; working as tenure-track and eventually tenured faculty in five different institutions; creating or directing Middle East Studies programs at two institutions; and participating in multiple professional capacities on AAA committees and section boards, MESA and AMEWS committees, journal editorial boards including the MERIP collective, and grant review committees for multiple government and private funding sources.

The positions we have held over our collective histories represent a diverse range of institutions, including (based on the Carnegie Classification of Institutions of Higher Education) very high research activity public and private universities, high research activity public and private universities, a liberal arts baccalaureate college, and a religiously affiliated institution. These institutions are located in urban and suburban environments on both US coasts as well as in the Midwest and range in size from tens of thousands of students to less than one thousand. It was the incredibly compelling nature of these cumulative experiences that led us to want to write this book. Although mostly not recorded in field notes of the classic sort, these experiences found their way into our previous publications, email archives, ongoing conversations, and interviews of one another. Sometimes interviews with our colleagues or archival and media research sparked memories that were then integrated into the analysis. We also benefited from our differing racial, national heritage, and class backgrounds, which allowed us to bring experiences that might be shared with a wider range of our interlocutors to bear on the project.

In order to understand how a particular world region gains definition, representation, and institutional presence within a discipline, we conducted archival research on academic associations. We focused on the archives of the American Anthropological

Association (AAA) which are primarily located in the National Anthropology Archives (NAA), as well as those of the two main MENA interest groups in American anthropological history: the Middle East Research Group in Anthropology (MERGA, active in the 1970s and 1980s), and the Middle East Section of the AAA (MES, active from the 1990s to the present). Most MERGA and MES materials were obtained directly from past leaders of those organizations. This archival research centered on key moments of US engagement with MENA since WWII and of anthropologists' engagement with their disciplinary association as elicited from interviews and reports in the AAA newsletter, *Anthropology News* (formerly *Anthropology Newsletter*). We also surveyed news stories on MENA anthropologists and anthropology, focusing on post–Cold War media including online and print academic media such as *Anthropology News*, *The Chronicle of Higher Education*, and *Inside Higher Ed*, right- and left-wing activist websites such as *Electronic Intifada*, *Jadaliyya*, *Campus Watch*, and *Front Page Magazine*, and national outlets from *The New Yorker* to major newspapers.

To assess the growth of the subfield, we examined job opening and funding patterns beginning in 1990 (pre-1990 data was elicited in interviews as well as secondary sources on academic funding since WWII). We gathered as much data as possible from various private and public funding agencies to see if there were patterns regarding when MENA anthropology was funded (and which topics were funded). This process was frequently—and unfortunately usually in relation to public funding sources—hampered by a range of bureaucratic factors including less accessible pre-internet records and lack of staff at agencies to produce data. Reviewing job advertisements allowed us to assess how, when, and if MENA anthropology became a desired area of hire in relationship to broader economic and political moments in the United States.

Much of our analysis is based on ethnographic interviews conducted in person, on the phone, or via Skype. While we personally conducted most of the interviews, in some cases we used a non-MENA anthropology graduate student as a research assistant—particularly for interviewing graduate students, who, we came to realize, were more comfortable speaking to a peer. We conducted over one hundred such interviews with cultural anthropologists of MENA currently studying at, employed in, or retired from accredited four-year institutions of higher education. Our interviewees had trained and/or held tenure-track academic positions in the United States, because we were interested in how working in the heart of empire shaped research and teaching in the context of political and economic attacks on the tenure system. We aimed for a broad sample across types of institutions (by size, public or private, and geographic area) as well as age, gender, race or ethnicity—speaking with retirees and people at the ends of their careers, graduate students, and many in-between.

To assess the validity of our sample, we compared our interviewee list with four other sources: the AAA website databases, the Middle East Section of the AAA's membership list, a massive bibliographic search we conducted for an *Annual Review of Anthropology* article of all publications in MENA anthropology since 1990,[1] and the websites of major cultural anthropology PhD programs. Comparing these sources led us to a list of 324 scholars. While this is not an exact number, it does indicate that we have interviewed approximately 33 percent of MENA cultural anthropologists employed full-time in academia, a percentage that quantitative researchers generally consider to be a solid sample. Our interviewees also reflected—to within a few percentage points—the same demographic variation as the larger subfield count.

To situate these conversations within the broader disciplines of anthropology and Middle East Studies, we interviewed a handful of archaeologists and biological anthropologists, discussed the project with MENA scholars from other disciplines, and presented our material in workshops with both nonanthropologist MENA scholars and cultural anthropologists who work in other regions. Additionally, we interviewed former and/or present officers, staff, and board members of the AAA to seek clarification on AAA-related policies, processes, and practices.

We note that there have always been MENA anthropologists who do not work in higher education and are instead employed by the US government, museums, NGOs and other development organizations, as well as those who change careers after receiving anthropology degrees. Where one ended up working sometimes had to do with personal career path or life circumstance choices, but we found anecdotal evidence of graduate school colleagues who had left academia because they were unable to land a job in four-year institutions for reasons related to factors including a limited job market, sexism, racism, and the topic of their research. We also note that our interviews included less than a handful of contingent faculty and those who teach in community colleges, a major lacuna due to the tighter political strictures on academic practice that scholars without the security of tenure face. More research is needed to more fully flesh out the different career paths of PhDs in MENA anthropology.

Interviews covered open-ended questions about how people became interested in both the discipline of anthropology and the MENA region, how they developed their specific areas and topics of interest (as well as theoretical orientation), any challenges they faced in any portion of their career that they believed were due to the fact that they worked in MENA, any work outside of academe that they undertook, and how (and if) they define themselves through prisms of race, ethnicity, gender, nationality, social class, and generation. In our interviews and analysis of them, we adopted some techniques from anthropological work on life histories.[2] Frequently interviewees would riff on academic politics on a more meta level, and their observations were critical both as data and analysis. All interviews and interview material are subject to the confidentiality ethics of the discipline of anthropology. The few cases where we have included scholars' names are situations written about in the press, situations about which the scholar has spoken publicly, cases where a scholar has requested that we name them, or cases where we have their explicit permission to do so. In addition to removing as many identifying aspects of a quotation or incident as possible while trying to preserve enough information to demonstrate patterns, any direct quotation or specific incident you read about in this book that is from an interview has been cleared for publication by the interviewee. We honored requests—made by approximately half our interlocutors—to edit their speech (e.g., to remove fillers like "you know" and to make grammatical corrections to their original statements). As a result, some of the quotes in this book read more formally than others.

Appendix B

AAA Motions and Resolutions*

1979 Resolution on the American-Iranian Crisis

Whereas recent events have led to a dangerous climate of hostility between the United States and Iran in which each side perceives itself as responding to injuries; and

Whereas the American Anthropological Association has traditionally urged that the cause of justice and peace is best served when events are understood and presented to the public in their historical and cultural context; and

Whereas the Association has traditionally spoken out against prejudice and bias against national and cultural groups, tending to lead to violence or discrimination; therefore,

Be it moved that the Association urge moderation and restraint on both sides and that it caution in the strongest terms that popular response to these events must not be inappropriately generalized to: (1) Individual Iranian guests in this country; (2) The Iranian people and their civilization as a whole; (3) Adherents to the Islamic faith here and abroad. And further,

Be it moved that this position be publicized at local and national levels, to provide a context for the efforts of individuals and groups to improve public understanding, prevent escalation of hostilities, and combat discrimination (and that the Association express the hope that the comparable aims will be pursued by the Iranian People.)[1]

1982 Resolution on Lebanon

Whereas the American Anthropological Association has long stood opposed to the destruction of peoples and cultures; and

Whereas what is occurring in Lebanon is a massive destruction of the Lebanese and Palestinian peoples and cultures by the Israeli and Lebanese militaries, and militias supported by both governments; and

*Published with the permission of the American Anthropological Association.

Whereas the recent massacres in Shatila and Sabra were part of a much broader pattern of destruction—for example, in recent weeks the entire Palestinian Red Crescent with 40 clinics and 9 hospitals which served poor Lebanese and Palestinians has been destroyed. The Palestine Research Center, a repository of Palestinian history and culture, has also been destroyed; and

Whereas the presence of American, French, and Italian troops is serving to aid the Israeli and Lebanese militaries, and militias supported by both governments, to continue rounding up, arresting, and detaining thousands of Lebanese and Palestinians, destroying their cultures,

We therefore move: that the American Anthropological Association (1) condemn the systematic and deliberate destruction of the Lebanese and Palestinian peoples and cultures; and that the American Anthropological Association call upon the American government to (2) end US military aid to Israel including military equipment and advisors; (3) end US military aid to Lebanon including military equipment and advisors; (4) use its offices to facilitate the earliest possible withdrawal of all foreign military forces from Lebanon; (5) withdraw support from any government in Lebanon which plays any role in the destruction of the Lebanese and Palestinian peoples and cultures.

And that the Association send copies of this motion to President Ronald Reagan and to the Israeli, Lebanese, French, and Italian governments.[2]

1982 Motion on Academic Freedom in the Israeli-Occupied West Bank

Whereas the American Anthropological Association has a long history of defending human rights and academic freedom;

Therefore, be it moved that the Association: first, condemn the work-permit restrictions on "foreign" professors, the expulsion of professors, the harassment of students, the censorship of books and teaching materials, and the closure of universities as suppressions of academic freedom by the present Israeli government on the occupied West Bank; and second, recommend that the Executive Board communicate this motion to the Secretary of State and Chairman of the Foreign Affairs Committees of the House and Senate of the US government and to the acting head of the Israeli administration on the occupied West Bank.[3]

1990 Resolution on the Persian Gulf Crisis (Original Text)

Whereas a U.S. invasion of Kuwait or Iraq would result in thousands of dead and wounded among American men and women in the U.S. Armed Forces deployed in the Persian Gulf; and

Whereas such an invasion would result in even greater loss of life and casualties among Iraqi troops, and among civilians and foreign nationals in Kuwait and possibly Iraq; and

Whereas such an invasion would result in widespread devastation and unforeseeable threats to the peace and stability of the Persian Gulf; and

Whereas the United Nations, member states of the United Nations, and countries of the Arab League continue to seek a diplomatic and peaceful resolution to the crisis; and

Whereas the continuing buildup of U.S. forces is leading to an escalation of tension without providing new opportunities for a diplomatic and peaceful resolution; and

Whereas the United States has no treaty obligations with Kuwait;

Whereas the United States is not in danger of attack; and

Whereas the people of the United States have given no mandate for a U.S. invasion of Kuwait or Iraq; and

Whereas the Anthropology profession is dedicated to fostering communication, understanding, and peaceful resolution of conflict among people of different nations, societies, and cultures;

Be it resolved that the American Anthropology Association call upon President Bush and upon Congress in a written communication to:

Pledge not to order a U.S. military offensive first strike in Kuwait or Iraq;

Pledge further to support actions to defend the national sovereignty of Kuwait by diplomatic and peaceful means only and abide by any international consensus in this regard;

Dramatically reduce the numbers of U.S. troops arrayed in Saudi Arabia to achieve a truly balanced multinational force under United Nations command for defensive purposes only;

Actively work toward securing a significant reduction of the arms buildup in the entire Middle East.[4]

1990 Resolution on the Persian Gulf Crisis
(Revised Text as Approved by Executive Board)

Be it resolved that the board of the American Anthropological Association calls upon President Bush in a written communication to:

Use all possible economic sanctions and diplomatic means to achieve a peaceful solution in the Gulf and avoid the use of military forces if at all possible;

Allow ample time for such sanctions and diplomacy to work;

Maintain and increase the contribution of other than US armed forces in the multinational military resources deployed in the Gulf crisis;

Actively work towards formal peace negotiations and a significant reduction of the arms buildup in the entire Middle East.[5]

1997 Resolution on Sanctions in Iraq (AAA Version)

Whereas the U.N. sanctions imposed on Iraq for seven years have caused the death of a million people and resulted in chronic malnutrition among a million of the country's most vulnerable civilians, the Iraqi children;

Whereas collective punishment is prohibited by international law;

Whereas punishment of innocent people violates universal principles of human rights;

Whereas starvation of civilians as a method of warfare is strictly prohibited by international law;

We the members of the AAA gathered in the city of Washington, D.C., the capital of the U.S.A. on November 20, 1997, hereby call for the immediate lifting of all trade and travel sanctions imposed on civilians in Iraq."[6]

1997 Resolution on Sanctions in Iraq (MES Version)

With urgent concern we, as members of the Middle East Section of the American Anthropological Association, and as professional anthropologists, researchers and educators of the region, resolve:

I. To call for an end to the systematic destruction of the people of Iraq with the sanctions. Since they were implemented in late 1990 the sanctions have caused the deaths of over 1.4 million Iraqis, including over 750,000 children under five years of age. Many more of the young ones are "wasted" and "stunted"—12% and 28% respectively in 1995—according to a report of the UN Food and Agricultural Organization, and each month brings a worsening of conditions.

II. To call for a comprehensive and immediate humanitarian intervention by the world community to save the lives of the Iraqi people and begin the rebuilding of the infrastructure so it will support healthy, productive living."[7]

2000 Resolution on the Second Intifada

Scholars, researchers and students of the Middle East are appalled and saddened at the latest round of provocation and violence in Palestine. Provocation has been followed by violence, including excessive use of force against Palestinians protesting occupation of their land. These are not separable, contrary to what the domestic press is prone to suggest. Attention must be directed at the media representations of the current situation that have moved with the news from provocations to responses which explicitly and implicitly blame the victims.

Whereas the underlying cause of the popular uprising is the Israeli Occupation;

Whereas most victims of the current crisis are Palestinians, many of whom are children;

Whereas the clashes are between an Israeli army and protesting, mostly unarmed, Palestinians;

Therefore, the Board of Directors of the Middle East Section urges the American Anthropological Association and the anthropological community at large to speak out in defense of the Palestinian people's humanity and against the excessive use of force against them, to recognize their legitimate grievances, and to support their right to international protection.

Moreover, the recent violence confirms the need for the United States to re-examine its foreign policy on the Middle East so that international protection is guaranteed for the lives, human rights and homes of the Palestinian people and thus respect for humanity and lives is extended to all people in the region."[8]

2003 Resolution on Graduate Assistance at Yale

Whereas an academic labor panel was convened on September 20, 2003, to consider charges of intimidating and coercive behavior by the Yale administration and some faculty. The panel consisted of: Fred Feinstein (chairman), former NLRB General Counsel; Cynthia Estlund, Professor of Law at Columbia University; Karl Klare, Professor of Law at Northeastern University; Adolph Reed, Professor of Political Science at the New School of Social Research; Robert Reich, University Professor at Brandeis University and former U.S. Labor Secretary; and Emily Spieler, Dean of the School of Law at Northeastern University.

And whereas the academic labor panel explains in the attached statement, "If the reports we heard of faculty, administration and campus police actions are true and representative, graduate student teaching assistants at Yale would clearly be justified in feeling threatened and intimidated."

And whereas the statement adds, "The fact that so many students reported threatening and intimidating experiences, including in relationships with their immediate academic supervisors, itself raises a serious concern. . . . Even if the reports we heard at the forum are exaggerated or mistaken, everyone connected with Yale should be alarmed by the apparent level of distrust, which cannot serve the interests of any segment of the community, and which is inimical to reasoned discourse."

And whereas the statement concludes, "we note with regret that the consequence of the administration's position, if sustained by the NLRB, is that the serious charges of intimidation and interference with expressional freedom raised by GESO's supporters will never receive any sort of adjudicative hearing."

Be it resolved that the Yale administration and GESO (the union of graduate teachers and researches at Yale) should work out a fair process for graduate teaching and research assistants to decide whether or not to unionize, in an atmosphere free from intimidation and coercion.

Be it further resolved that the Yale administration and GESO should, as recommended by the aforementioned statement, find a mutually acceptable forum for reaching some understanding about conduct that members of the Yale community regard as a genuine threat to their freedom of belief and expression. That forum could be the NLRB if all parties conceded its jurisdiction; or it could be another forum devised by the parties.[9]

2003 Resolution on Academic Freedom

Whereas, as anthropologists we are deeply concerned about recent legislative attacks on intellectual freedom and the general discouragement of open public debate that have accompanied patriotic fervor and the war on terror in the United States since September 11, 2001; and

Whereas, the freedom to disagree and to debate issues from a wide range of perspectives is one of the foundations upon which the United States is built, and this foundation, along with the possibilities for the open intellectual inquiry and democracy for which this country is renowned, are deeply threatened by the current U.S. administration; and

Whereas, the U.S. House of Representatives (currently) and Senate (in early 2004) are considering H.R. 3077, which will create an "International Education Advisory Board" charged with linking Title VI funded institutions with national security and intelligence, and that will oversee curricula, course materials, and faculty hires in institutions that accept Title VI funding, giving government security agencies undue influence over academic issues and potentially putting our interlocutors at risk in their home societies; and

Whereas, the USA PATRIOT Act has had severe consequences on both our scholarship and our teaching, due to the ability of federal agencies to request records from libraries and bookstores in order to monitor what we read, and due to the removal of books and CD-ROMs from Federal depository libraries and the closing of websites, based upon "presumed terrorist ties;" and

Whereas, the recent limitations of the Freedom of Information Act undermine our rights as citizens and scholars to access government information, information necessary both to scholars of American history and policy and to citizens who want to formulate informed decisions about government policies; and

Whereas, restrictions on international students and scholars from Muslim-majority countries, including the increased difficulty in obtaining visas, FBI and Homeland Security monitoring of international students on campuses, and the exclusion of international students and scholars from government funded research projects, all contribute to a climate of intimidation and suspicion on our campuses that thwart the democratic exchange of ideas and impede the development of research and knowledge both in the U.S. and in the world at large; and

Whereas, intimidation of faculty and researchers is on the rise, as university administrators have come under pressure to silence members of their communities whose political positions are unpopular and organizations like Campus Watch have published lists of faculty and students critical of US foreign policy in the Middle East,

Therefore be it resolved that, the American Anthropological Association at its annual business meeting of November 21, 2003, calls upon the leaders and administrations of colleges and universities to fulfill their responsibility to uphold academic freedom on our campuses; and

That, the AAA urges the three branches of government to repeal the PATRIOT Act, fully re-instate the Freedom of Information Act, and vote against H.R. 3077,

That, the AAA calls upon university administrators and leaders to protect equal rights and due process for international students and scholars by challenging federal requests for information, refusing restrictive government grants, and supporting the intellectual exchange that international students and scholars bring to campus life,

That, the AAA calls upon university administrations to resist external pressure to curtail academic freedom and to support faculty and researchers who come under attack for their ideas, in the interest of preserving a space for open public debate in this country,

That, the AAA reaffirms its commitment to the principles that critical and open debate is a crucial aspect of university life and that individuals have equal rights to participate in that debate freely no matter what their personal status, country of origin, religion, or ideas about politics and policy.[10]

2003 Resolution on Iraq

Whereas the invasion and occupation of Iraq by the United States and Britain which began in March 2003 is in violation of international law and the United Nations Charter to which all three countries are signatories; and

Whereas international law requires that a state using force unlawfully should pay reparations for the damage caused (as was required of Iraq, which paid billions of dollars to Kuwait and others for its unlawful invasion of that country in 1990); and

Whereas the United States policy behind the invasion, the doctrine of preemptive force, challenges the international legal system and sets a dangerous precedent and has resulted in an unnecessary and excessive loss of human life for primarily Iraqis, but also Americans, Britons and others; and

Whereas the United States used depleted uranium weapons (DU) in Iraq both in 1991 and in 2003, weapons which release high levels of radiation and are implicated in the high levels of birth defects and cancer (among other diseases) present in Iraqis and US military personnel; and

Whereas the conduct of the United States and the United Kingdom is governed by the Geneva Conventions and the Hague Regulations which require that the occupying power maintain law and order (Hague, art. 43), secure the basic human needs of the population (Geneva, art. 55 and 56), manage resources under law of usufruct and to prevent waste (Hague, art. 55), and not enrich itself from the resources of the occupied territory; and

Whereas the US Department of State's Memorandum of Law (Oct. 1, 1976) takes the position that "international law does not support the assertion of a right in the occupant to grant an oil development concession;" and

Whereas an unlawful belligerent occupant has no legal authority to make international agreements for Iraq on debts or any other matters, according to international law and its precedents; and

Whereas as anthropologists we share concerns for the preservation of human life and diversity that are an essential part of our professional and ethical standards;

Therefore Be it Resolved:

That the AAA condemns the U.S. invasion and occupation of Iraq and asks

That the US Government quickly and effectively restore Iraq's infrastructure including power, water, and health-care for all Iraqis in accordance with international law, in such a way that benefits Iraqi business, not American ones; and

That the restoration of Iraq be undertaken at the expense of the powers that destroyed the Iraqi infrastructure (namely the US and Britain) and not be transferred to the Iraqi people, and neither should the US grant oil development concessions to pay for the occupation. The reconstruction should be accomplished in accordance with all international laws and under United Nations authority, in the process guaranteeing human rights for all Iraqis and protecting the cultural heritage of Iraq by adhering to the 1954 Hague Convention for the Protection of Cultural Property in the Event of Armed Conflict and its Protocol, including especially Chapter I, Article 4 of the Convention; and

That the US government, following the effective and quick reconstruction of the country, unilaterally end the occupation of Iraq and support the democratic election of a new Iraqi leadership that represents all Iraqis; and

That the US government support the establishment of a UN authorized war crimes tribunal such as the International Criminal Tribunals for Rwanda and the Former Yugoslavia (ICTR and ICTY) or a Truth and Reconciliation Commission as in South Africa with the purpose of punishing those responsible for the oppression under the former Ba'athist Regime and for war-crimes under the current occupation, and of working towards the reconciliation of all Iraqis.[11]

2003 Resolution in Support of Civil Liberties in the Aftermath of September 11th

Whereas, The Federal Government has used the heinous attacks of September 11th as a justification for a series of attacks against persons perceived to be Arab, South Asian, and/or Muslim; and

Whereas, Since 9/11, the Federal Government has dramatically expanded its power at the expense of our basic liberties; and

Whereas, The Federal Government has detained and deported countless immigrants without due process, spied on political and religious meetings, and given the FBI access to all of our financial, medical, and other personal records; and

Whereas, The United States Constitution guarantees all persons living in the United States fundamental rights including freedom of religion, speech, assembly and privacy; protection from unreasonable searches and seizures; due process and equal protection to any person; equality before the law and the presumption of innocence; access to counsel in judicial proceedings; and a fair, speedy and public trial; and

Whereas, Examples of the provisions of the USA PATRIOT Act and Executive Orders that may violate the Constitution and rights and civil liberties are as follows: A) Significantly expands the government's ability to access sensitive medical, mental health, financial and educational records about individuals, and lowers the burden of proof required to conduct secret searches and telephone and internet surveillance; B) Gives law enforcement expanded authority to obtain library records, and prohibits libraries from informing patrons of monitoring or information requests; C) Gives the Attorney General and the Secretary of State the power to designate domestic groups, including religious and political organizations as "terrorist organizations;" D) Grants power to the Attorney General to subject citizens of other nations to indefinite detention or deportation even if they have not committed a crime; E) Authorizes eavesdropping of confidential communications between attorneys and their clients in Federal custody; F) Limits disclosure of public documents and records under the Freedom of Information Act; and

Whereas, The Department of Justice interpretation of this Act and these Executive Orders particularly targets Muslims, persons of Middle Eastern and South Asian descent and citizens of other nations, and thereby encourages racial profiling by law enforcement and hate crimes by individuals in our community; and

Whereas, the USA PATRIOT Act signed by President George W. Bush on October 26, 2001 has a number of provisions that contradict the above mentioned inalienable rights and fundamentally alters the nature of our civil liberties while doing little to increase public safety; therefore

Resolved, That the Federal Government's targeting of Arabs, South Asians, and/or Muslims and its attacks against our civil liberties do not have our support.

Resolved, That the American Anthropological Association calls upon our United States Representatives and Senators to monitor the implementation of the Act and Orders cited herein and actively work for the repeal of the Act and those Orders that violate fundamental rights and liberties as stated in the United States Constitution and its amendments.

Resolved, That the American Anthropological Association affirms that any efforts to end terrorism not be waged at the expense of the fundamental civil rights and liberties of any individual or racial/ethnic/national group.

Resolved, That the American Anthropological Association also affirms the rights of all people, including United States citizens and citizens of other nations, living within the United States, in accordance with the Bill of Rights and the Fourteenth Amendment of the United States.

Resolved, That the American Anthropological Association calls upon all researchers and educators to demonstrate similar respect for civil rights and civil liberties, especially but not limited to conditions of free speech rights.[12]

2003 Resolution on Israel-Palestine

Whereas, in the course of the current violence in Palestine in Israel [*sic*], excessive use of force and collective punishment measures, illegal under international law, has been directed against Palestinian civilians protesting the military occupation of their land. Given that one of the guiding principles of anthropological work has been to oppose all forms of colonialism and racism throughout the world, it is the anthropological community's responsibility to take a principled stand against Israel's subjugation of the Palestinian people. Critical attention must also be directed at media representations of the situation, because they lack the political, historical, and cultural contextualization that an anthropological approach to such conflicts provides; and

Whereas the underlying cause of the popular uprising is the Israeli Occupation and the structural violence implicit in it; and

Whereas most victims of the current crisis are Palestinian civilians, many of whom are women and children; and

Whereas the violence involves a powerful state army against Palestinian protestors and innocent civilians;

Therefore be it resolved, that the American Anthropological Association speak out in defense of the Palestinian people's human rights as guaranteed under international law, and support their right to self-determination.

Resolved, that the American Anthropological Association publicly condemns the excessive use of force against Palestinians, and demands the application of all relevant international laws and U.N. resolutions.

Resolved, that the AAA deplores and calls for an immediate halt to the killing of Israeli civilians by Palestinian combatants, as well as the killing of Palestinian civilians by the Israeli military and settlers.

Resolved, that the AAA calls on the United States government to develop a foreign policy in the Middle East that promotes the security and human rights of Palestinians, Israelis, and U.S. citizens at home and abroad.

Resolved, that the AAA calls for the respect for the humanity of all people in the region, and their right to live in peace.[13]

2004 Resolution on Israel's Wall

Whereas, Israel has built and is continuing to build a barrier through Palestinian territory, illegal under international law, a fact reconfirmed by the International Court of Justice advisory decision in July 2004 in a vote of 14–1. Given that the wall is being built deep within the West Bank, rendering impossible the continuity of daily economic and social life in the region, causing Palestinian communities to lose land, water, and resources which provide their sustenance, as well as the destruction to personal property, disrupting Palestinians' access to crucial basic services, demolishing the economies of many areas, trapping thousands of Palestinians in ghettos between the wall and the Green Line, preventing children from reaching their schools and the ill from accessing medical care, while also separating farmers from their lands and families from one another. Given that one of the guiding principles of anthropological work has been to oppose all forms of colonialism and racism throughout the world, it is the anthropological community's responsibility to take a principled stand against this wall and Israel's continual dispossession of the Palestinian people of their land by means of its construction, and clear and continuing grave breaches of the Geneva Conventions, to which Israel is a signatory;

Whereas, The wall's location deep within Palestinian territory (in some places ten miles into that territory) and around large and illegally built Israeli settlements indicates that the wall is not being constructed to protect Israeli security but to seize Palestinian land and water and entrench settlements on it;

Whereas, Most victims of the wall's incursions into Palestinian lands are Palestinian civilians;

Whereas, The wall is an act against Palestinian national aspirations and right to self-determination;

Whereas, The wall is also a tool to effect the creeping "transfer" of the Palestinian population, as people are being forced out of their homes and into ever smaller cantons; and

Whereas, Anthropology as a profession is committed to the promotion and protection of the right of all peoples to the full realization of their humanity. When any government denies such opportunity to anyone, the American Anthropological Association has an ethical responsibility to protest and oppose such deprivation; therefore, be it

Resolved, That the American Anthropological Association speak out against the construction of this wall, and in defense of the Palestinian people's human rights as guaranteed under international law.

Resolved, That the American Anthropological Association publicly condemns the construction of this barrier in Palestinian territory, and demands the application of all relevant international laws and U.N. resolutions.[14]

2004 Letter to a U.S. Government Official from the AAA Middle East Section and Committee for Human Rights about Falluja, Iraq

As Chairs of the Middle East Section and Committee for Human Rights of the American Anthropological Association, we are writing to urge you to move more quickly to bring normalcy back to Falluja and its people by expediting delivery of relief through safe corridors. Furthermore, we ask that you recognize the debilitating effects that the operations in April and November have had on the fabric of social life in Falluja, and therefore make your actions to rebuild the city culturally sensitive and appropriate. Finally, we ask that you promptly and publicly recognize that following international humanitarian law is not an option for the U.S., but an obligation to which this country is committed.

As you know, relief has only just arrived to the city. Eyewitnesses report unbelievable destruction to homes, schools, and mosques. There has been no water for a month. Illness is mounting, and civilian corpses lie in the streets. There needs to be immediate action to ensure the continued safe access of independent humanitarian aid in Falluja, to allow the thousands of refugees to return safely to their homes, and to quickly rebuild what is now destroyed. Safe corridors and areas can and must be immediately created so that people can get the basic aid that they need, and so that they can begin to pick up the pieces of their lives.

The ordinary men, women, and children of Falluja have suffered a major breakdown in their families and communities because of this conflict. It is very hard for a community with little resources to rebound from two major urban battles that resulted in large numbers of civilian casualties, the destruction of culturally important buildings, and tremendous damage to infrastructure. Attention needs to be placed on providing the social services needed for people to rebuild their community, and to give them control over rebuilding it according to their own priorities. It is imperative that the people of Falluja be able to return as quickly as possible to some semblance of normalcy. This is not just about water, food, rebuilding homes, and providing compensation to families who lost relatives, though these basics should be a priority. This is also about creating a sense of stability and respect that comes from having control of one's movements, places of worship, and family life.

The administration needs to make and keep a public promise to abide by international humanitarian law. The administration's claims that it is concerned with the humanitarian situation in the region ring hollow in the Arab world. The coalition forces are not observing the basic requirement under the Geneva Convention that the warring parties provide for the sick and wounded and ensure that basic food, water, and medicine is not cut off. Neither refugees nor civilians remaining in the city are receiving enough basic aid. The situation in Falluja resembles the Israeli assault on Jenin refugee camps in April 2002, in which aid workers were also prevented from entering to provide humanitarian relief from the Israeli incursion. Falluja, like Jenin, was a serious violation of international humanitarian law. The United States has a legal and moral obligation to follow international humanitarian law, which was created so that human cultures and societies do not get ripped asunder by political and military conflicts.

If the United States does not meet this obligation quickly and thoroughly, then the long-term effects of this conflict on Fallujan society, and on Iraqi society in general, will be grim indeed. As experts in human societies and cultures, we cannot stress this point enough.[15]

2006 Resolution on the U.S. Occupation of Iraq

Whereas the U.S. Government led an invasion and occupation of Iraq in violation of Chapter VII of the United Nations Charter in March 2003; and

Whereas over the past 32 months more than 2700 U.S. troops and an estimated 655,000 Iraqis (the vast majority civilians) have been killed in the subsequent violence; and

Whereas the U.S. military is holding in detention approximately 15,000 Iraqis without charge; and

Whereas U.S. military and intelligence personnel and U.S. Government subcontractors have tortured and abused detainees at Abu Ghraib and other Iraqi prisons in violation of the Geneva Conventions; and

Whereas much of Iraq's historical, cultural, and archaeological heritage was looted or destroyed following the U.S.-led invasion while occupying forces made no effort to protect it; and

Whereas the U.S. Coalition Provisional Authority, under the leadership of Paul Bremer, created a set of edicts (codified into the Iraqi constitution in violation of international law) that has facilitated the plunder of Iraq's national industries and natural resources by multinational corporations; and

Whereas the U.S. military presence in Iraq has undermined the political stability of that country and the Middle East region;

Be it moved that the American Anthropological Association condemns the U.S.-led invasion and occupation of Iraq and urges the U.S. Congress and President George W. Bush to:

Immediately withdraw all U.S. military personnel, intelligence agents, and subcontractors from Iraq; and

Cease all U.S. military operations and vacate all U.S. military bases in Iraq; and

Make payments for the removal and cleanup of depleted uranium, unexploded cluster bombs, and other residual waste left from munitions; and

Prosecute all individuals who have committed war crimes against Iraqis; and

Fund the creation of a United Nations peacekeeping force to assume peacekeeping duties in Iraq.[16]

2006 Resolution on Torture

WHEREAS over the past 32 months, documentary and photographic evidence of widespread physical and psychological torture and abuse of prisoners in the Middle East, Central Asia, and Guantanamo Bay at the hands of U.S. military and U.S. intelligence personnel and subcontractors has appeared; and

WHEREAS at least 98 prisoners have died while in custody of U.S. military and U.S. intelligence personnel in Iraq and Afghanistan, including 45 suspected or confirmed homicides; and

WHEREAS the Britons Moazzam Begg, Asef Iqbal, Shafik Rasul, and Ruhal Ahmed have alleged that they and others were tortured by U.S. military or U.S. intelligence personnel while imprisoned in Afghanistan and Guantanamo Bay; and

WHEREAS U.S. Central Intelligence Agency officials have assembled an overseas network of secret prisons not accessible by the International Committee of the Red Cross or by other international bodies charged with monitoring compliance with the U.N. Convention Against Torture; and

WHEREAS U.S. Central Intelligence Agency officials have, since the early 1990s, been abducting foreign nationals for detention and interrogation as part of an "extraordinary rendition" program violating the U.N. Convention Against Torture; and

WHEREAS U.S. Central Intelligence Agency personnel and subcontractors have used "waterboarding" (in which the prisoner is made to believe he is drowning) and other techniques violating the U.N. Convention Against Torture; and

WHEREAS the U.S. Government has, since 1988, narrowed the legal definition of torture to exclude sensory deprivation, self-inflicted pain, disorientation, and other forms of severe psychological abuse; and

WHEREAS in September 2006 the U.S. Congress passed into law the Military Commissions Act, which includes provisions that would in many cases grant retroactive immunity for government officials who authorized or ordered illegal acts of torture or abuse;

Be it moved that the American Anthropological Association unequivocally condemns the use of anthropological knowledge as an element of physical and psychological torture; condemns the use of physical and psychological torture by U.S. military and intelligence personnel, subcontractors, and proxies; and urges the U.S. Congress and President George W. Bush to:

Comply fully with national and international anti-torture laws, including the Geneva Conventions, the U.N. Convention Against Torture, the 1996 U.S. War Crimes Act, and U.S. Criminal Code, Sections 2340-2340A; and

Ban all interrogation techniques—including physical and psychological torture—that violate the broad universal humanitarian standard outlined in the U.N. Convention Against Torture; and

Restore the legal definition of torture to include sensory deprivation, self-inflicted pain, and disorientation, and other forms of psychological abuse; and

Comply fully with the U.S. Supreme Court's *Hamdan v. Rumsfeld* decision of 2006, in which the majority opinion states that even during times of war, "the Executive is bound to comply with the Rule of Law;" and

Repeal the 2006 U.S. Military Commissions Act; and

Terminate the "extraordinary rendition" program and halt the transfer of detainees to countries with a history of prisoner abuse and torture; and

Close all U.S. overseas prisons and release all prisoners being held without charge in U.S. prisons (including overseas prisons); and

Release the names of all prisoners being held in U.S. prisons (including all overseas prisons); and

Pay reparations to all victims who have suffered physical or psychological torture at the hands of U.S. military and intelligence personnel, subcontractors, and proxies; and

Grant the International Committee of the Red Cross and other international monitoring agencies full access to all U.S. overseas prisons; and

Prosecute to the fullest extent of the law all individuals—including current and former Bush administration officials—who have authorized or committed war crimes or who have violated laws prohibiting torture.[17]

2009 AAA Committee for Human Rights Statement
Regarding Israeli Attack and International Siege on the Gaza Strip

The Committee for Human Rights of the American Anthropological Association (AAA) would like to express its deep concern about the ongoing siege of the Gaza Strip, and the humanitarian consequences of the 22-day-long attack by the Israeli army. Our concern speaks to the AAA's disciplinary and professional commitment to furthering and defending the cultural, political and human rights of the world's peoples. The AAA, which currently has over 11,000 members, is the largest professional organization of anthropologists in the world.

The three weeks of Israeli bombardment were a disproportionately violent attack on an occupied territory approximately twice the size of Washington D.C., home to some 1.5 million Palestinians, two-thirds of whom are refugees. The repercussions of these assaults will be felt by the region's peoples for decades to come. The UN states that as of January 19, 1,314 Palestinians have been killed. Of those, some 580 were women and children. More than 5,300 have been injured, and half of those sustained severe injuries such as fractures, amputations, burns and head wounds that will require rehabilitation to prevent permanent disability. More than 66,000 Palestinians have not been able to return to their homes, and many are without running water. The massive airstrikes against Gaza targeted military and civil installations, included civilian police, the education ministry, culture ministry, universities, as well as private houses, hospitals, and mosques. Much of the basic infrastructure of the small strip of land has been destroyed, including the systems that provide water, electricity, and sanitation. Supplies of basic foodstuffs and fuel, and the provision of medical, water and sanitation services remain critical.[18]

Of particular concern is the targeting of civilian residents and civilian institutions, including UNRWA schools, and the use of white phosphorous on civilians by the Israeli Defense Forces (IDF).[19] Military operations, including aerial bombing in civilian populations, is in direct violation of Israel's legal requirement as a signatory of the Geneva Convention to take all feasible precautions to avoid harming civilians during military operations. The Fourth Geneva Convention also prohibits collective punishment, without exception. (Art. 33). Many believe that the use of white phosphorous violates the ban on incendiary weapons in the international Convention on Conventional Weapons. (Art. 1, Protocol III). Although Israel is not a signatory to this Convention, its use of such weaponry, which has been banned by the international community, including most recently the United States, violates international standards of human rights and the requirement to protect civilian populations during military operations.[20] Amnesty International reports that evidence of war crimes and crimes against humanity is mounting daily.[21]

The attack on Gaza comes on the heels of the 18-month blockade that Israel and its allies have imposed on the Gaza Strip since 2006. The siege has contributed to severe shortages of medical supplies and food. The number of households in Gaza below the poverty line reached an unprecedented high of nearly 52 per cent in 2007. Joblessness in Gaza between July and December 2007 reached 45.3 per cent (UNRWA 2008, OXFAM 2007). The U.N. special rapporteur on the right to food has found that acute malnutrition in Gaza is on the same scale as in the poorest nations in the southern Sahara, with more than half of all Palestinian families eating only one meal a day. Eighty per cent of families in Gaza rely on humanitarian aid (OXFAM 2008).

We recognize that every state has a right and a duty to protect its citizens. This fact does not, however, in any way absolve the Israeli government and military from the requirement that they be held accountable to the norms of international humanitarian and human rights laws for their actions in Gaza. Just as Israelis have a right to live in peace and security, so do the Palestinians. But they are not. Throughout the occupied territories of the West Bank, Gaza Strip, and East Jerusalem, Palestinians live in ceaseless all-encompassing insecurity and unfreedom.

Given the above, we, the AAA Committee for Human Rights, request the following:

1. that Israel and the international community immediately lift the siege on Gaza to allow vital medical and humanitarian supplies to get through to civilian populations and to allow the free movement of civilians in and out of Gaza;

2. that the United States and the European Union establish an independent and impartial investigation of abuses of international human rights and humanitarian law, including and especially Israeli attacks directed at civilians and civilian buildings in the Gaza Strip;

3. that the High Contracting Parties to the Fourth Geneva Convention comply with its legal obligations detailed in Article 146 of the Convention to search for and prosecute those responsible for grave breaches, including war crimes and the misuse of weapons such as white phosphorus;

4. that Israel allow free access to Gaza for media and members of the international and Israeli human rights communities;

5. that Israel grant academic freedom and freedom of movement to students and scholars in Gaza, East Jerusalem and the West Bank.[22]

Notes

Introduction

1. The more publicized cases related to the Middle East include Steven Salaita's unhiring by the University of Illinois at Urbana-Champaign, Thomas Abowd's denial of contract renewal by Wayne State University, Norman Finkelstein's tenure denial at DePaul University, and the drawn-out but eventually successful tenure battles of Nadia Abu El-Haj at Barnard/Columbia University and Joseph Massad at Columbia University.

2. We focus on cultural anthropology of the Middle East and North Africa (MENA), with occasional comparative consideration of other anthropological subfields, especially archaeology. We also focus on MENA anthropology as practiced in academia; future studies could examine its practice in applied contexts from government to NGOs and corporations.

3. Throughout this book, we use MENA (Middle East and North Africa) to denote the region and describe the anthropological subfield, unless one of our interlocutors or secondary sources uses the term "Middle East" without appending North Africa. As a world region, MENA refers to the Arab League states, plus Iran, Turkey, and Israel; as an anthropological subfield, it includes Israel when the anthropologist working there identifies as a MENA anthropologist (via membership in the Middle East Section of the AAA or by listing "Middle East" in the AAA membership directory). We also include Afghanistan. Our focus is primarily on global politics related to the region. While we recognize that politics specific to various MENA national contexts and their study (e.g., Iranian Studies, Turkish Studies, Lebanese politics) also impact scholars, their analysis falls beyond this book's scope.

4. There are, of course, numerous other military actions in the region—overt and covert—in which the United States has played a leading role since 1990.

5. This insight grew from discussions questioning the value of area studies, as well as new work on globalization. For more on these debates vis-à-vis the Middle East, see Mirsepassi, Basu, and Weaver 2003.

6. Florida governor Rick Scott singled out anthropology as a useless major. http://www.huffingtonpost.com/2011/10/12/rick-scott-anthropology-major-daughter-jobs

_n_1007900.html. *Forbes* magazine recently wrote that anthropology topped the list as the worst college major in economic terms. http://www.forbes.com/sites/jennagou dreau/2012/10/11/the-10-worst-college-majors. Anthropology may be singled out because of its stereotypical reputation as focused on primitive cultural others deemed either irrelevant or obstacles to social and economic progress.

7. Our work is in conversation with, but adds an ethnographic dimension to, key works in the historiography of anthropology including those by Darnell 2001; di Leonardo 2000; Nader 1997; Price 2004b, 2008, and 2011; Stocking 1968 and 1992; Wax 2008; and, especially for MENA, Anderson 2013; Hafez and Slyomovics 2013b; and Slyomovics 2013. Eickelman 2012 discusses the special challenges facing MENA scholars. We also view our work as in dialogue with anthropological work on intellectuals, especially but not exclusively as "artisans of nationalism" (Boyer and Lomnitz 2005), and sociological studies of the academy (e.g., Bourdieu 1988; Gumport 2007; Kennedy 2015). For another example of how academic disciplines are formed in relation to specific geographic foci, see Pomeranz and Segal's 2012 discussion of how, in the mid-twentieth century, "the West" was viewed as the discipline of history's domain while the non-Western world remained the domain of anthropologists.

8. Hancock 2008: 173.

9. Haraway 1988.

10. We thank Flagg Miller for poison chalice.

11. For example, Bok 2004; Donoghue 2008; Ginsberg 2011; Taylor 2010.

12. Bureau of Labor Statistics, 2012. http://www.bls.gov/ooh/education-training-and -library/postsecondary-teachers.htm.

13. This is happening in a climate of economic instability that may cause parents to feel anxious about whether or not their "investment" translates into their children learning skills necessary to lead an economically successful postgraduation life.

14. Government authority also affects private institutions, especially via federal financial aid and accreditation regulations, even when the latter processes are outsourced to private organizations (e.g., the Western Association of Schools and Colleges). Part of the administrative bloat in higher education is due to institutions hiring staff to manage the increasing reams of federal and state regulations on teaching and research that result from the particular kind of technocracy attendant to neoliberalism. See Harvey 2005; Mitchell 2002; Sharma 2013.

15. According to the American Association of University Professors (AAUP), more than 50 percent of faculty in the United States do not hold tenure-line jobs, and 76 percent of all appointments are made outside the tenure track. The AAUP estimates that the total number of contingent faculty has risen from 43 percent in 1975 to 57 percent in 1993 and 70 percent in 2011. See http://www.aaup.org/issues/contingent-faculty/ resources-contingent-appointments. See also http://www.aaup.org/issues/contingency/ background-facts.

16. Schrecker 2010: 60. Not coincidentally, the trend toward hiring more adjuncts occurred at the same time as women's and ethnic studies programs were beginning to challenge the white patriarchal status quo in theory, methods, and demographics. See http://www.lowendtheory.org/post/112138864200/theses-on-adjunctification.

17. See the report at http://www.aaanet.org/resources/departments/upload/job-sur
vey-for-web.pdf. The AAA Committee on Labor Relations has also conducted an analysis
of data from the subset of anthropologists who responded to a 2010 survey by the Coalition on the Academic Workforce (full survey here: http://www.academicwork force.org/
survey.html; AAA analysis available from the AAA executive director upon request). It
found that 42.1 percent of anthropology respondents were employed part-time at one
or more institutions; 22.9 percent were employed in a full-time non-tenure-line position; 82 percent described contingent employment as "essential" or "very important"
to their total income; yet only 10.6 percent said that they "preferred" non-tenure-line
employment.

18. Contingent faculty face even tighter political strictures on academic practice
than do those with the security of tenure. A recent survey by the Middle East Studies Association revealed that 41.5 percent of contingent faculty modify their courses to
avoid controversial topics (presented by Amy Newhall, MESA Executive Director at the
2013 MESA meetings). This is also gendered, as women make up the majority of contingent faculty labor. As Schrecker notes, "When student complaints can lead to unem-
ployment, a vulnerable instructor will think twice before saying something that might
upset a Christian fundamentalist or religious Zionist" (2010: 214).

19. See Hollinger 1996 on the importance of the GI Bill, alongside the discrediting
of anti-Semitism, for the increase in Jewish faculty members across academic disciplines
between the 1930s and 1960s.

20. Classifying class is frequently a challenge, particularly in the United States,
where people tend to think it is irrelevant, or flexible and shifting. The academy, from
many working class scholars' perspectives, is a "class-phobic professional environment"
(Anthony 2012: 305) in that discussions of class are marginalized in favor of race and
that working class scholars experience discrimination. Organizations such as the Association for Working Class Academics (http://awcaonline.org/wordpress) and numerous blogs on the topic also indicate that class discrimination occurs in academia. Two
of our interlocutors from working class backgrounds expressed feeling like outliers in
academia because of their class difference. The intersections of class and race also affect
many scholars' lives (Brodkin, Morgen, and Hutchinson 2011). Yet class was not spontaneously mentioned in the vast majority of our interviews, and at first, we simply did
not ask about it. When we realized our error, we sent a follow-up email to our interlocutors, asking them (in anthropological fashion) to describe their class backgrounds in
their own terms. Many respondents asked us to define what we meant by class and/or
discussed how difficult it was to determine their social class. Our careful analysis of the
over one hundred often lengthy and rich qualitative responses we received—attending
to descriptions of class background, parent and grandparent occupations, geographic
location, and possession of economic, educational, and cultural capital—showed the diversity of the subfield's class composition. There was a strong clustering of anthropologists in the middle (39 percent) to upper-middle classes (27 percent), with a notable
15 percent from the working classes, and another 14 percent from the precarious lower-
middle classes (3 percent were from upper-class and 2 percent from poor backgrounds).

21. We use "region-related" to include "native" scholars who immigrated to the

United States for graduate school or before, and "heritage" scholars like Arab American or Iranian American anthropologists (who have one or both parents or grandparents from the region). This latter term also includes what many refer to as "halfie" scholars, those who are "between cultures, the West of their upbringing, one parent, or training, and the culture of their origin, their family's origin, their other parent's, or some part of their identity" (Abu-Lughod 1990: 26). "Region-related" is our term and includes the Arab League states, Iran, Turkey, and Israel. Our interlocutors usually used the terms *native, heritage,* and *halfie* in ways that align with our definitions. We understand region-related anthropologists to be racial or ethnic minorities in the United States and in the US academy in particular. A number of scholars have discussed the myriad ways in which Arabs and others of Middle Eastern (and/or Muslim) descent are racialized in the United States (Abraham 1989; Gualtieri 2009; Naber 2000; Jamal and Naber 2008; Rana 2011; Salaita 2006; Saliba 1999; Samhan 1999; Stockton 1994). Arabs, like Iranians and Muslims (especially of Middle Eastern and South Asian background), are frequently presumed to be "different than and inferior to whites" due to "culturalist and nationalist logics that assume that 'they' are intrinsically unassimilable and threatening to national security" (Naber 2008: 31). Thus, the entire US military-industrial-security-oil complex, after World War II but especially after 9/11, has been a major force in the racialization of those with MENA and/or Muslim heritage, even if US censuses have often classified them as white. They may not self-identify as such. Our data show that this racialization occurs frequently in the US academy (see also Hagopian 2004; Salaita 2006). Understanding these scholars as both members of ethnic minorities and as racialized allows us to better understand their described experiences and understandings. Finally, these categories are not fixed. People are often placed (or place themselves) in different or multiple categories situationally. And experiences are often discipline-specific: an interlocutor trained as an anthropologist who works in a different disciplinary context reminded us that anthropology is better than some fields in relation to racist and other discriminations. For more on racism in the academy, and in anthropology in particular, see the report *Racism in the Academy: The New Millennium,* available at http://www.aaanet.org/cmtes/commissions/Racism-in-the-Academy-New-Millennium.cfm.

22. Within the category of region-related anthropologists we see increasing numbers of male scholars, with more region-related men than white men entering the field in the last two decades. Perhaps anthropology is becoming a more acceptable career among region-related men, or they are growing more likely to challenge family expectations regarding traditional professional paths (e.g., engineering and medicine). Over time, more people from working class backgrounds have entered the subfield; class did not significantly correlate with gender. Also, the relative proportions of interlocutors from working class and middle-class backgrounds are very close to the overall ethnic/racial breakdown of our sample. Nonwhite, non-region-related interlocutors were more likely to be from working class backgrounds (12.5 percent, versus 8 percent of all interlocutors). The largest racial/ethnic contrast is between the lower-middle classes, (86.6 percent white versus 6.7 percent region-related) and the upper-middle class (55 percent region-related versus 38 percent white). The general clustering of region-related scholars in the middle to upper-middle classes suggests that relative economic stability for

immigrant groups plays a role in choosing anthropology as a career path. Several region-related scholars were also raised (or partly raised) in MENA, adding another layer of complexity to their class positions and understandings. Quite a few lower-middle- and middle-class people of all ethnic and racial backgrounds mentioned having much higher cultural or educational capital than economic capital. Possession of cultural or educational capital was a crucial aspect of their class self-definitions, perhaps due to political leanings that might lead one to downplay economic privilege.

23. These numbers reflect larger disciplinary patterns: according to an unpublished AAA analysis of the 2012 NSF Survey of Earned Doctorates (available from the AAA executive director upon request), Black graduates received only 3 percent of doctorates in anthropology in 2012, while Hispanic graduates received only 7.2 percent.

24. Women comprised 65.9 percent of doctorate recipients in anthropology in 2012 (as compared to 46 percent of all doctorates that year). Ibid.

25. Abu-Lughod 1990: 27.

26. On the ways that anthropology departments remain "white public spaces" despite some demographic shifts, see Brodkin, Morgen, and Hutchinson 2011.

27. A term specific to US educational institutions that currently includes African Americans, Mexican Americans, Native Americans, Pacific Islanders, and mainland Puerto Ricans.

28. Gutiérrez y Muhs et al. 2012.

29. The AAA Commission on Race and Racism in Anthropology found that there was a "steep growth spurt" in minority faculty hires in anthropology between the late 1970s and 1980s, which prefaced a smaller growth in minority PhDs beginning in the mid-1990s. Yet there was no growth of minority faculty between 1988 and 1998. Contemporary data are sparse and unreliable (see Brodkin, Morgen, and Hutchinson 2011).

30. Constantine and Dorazio 2008: 1290. The term microaggression is generational, an example of a term taken up by recent scholars to describe what have been previously called everyday discriminations.

31. Homophobia and heterosexism also affect academe, and queer and queer-allied scholars have long histories, including in anthropology as a whole, of confronting those discriminatory discourses and practices. We do not discuss these dynamics for two reasons: because queer studies has only recently intersected with MENA anthropology and its influence has yet to be strongly felt in the subfield, and because issues related to sexuality came up in so few of our interviews that discussing them ethnographically would reveal those interlocutors' identities.

32. McAlister 2001: 2.

33. Said 1978: 2.

34. On this Christian Zionism, see Wagner 1995 and Weber 2004.

35. Archaeologists faced a different but related set of political issues related to access. Wars or the breakdown of diplomatic relationships can have a greater effect, as their projects are usually multiseason and require a local infrastructure. Excavating in both Israel and in majority Arab countries was again facilitated by Oslo and has become more difficult since the second intifada. National governments also vary in their permissions to remove objects or remains. Working with human skeletal remains in Israel

is difficult due to restrictions related to Orthodox Jewish law. Jordan has no restrictions on human skeletal remains but regulates other artifacts strictly. Egypt's regulations lie in between, with some limitation on the study of human remains in part to avoid challenges to the idea that modern and ancient Egyptians are related to one another. The nationalization of archaeological work in some places, like Turkey, has made access more difficult for noncitizen scholars. And finally, archaeological projects are often entangled with contemporary politics. Excavating in the Biblical periods and in Israel more generally is the most obvious example, with ramifications for nationalist claims (Abu El-Haj 2001). An interlocutor learned "the importance of archaeology as a modern political tool" in another region when the local community opposed cultural preservation rescue excavations in an effort to halt the development project that necessitated those excavations in the first place. On global politics' effects on MENA archaeology, see Emberling 2008 and Luke and Kersel 2013.

36. Access issues are not unique to MENA; other anthropologists have had research plans derailed by coups, State Department travel bans, or natural disasters. Due to the pace of political shifts in MENA, in every generation, multiple scholars have had to relocate (and reenvision) their projects. Our interlocutors' field plans were thwarted by almost every major revolution, coup, or war in the region since the 1950s. Local violence, including a government crackdown on village smuggling, the murder of a foreign aid worker, and a car bomb, have also forced research changes.

37. Iran is a special case: While non-Iranian scholars lost access to the country for research after 1979, the situation was more complex for those of Iranian heritage. After 1997, several such anthropologists conducted fieldwork in Iran. They told us they believed this was possible because of the Khatami government's (1997–2005) relative openness but that field opportunities were limited again under Ahmedinejad (2005–2013). Even under Khatami, several were unable to return to Iran following their books' publications because their ethnographies were at odds with the regime's portrayal of Iranian society. One anthropologist also described concerns about leaving Iran with ethnographic data that could potentially be used to pressure interlocutors.

38. The few scholars who have conducted research in Syria deliberately chose topics less obviously related to formal politics, pushed their projects back in time so that they wouldn't "implicate any living community or any living person," as one scholar put it, and/or worked within communities where they already had long-standing relationships.

39. Feldman 2008: 4. We did not ask about the well-known security hassles scholars conducting fieldwork in the occupied Palestinian territories face at the Israeli border, as our focus was the effects of US state practices. Depending on the scholar's citizenship, as well as religious identity, crossing those borders can include everything from hostile questions to hours-long body and property searches. Exiting Israel or the occupied Palestinian territories can be equally problematic, with the potential for confiscation of computer and/or field notes, the compromising of interlocutors' identities, and even travel bans to Israel. It is taken utterly for granted by these scholars that Israeli border security is, at best, a hassle, and at worst, a hindrance, to research. That said, it is worth noting that a senior anthropologist who has long worked in Palestinian communities no longer plans to do so because crossing the border has become so "horrific."

40. The Oslo Accords, signed in Washington DC in September 1993, established mutual recognition of Israel and the PLO, which then formed the Palestinian Authority in 1994. It also initiated a negotiation process that collapsed in 2000 as it became apparent that the accords institutionalized and normalized the Israeli occupation of the West Bank and Gaza and continued Israeli colonization and expansion, and folded Palestinian communities into a neoliberal economic order. See Farsakh 2002; Hanieh 2013; and also the excellent primer produced by the Middle East Research and Information Project, available here: http://www.merip.org/primer-palestine-israel-arab-israeli-conflict-new.

41. On these stereotypes, and the shift to "terrorist" from earlier representations of Middle Eastern men as "desert oil sheikhs," as well as the parallel shift in stereotypes of Middle Eastern women that moved from eroticized to oppressed, see Jarmakani 2008.

42. Before 9/11, the 1990 Gulf War marked perhaps the most intense period of anti-Arab and anti-Muslim racism and violence in US history (Hagopian 2004; Naber 2014).

43. Slyomovics 2013: 9.

44. Fulbright funded between 1 and 5 MENA anthropology research grants each year from 1993–2001, and between 3 and 8 per year from 2002–2012. Nonanthropology MENA Fulbright research grants increased far more: from a range of 28–51 per year from 1993–2001 to 47–96 per year from 2002–2012. Between 1993 and 2012, there were fourteen Fulbright offices (at various times): Bahrain, Egypt, Israel, Kuwait, Jordan, Morocco, Oman, Saudi Arabia, Syria, Tunisia, Turkey, the United Arab Emirates, the West Bank, and Yemen. We were only able to obtain Fulbright data from 1993–2012, as the regional program officer told us that data prior to 1993 were not publicly available.

45. The IDRF replaced SSRC's earlier area-based committees in 1997, although SSRC also maintained for a time a MENA-specific predissertation and dissertation field grant program. IDRF funding for MENA projects (in all disciplines) went from between 3 and 7 grants per year from 1997–2001 to between 4 and 15 grants per year from 2002–2012, with over 10 grants awarded in four of those years. In comparison, Latin America IDRFs for all disciplines remained steady between 10 and 17 grants per year, with the exception of four years during that period when they dipped below that number. SSRC-IDRF information is from http://www.ssrc.org/fellowships/idrf-fellowship. For Wenner-Gren, between 1990-2001, the range was 0 to 7 grants/year, while from 2002–2012, it was between 2 and 19 grants per year, with five years having over 10 MENA grants. Wenner-Gren information from 2001–2012 is available at http://www.wennergren.org/about-grantees.

46. Anthropology-specific SSRC-IDRF grants for MENA research only rose from between 0 and 3 grants per year from 1997–2001 to between 0 and 5 per year from 2002–2012. And from 2003–2012, the National Security Education Program's (NSEP's) Boren Fellowships were awarded to between 17 and 31 graduate students studying MENA languages each year, but *anthropology* graduate students rarely received them (none in five of those years and only one in three of those years). This is not only a reflection on ideas about disciplinary utility for state-sponsored research, but also suggests that anthropology graduate students were less likely than those in other disciplines to apply for this "strings-attached" funding.

47. At least one scholar working in Iran received a private foundation grant but had

to wait five months for permission from the US Office of Foreign Assets Control before they were allowed to spend any money in the country.

48. As Talal Asad wrote in 1973, "The powerful who support research expect the kind of understanding which will ultimately confirm them in their world" (91).

49. See Price 2011 for detailed discussion of this shift, its new funding programs, and its consequences for scholarship. See also Wax 2008. Similar changes affect undergraduate education, with financial aid and other funding from the Department of Homeland Security, the CIA, and other security and intelligence agencies.

50. For example, Lara received an invitation (which she ignored) to join a major multicountry Minerva project, led by a researcher at the Naval Postgraduate School, on "supporters of violence" that essentially sought to use dominant political science frameworks to assert categorical reasons (e.g., "religious" versus "ideological") why certain people support groups that the project (following US government designations) deemed to be "terrorists," including Hizbullah, the IRA, and others. On Minerva, see Glenn 2009 and Price 2011.

51. On the role of anthropology professor Felix Moos in the establishment of the Pat Roberts Intelligence Scholars Program, see Glenn 2005.

52. https://www.borenawards.org/boren_fellows_service.html. Despite this stipulation, as one of our reviewers pointed out, it seems that few recipients actually end up in such positions, both because there are not very many available and because they are not necessarily qualified for them.

53. Much of this funding is for language study; far less is allocated for research projects. On the extraordinary increase in "strings-attached" and other forms of defense-related government funding for Arabic, see Chris Stone's April 11, 2014, *Jadaliyya* piece, "Teaching Arabic in the US After 9/11." Available at http://www.jadaliyya.com/pages/index/17286/teaching-arabic-in-the-us-after-9-11. We also heard about graduate students studying the Middle East with "invisible means of support" related somehow to "CIA training." As one faculty member explained, "it was above my pay grade to know what was involved with these students."

54. During most years between 1996 and 2001, there was at most one search dedicated to hiring a MENA anthropologist and one or two where MENA was one of several preferred regions. These numbers doubled in 2002 and then growth slowed until 2006, though job ads continued to include MENA as one of several possible areas. A major jump took place from 2006–2008, when there was an average of thirteen possible positions a year, several of which were dedicated specifically to the Middle East. These increases are less than those in other fields, perhaps partly because anthropology is a relatively smaller discipline than history and political science.

55. The number of job advertisements posted through the online AAA Career Center (where nearly all anthropology jobs are announced) declined by 19 percent from 2007 to 2008 and by a further 22 percent in the first six months of the 2008–2009 academic year (see http://www.aaanet.org/resources/departments/upload/job-survey-_for-web.pdf). For MENA-specific jobs, from 2011–2013 the trend returned to only one or two tenure-track anthropology positions per year dedicated to the region. While not

limited to MENA, these years also saw at least one tenure-track anthropology position that specified Islam and often one or two interdisciplinary positions in Islamic Studies.

56. For more on the major intellectual trends in MENA anthropology since the end of the Cold War, see Deeb and Winegar 2012.

57. Edwards 2005; Little 2003; Lockman 2004; McAlister 2001; Said 1978. Orientalism also has significant traction within Israel in legitimating that state's actions against Palestinians; see Abu El-Haj 2001.

58. Said 1978: 3.

59. By post-Orientalist, they meant an anthropology in which Orientalist approaches to MENA were no longer dominant and where critiques of Orientalism were taken for granted such that they did not need to be continually rehearsed. A few of our interlocutors instead found the critique of Orientalism to be stifling for anthropology.

60. Chatterjee and Maira 2014b: 6. See also Abraham 2008 and Schrecker 2010.

61. While our interlocutors did not address homophobia directly in relation to these attacks, public examples include the homophobic language used to denounce some of the scholars on the "Dirty 30" blacklist of UCLA faculty and homophobic attacks on the American Studies Association leadership following that association's adoption of the academic boycott against Israeli institutions.

62. Chatterjee and Maira 2014b: 22, 24.

63. On these culture wars in relation to academe, see Schrecker 2010.

64. Such debates were very robust in the museum world, that epicenter of cultural representational work, as activists, museum professionals, and academics gathered to rethink museum practices. See Karp and Kratz 2014.

65. Schrecker 2010: 122.

66. Ibid.

67. See Abowd 2014; Abraham 2008; Beinin 2006; Chatterjee and Maira 2014b; Doumani 2006b; Gonzalez 2004; Price 2011; Schrecker 2010. For more on assaults on academic freedom during the McCarthy era from the perspective of anthropology, see Price 2004b.

68. Hafez and Slyomovics 2013b: xiv.

69. In this regard, Israel-Palestine replaced Vietnam as the most contentious foreign policy issue among faculty. While scholars do face other kinds of political pushback, nothing approaches the level of career damage that has followed criticism of the Israeli state in some cases. As Corey Robin titled a post on Salaita's unhiring: "There is a Palestinian exception to the First Amendment." See http://coreyrobin.com /2014/09/09/a-palestinian-exception-to-the-first-amendment.

70. On the ways Israel-Palestine politics and especially Zionist pressures have affected academia, see Abraham 2008; Aruri 1985; Chatterjee and Maira 2014b; Nader 2002; Salaita 2014; Schrecker 2010; and specifically for Middle Eastern Studies, Lockman 2004. On experiences of Zionism from a Palestinian intellectual's perspective, see also Said 1980.

71. On this alignment, see Khalidi 2013; Mansour 1994; Smith 2005 (writing from a US policy perspective); Spiegel 1985 (writing from a pro-Israel perspective); Terry 2005; Toensing 2013; Walt and Mearsheimer 2008; and, in relation to Christian

Zionism, Wagner 1995 and Weber 2004. On the political lobby's deliberate extension into academe, see Aruri 1985 and note the publication of *The AIPAC College Guide* (Kessler and Schwaber 1984).

72. In addition to our interviews and media discussion, see Abowd 2014; Abraham 2008; Beinin 2006; Chatterjee and Maira 2014a; Nader 2002.

73. We take this phrase from Cable n.d. On Zionism's broad cultural influences in the United States, see McAlister 2001 and Kaplan 2013.

74. This definition of the form of Zionism that has become compulsory is on the website of the Jewish Virtual Library, a project of the American-Israeli Cooperative Enterprise: http://www.jewishvirtuallibrary.org/jsource/Zionism/zionism.html.

75. Lockman 1996, 26. See this text for a sophisticated historical analysis of the many different strands of Zionism.

76. Colleagues in other disciplines have also described similar experiences with compulsory Zionism, as well as compulsory US patriotism.

77. Umayyah Cable does just this in relation to Arab American film festival organizers' experiences of compulsory Zionism (n.d.).

78. Kates 2014; Naber 2014. There is mounting evidence that undergraduate students supporting Palestinian rights face intense pressure and surveillance from other students, faculty, and administrations, and are learning to police themselves as a result.

79. See http://www.insidehighered.com/news/2014/08/06/u-illinois-apparently-revokes-job-offer-controversial-scholar; https://www.insidehighered.com/news/2014/08/25/u-illinois-officials-defend-decision-deny-job-scholar-documents-show-lobbying; and http://coreyrobin.com/2014/08/25/follow-the-money-at-the-university-of-illinois.

80. http://www.davidproject.org/about/our-campus-approach.

81. These organizations do not concern themselves with critical perspectives on other states in the region, which exist to an equal if not greater extent in MENA scholarship.

82. In a survey we conducted in 2012 of Campus Watch—the most thorough of these watchdog sites—we found that the vast majority of articles related to MENA anthropology or anthropologists concerned Israel-Palestine in general (nearly 100 articles), followed by Nadia Abu El-Haj's tenure case (80 articles), and then by Columbia University's Israel-Palestine controversies more broadly (58 articles). Anthropologist Richard Antoun's murder by a mentally ill graduate student garnered 36 articles. The remaining themes or anthropologists had fewer than 20 mentions on the site each (William Beeman, Lila Abu-Lughod, Sondra Hale, Thomas Abowd, the Task Force on Middle East Anthropology's teaching handbook, the AAA, and its report on the US military's Human Terrain Systems program). Israel-Palestine was also *the* main issue at stake for Discover the Networks and for the David Horowitz–sponsored Students for Academic Freedom websites.

83. Schrecker 2010: 147.

84. See these organizations' websites: http://discoverthenetworks.org; http://www.campus-watch.org; http://spme.org; http://www.davidproject.org. Discover the Networks is an academia-focused group linked to *FrontPage Magazine*; both are projects of the David Horowitz Freedom Center.

85. http://www.davidproject.org/resources/white-paper.

86. See Chatterjee and Maira 2014b; Schrecker 2010: 146–147; and the websites for these organizations: http://www.standwithus.com/campus; http://israelcc.org; http://www.hasbarafellowships.org; http://www.amchainitiative.org. See also the white paper "Tenured or Tenuous" published by the Israel on Campus Coalition and available here: https://www.jewishvirtuallibrary.org/pub/Tenured_or_Tenuous.pdf. Many of these organizations are also linked via a small group of funders. See http://www.ijan.org/resources/business-of-backlash/.

87. See http://emetonline.org.

88. Attacks by Zionist groups on Middle East Studies departments and centers, including efforts to pressure public officials and interfere with centers' funding, have occurred since at least the 1970s (Aruri 1985). Recent efforts have been led by the Louis D. Brandeis Center for Human Rights Under Law, which produced a white paper (available at http://brandeiscenter.com/images/uploads/practices/antisemitism_whitepaper.pdf) that has been influential in policy circles. See http://www.defendingdissent.org/now/news/congress-under-pressure-to-defund-university-middle-east-programs.

89. Many have made this point; recently Rebecca Vilkomerson, Executive Director of Jewish Voice for Peace, stated it quite clearly on a December 4, 2014, public policy panel at the annual meeting of the American Anthropological Association in Washington, D.C. In case the distinction is not clear: anti-Semitism is racism and discrimination against a people (and should be opposed); anti-Israel or anti-Zionist positions are criticisms of a nation-state or a political ideology (and should be allowed).

90. For example, Butler 2012; Chomsky and Pappe 2010; Finkelstein 2005; Gordon 2008; Pappe 2006; Roy 2002; and Henry Siegman's articles in venues such as *The Nation* and the *London Review of Books*.

91. See http://www.usacbi.org.

92. Sexuality is notably missing from this list, because the number of sexual minority or self-identified queer anthropologists in our sample was so small that to write in any meaningful way about how this factor shaped academic practice would reveal their identities. We do have evidence of experiences of homophobia and heterosexism, especially in Middle East Studies. Similarly, the number of anthropologists who practice religion is so small that to foreground that aspect of analysis would violate confidentiality. Most people—with the exception of converts—did not mention religious practice in their interviews as shaping their academic practice. Where possible and relevant, we took into account interlocutors' geographic backgrounds. On intersectionality as an analytic approach, see Blackwell and Naber 2002; Chatterjee and Maira 2014b; Crenshaw 1991; Collins 2000; Gutiérrez y Muhs et al. 2012. For critiques of identitarian uses of intersectionality, see Ahmed 2006 and Puar 2007.

93. Stocking 1968.

94. Darnell 2001: 1.

95. Mannheim 1952: 291.

96. See, for example, Cole and Durham 2007 and 2008; Deeb and Harb 2013; Christiansen, Utas, and Vigh 2006; Winegar 2006. We find especially useful Cole and Durham's concept of "regeneration," which addresses "the mutually constitutive interplay

between intergenerational relations and wider historical and social processes" and thus can reveal how generations are critical agents and interpreters of social change (Cole and Durham 2007: 17).

97. Some of our interlocutors did not feel a sense of belonging to a generation or did but expressed hesitancy around such classifications. Such positions themselves were generational, which highlights the importance of using generation as an analytic even in the absence of "native" notions of it. Those who received their PhDs before 1980 and expressed such hesitancy did so partly because they felt that there was no coherent MENA anthropology at the time around which to coalesce. Those trained in the 1980s were furthest from a sense of generation: a couple people said that they felt isolated from broader scholarly networks in Middle East Studies and/or anthropology because the area studies and disciplinary frameworks were not yet strongly linked. Those trained in the 1990s had stronger feelings of generation than those in the 1980s (but not the 1960s), especially as related to the end of the Cold War and the rise of MENA as the main geopolitical "problem" for the United States. People in this group who expressed generational hesitancy usually worked in MENA's geographic margins. Some who worked in Palestine felt that Palestine rather than scholars constituted the core of their academic community (due to shared fieldwork and political struggles). Finally, generational identifications were most consistently present for scholars trained in the 2000s, likely because there are more of them and the internet has connected them consistently throughout their careers. A few people did not identify with a generation because there were few MENA students in their graduate programs or because they were biologically older than their cohorts, and a few said that our research, and/or our questions in the interviews, actually prompted their generational identification.

98. Mannheim 1952: 293.

99. Cole and Durham 2007.

100. They described the latter in terms that Mannheim would describe as a "trigger action," or "crystallizing agent" of generational consciousness (1952: 310).

101. Certainly there are no strict boundaries around these generational categories, and there are scholars who bridge certain categories or whose experiences are exceptions to these general patterns. Rather than label specific generations, we gesture to them by noting characteristics relevant to any particular discussion (e.g., "those who were trained in 1990s"). There were a few cultural anthropologists of MENA prior to this period; our categorization is based on our sample of living anthropologists.

102. Dean 2009.

103. Of the approximately 324 MENA anthropologists we found that are currently working or studying in four-year colleges and universities, 75 entered graduate school after 1990 and 135 entered graduate school after 9/11.

104. For a more detailed analysis of this generation, see Deeb and Winegar 2013a.

105. For many, this meant a renewed commitment to deep ethnographic fieldwork and mastery of MENA languages to revivify (and improve upon, especially in terms of language skills) what was valued in earlier approaches while also counteracting what many viewed as the thinness, self-centeredness, and ultimately depoliticizing aspects of the postmodern turn. Some also made similar critiques of Geertzian anthropology, po-

sitioning themselves theoretically as after it. This is a theoretical strain of anthropology influenced by Clifford Geertz that took an interpretive and symbolic approach to social life, which many critiqued as devoid of political economy.

Chapter 1

1. As one of our reviewers suggested, some of our interlocutors may have narrated, retrospectively, the centrality of Israel-Palestine politics in their academic trajectories as a way to organize an idiosyncratic personal trajectory into a common geopolitical one. Whatever the cause, the centrality of the issue in so many interviews is notable.

2. CASA opened a branch in Damascus for a brief time; it closed after the civil war in Syria began in 2011. The Arabic Summer Immersion Program at the University of Texas at Austin has also begun to compete with Middlebury and CASA for popularity.

3. See Anderson 2013. Luke and Kersel (2013) describe some of these institutions, including the American Schools of Oriental Research, including the WF Albright Institute of Archaeological Research, and the Council for American Overseas Research Centers (CAORC) in several MENA counties. They note that, with the possible exception of the one in Jordan, these centers are used by archaeologists more than cultural anthropologists.

4. On the growth of study abroad after the Cold War, see Keller and Frain 2010. On its expansion into MENA, among other world regions, see Ogden, Soneson, and Weting 2010.

5. Self-representations of anthropologists feeling like outsiders alienated from their own societies are not limited to those whose research focuses in MENA. See Caton's discussion (1999: 146–147) of this discourse in the work of Claude Lévi-Strauss (1955), Clyde Kluckhohn (1949) and Hortense Powdermaker (1966).

6. Caton 1999: 146–147.

7. We were primarily concerned with analyzing patterns across our interviews, rather than focused on analyzing the narrative form that emerged within each one. That said, we maintained an awareness of how narratives are constructions of one's "subjective involvement in the world," provide both particular temporal ordering and perspective (Ochs and Capps 1996: 21), and reflect a person's present as much as their past (Honig 1997) and their consciousness as much as their experiences (Weber 1989).

8. Said 1993: 116. Said's discussion reminds us that this sense of exilic outsiderness or marginality is not specific to anthropology and can be cultivated as a productive space from which to think and theorize phenomena as contingent and interconnected.

9. Caton 1999: 142.

10. Caton 1999: 143.

11. By identity politics, we mean the rights-based political movements and discourses that made claims related to the oppression of specific social groups (e.g., the civil rights, gay liberation, and second-wave feminist movements). By the late 1980s, both discourses about identity-based rights and backlash to them had consolidated. These movements and their later instantiations both facilitated political organizing for rights and excluded those who did not fit easily into the categories deployed.

12. For an excellent overview of the racialization of Arabs in the United States, see

Naber 2008. For discussion of how, despite US Census classifications of them as white, Arabs have been viewed in the United States as nonwhite and inferior to whites (prior to 2001), see Naber 2000; Samhan 1999; Saliba 1999.

13. Further research is needed to explore this phenomenon, as our framing of our interview questions and project overall provide only a partial possible explanation. We did not ask explicitly about these aspects of experience, but we did not ask explicitly about race, ethnicity, or moving during childhood either. It is, however, possible that our stated interest in understanding why people became anthropologists of MENA as opposed to, say, anthropologists of gender and sexuality shaped the sorts of responses we received. The dominance of narratives of mobility, race, and national heritage in our data may also be a particularly North American formation, inasmuch as these themes are more central to dominant discourses in the US than those of class.

14. See Abu-Lughod 1991; Clifford and Marcus 1986; Clifford 1988; Marcus and Fischer 1986. Note that Talal Asad's influential edited volume *Anthropology and the Colonial Encounter* was published over a decade earlier (1973), but is not often included in this group of disciplinary critiques, perhaps because he was writing from Britain or from a postcolonial perspective.

15. Liss 1998.

16. Given this association, the relative rarity of this discourse among our interlocutors is interesting. On the long and varied relationship of US anthropology to Native America, see Strong 2004; Starn 2011.

17. The framings of Native Americans as the paragon of (internal) difference reflects widespread discourses in US society that are not unique to academic anthropologists. See Deloria 1999.

18. Abu-Lughod 1990: 26.

19. Based on our conversations with colleagues outside the United States, there seems to be an unsurprising pattern of anthropologists from countries with colonial histories, like France and Germany, going to "other" places for fieldwork, while anthropologists from countries like Turkey and Greece tend to conduct fieldwork at home. A Turkish scholar suggested that one reason for this in Turkey was that learning additional languages other than English is very difficult. Another colleague suggested that prestige, funding, and intellectual trajectories tend to lead French anthropologists outside France for fieldwork and that in Greece the furthest an anthropologist was likely to go was Turkey or the Balkans.

20. On these US Orientalisms, see McAlister 2001; Jarmakani 2008; Little 2003. Edwards (2005) examines how Orientalism's framework of distancing, generalizing, ahistoricizing, and depoliticizing shaped the work of early US anthropologists of Morocco in particular, in relationship to the larger context of Vietnam and civil rights politics.

21. See hooks (1992, especially "Eating the Other") on difference as seductive for mainstream white society in relation to imperialist nostalgia, racism, and consumerism in the United States. On travel writing in imperial and neoimperial contexts, see Pratt 2007.

22. For more on the 1980s culture wars and their impact on academic freedom, see Schrecker 2010 and Chatterjee and Maira 2014b.

23. On the invisibility of "whiteness" as a racial category in the United States, see

Tochluk 2007, and especially among white liberals, see hooks 1992, especially "Madonna: Plantation Mistress or Soul Sister?"

24. *The Source* is a popular biblical-historical novel that draws on a Zionist framing of Jewish history in relation to the modern state of Israel, first published by James A. Michener in 1965.

25. And in an interesting and perhaps unsurprising reversal, Lebanese anthropologist Fuad Khuri's memoir mentions that his "fascinat[ion] with the adventure and romance of American films," including westerns and *Gone with the Wind*, contributed to his decision to do graduate work in anthropology in the United States (2007: 12).

26. Caton 1999: 147.

27. We should not forget that there are, obviously, anthropologists of Middle Eastern background who never work in the region and have focused their research elsewhere in the world. Also, many heritage scholars do not situate their research in their "home" communities or even necessarily in their countries of origin.

28. On the relationship between feminism and anthropology, see Strathern 1987. On situated knowledge, feminism, and critiques of objectivity in social science, see Haraway 1988. For a prediction of this shift in anthropology as related to increasing feminist and halfie anthropologists, as well as discussions of converging critiques of objectivity in anthropology and feminist scholarship, see Abu-Lughod 1990.

29. The growth of ethnic studies departments at this time is a good example of the institutionalization of concerns about the racialized nature of knowledge production.

30. Mannheim 1952: 310.

31. See Dale Eickelman's argument for a "balance between partisanship and scholarship" as found in the work of Pierre Bourdieu, Ernest Gellner, and Abdellah Hammoudi (2012: 220). See Wax 2008 on male scholars' invocation of science and objectivity.

32. This discourse also contains echoes of a gendering of theory versus ethnography in anthropology, where female scholars have been accused of not being theoretical enough. This gendered assumption is related to the valorization and gendering male of theory on the one hand, and the feminization of ethnography as experiential knowledge on the other. See Lutz 1995.

33. The importance of the anti-apartheid movement to the political consciousness of many scholars trained in the 1990s appeared in the burst of social media activity when Nelson Mandela passed away, with a striking number of people explicitly describing how his example was important to them because it was through the anti-apartheid movement that they learned politics, and often specifically Palestine politics.

34. This concern is reflected in the growth of anthropological scholarship on Muslim women in particular that aims to debunk and complicate these stereotypical images, as we discuss in Deeb and Winegar 2012. There is also a growing literature, much of which is written by region-related anthropologists, that explicitly addresses how stereotypes about Muslim women are deployed in US political machinations. Just a few examples: Abu-Lughod 2002 and 2013; Adely 2009; Hirschkind and Mahmood 2002; and Mahdavi 2013.

35. It is difficult to overemphasize Foucault's impact on graduate training after the translation of and adoption of his work into the majority of curricula.

36. "A Veteran Presence." *The GSAS Bulletin,* Jan. 27, 2012. http://www.gsas.harvard
.edu/scholarly_life/a_veteran_presence.php.

37. We address these theoretical and topical shifts in anthropology of the region in
Deeb and Winegar 2012.

Chapter 2

1. In a less known and related case, Mehrene Larudee was denied tenure at DePaul,
and many believe this is because she supported Finkelstein's case there. See http://eng
lish.sxu.edu/sites/kirstein/archives/900.

2. Some material from this and the next chapter has previously appeared in Deeb
and Winegar 2013a.

3. See our Introduction and 214n73.

4. For an overview of academic freedom issues in higher education in the United
States over time, see Schrecker 2010.

5. On women's experiences in the sciences during this era, see Rossiter 1995.

6. As one of our reviewers pointed out, it is indeed notable that such a supposedly
objective stance would be directed more at women than at men and likely also stems from
older racist notions about the importance of endogamy for women.

7. Rabinow 1977.

8. See Mamdani's related discussion of "good Muslim, bad Muslim" as a persistent
binary logic structuring US foreign policy (2004).

9. On the racialization of Arabs and other Middle Easterners and Muslims in the
United States, see Introduction, 207n21.

10. Readers may wonder about the experiences of graduate students wearing Islamic dress; unfortunately, their numbers are so few that there is no way to discuss this
without revealing their identities.

11. See http://mondoweiss.net/2014/04/reforming-education-programs.html and
http://emetonline.org/event/politicizing-education-title-vi-higher-education-act.

12. American tourists in places like Bethlehem and Jerusalem even assumed that
the living Palestinians they encountered represented life at the time of Jesus. See McAlister 2001. Daniel Segal's 2005 discussion of a "Western Civilization" textbook from 1995
also notes how the Middle East continues in such textbooks to be positioned as part of
the "ancient" world. That particular text juxtaposed an image from Abu-Lughod's 1986
ethnography *Veiled Sentiments* with a painting from ancient Egypt and essentially states
that little has changed in the region since "early civilization."

13. See Fabian 1983.

14. See Jarmakani 2008; McAlister 2001; Shaheen 2014.

15. However, their Jewishness continues to be scrutinized, particularly if they adopt
positions sympathetic to Arabs, Muslims, and especially Palestinians.

16. See Deeb and Winegar 2012.

17. Archaeologists reported similar self-censoring; some chose to research less politicized eras (meaning not the biblical period). We also have anecdotal evidence that
some students in other disciplines are still being told not to study Israel-Palestine.

18. The persistence of these hierarchies (and what some colleagues describe as "im-

poster syndrome") in our conversations with female graduate students highlights for us the importance of calling out the persistent *structural dynamics* of sexism and racism that underlie such feelings of inadequacy.

19. While these assumptions may be true for some region-related anthropologists, there are many who did not have personal connections facilitating entry into their research communities and many who learned MENA languages in college or graduate school classrooms.

20. We are not suggesting that white scholars are necessarily conscious of this process.

21. Yet as their work shows, such a position can also have advantages in fieldwork (see also Ghosh 1993).

22. See Jane Kramer, "The Petition: Israel, Palestine, and a Tenure Battle at Barnard," *The New Yorker*, Apr. 14, 2008, p. 10.

23. Several US citizen region-related anthropologists also experienced difficulties with fieldsite access, challenging some white interlocutors' assumptions that their colleagues somehow had it easier because they were "from" the region.

24. She has written about this experience (Sawalha 2010).

25. http://www.icahd.org.

26. See Harvey 2005; di Leonardo 2008.

27. Peteet also discussed these experiences in her presentation during the 2014 AAA conference. For more on job market problems Palestine scholars faced at this time, see Nader 2002.

28. Faculty asking politically inflected questions that reflected a Zionist perspective during campus visits were sometimes archaeologists or biological anthropologists.

29. Navarro, Williams, and Ahmad 2013: 449.

30. It is unlawful to use religion as a basis for a hiring decision. Asking a candidate about their religion may be evidence that one is using religion as a factor in that decision.

31. ISIS is the media term referring to the Islamic State in Iraq and Syria.

32. Most Palestine anthropologists trained in the 1990s obtained tenure-track positions; the jury remains out for those trained in the twenty-first century.

Chapter 3

1. We faced this with a few male colleagues in the course of working on this project.

2. Lutz 1995.

3. One doubts whether academics would similarly refuse assertions of atheism by people of Christian or Jewish background.

4. One of those shocking cases took place when administrators at the University of Connecticut overturned the anthropology department's decision to hire Egyptian anthropologist Soheir Morsy in 1993. Morsy, as well as several anthropology professors in that department, suggested that her national origin was the reason the job offer was rescinded. See http://articles.courant.com/1994-08-02/news/9408020187_1_graduate-students-anthropology-faculty.

5. See Abowd 2014.

6. Kramer 2008.

7. Such settlements are also illegal under international law.

8. The document is posted on the AAA website and titled "AAA Responds to Barnard College Tenure Debate."

9. As Naseer Aruri stated in an article about such attacks on professors in the 1970s and early 1980s, "The available evidence suggests that Professor Fluehr-Lobban's written work, which legitimized the Palestinian struggle, was elevated to a significant issue in the recruitment process" and that questions remain as to whether or not her chances were already damaged before she arrived on campus for the interview (Aruri 1985: 9).

10. For discussion of recent cases outside anthropology where scholars were denied tenure (Norman Finkelstein), fired from tenured positions (Ward Churchill, Sami al-Arian), or fired from contingent teaching positions (Mohammad Yousry, Elizabeth Ito) as a direct result of external political pressure related to their views on US foreign policy and Middle East politics (especially Israel-Palestine), see Schrecker 2010. See Aruri 1985 for cases in earlier eras.

11. Kramer 2008: 52.

12. Another incident is the pressure put on Brooklyn College to cancel a panel discussion on the movement to boycott, divest from, and sanction Israel until it ends the occupation. This pressure came from the Anti-Defamation League, some New York legislators, and prominent alumnus Alan Dershowitz, who supports current Israeli state policies and actions towards the Palestinians and who also played a key role in Norman Finkelstein's tenure denial at DePaul University. Then-mayor Michael Bloomberg defended academic freedom and rights to free speech at Brooklyn College, even though the event contradicted his personal views on Israel.

13. Some pundits have suggested that this support is waning in light of Israeli state violence. See http://www.counterpunch.org/2014/09/29/christian-evangelicals-increasingly-support-palestinian-human-rights.

14. Aruri 1985.

15. This app is a joint project by Hillel International and the Simon Wiesenthal Center, which recently built its Museum of Tolerance on top of a Muslim cemetery. http://www.hillel.org/about/news-views/news-views---blog/news-and-views/2014/12/11/hillel-international-partners-with-simon-wiesenthal-center-to-combat-anti-semitism-on-more-than-550-college-campuses.

16. We found this gendered pattern among our anthropologist interlocutors. It is possible, and was suggested to us, that it might not obtain for other disciplines.

17. Individual employment situations, particularly whether or not the white male scholar has tenure, matter here.

18. Not receiving tenure leads to losing employment; for non-US citizens, residency in the United States often depends on visas linked to employment.

19. One of our reviewers suggested that this difference was due to the long-lasting effects of 1950s McCarthyism that largely killed Marxist politics in the US academy, depoliticizing the professoriate in ways that never happened in the United Kingdom or France. Hilary Aked finds otherwise, and traces similar processes in the UK. See https://www.opendemocracy.net/ourkingdom/hilary-aked/so-much-for-free-speech-southampton-university-and-proisrael-lobby.

20. Nader 2002: 163.

21. This incident is documented both in a set of testimonies written at the time and in oral testimonies shared with us by some of those involved.

22. The file we have on this incident includes some of these student papers, which include these quotes from the rabbi and also confirm that students were told that he had decided Hillel members would not participate in the assignment.

23. Available at www.meanthro.org and http://www.aaanet.org/sections/mes/wp -content/uploads/2014/02/Academic-Freedom-and-Professional-Responsibility-A -Handbook-for-Scholars-and-Teachers-of-the-Middle-East.pdf.

24. They may have been more inclined to do so if they had read our aforementioned handbook.

25. The Task Force on Middle East Anthropology, of which we are founding members, organized this workshop.

26. For example, an anthropologist whose research is not about Islam had to explain why no Muslims attended a brown-bag lunch faculty forum held during Ramadan to discuss Pope Benedict's anti-Islam comments.

27. Amahl Bishara makes a compelling argument for media engagement in her January 2007 *Anthropology News* article, "Anthropologists Must Enter the News about the Middle East and Expand Its Limits" (8–9).

28. These organizations include the Anti-Defamation League, The American-Israel Public Affairs Committee, the Jewish Defense League, Campus Watch, The David Project, as well as the David Horowitz Freedom Center's projects: *FrontPage Magazine* and Discover the Networks. Hillel International can also be placed in this category, as it is independent of college administrations (although on some campuses it is entirely student-run and/or a Hillel-funded rabbi also serves as a college chaplain). Hillel also coordinates with some of these other external organizations in training Zionist student activists. Recently, the student-led Open Hillel movement has challenged the Zionist requirement for Hillel activities and membership, arguing that Jewish students need a space where all political viewpoints are accepted. See http://www.openhillel.org.

29. The three scholars who disagreed with this analysis of the climate were tenured white men trained prior to the 1990s, one of whom thought that Palestine politics had improved in the twenty-first century because we no longer have the "generation that had this sort of knee-jerk pro-Israel, can't talk about Palestine stuff. I think they just like went away, they retired." Another thought that the twenty-first-century leaders of organized political attacks were not taken seriously and "don't really have the power to seriously mess you over" the way they could in the 1980s and 1990s.

30. As one of our reviewers noted, there was also an increasingly negative image of hard-line Zionism of the sort that led to the assassination of Israeli Prime Minister Yitzhak Rabin for being supposedly too generous with the Palestinians during the Oslo Accords.

31. And occasionally, hostile questioning was related to internal MENA national politics.

32. This situation also highlights the importance of context: the lecture series was

already being monitored by this local community and had come under prior attack. http://jh vonline.com/ableminded-volunteers-badly-needed-tuesday-april-p3817.html.

33. Some of our interlocutors thought that Northern California was a focus due to some early classes on Israel-Palestine at UC Berkeley, as well as a lecture series there that included some Palestinian academics.

34. This event is detailed in Aruri 1985. The ADL eventually said it was an "unfortunate incident" that would not be repeated. See also Colin Campbell, "Middle East Group Wants Anti-Defamation League to Disown List," *New York Times*, Jan. 30, 1985, p. B7.

35. Wax 2008: 12.

36. See Beinin 2006. Horowitz has also produced a three-volume *Black Book of the American Left*.

37. This episode is described in http://www.thenation.com/article/uclas-dirty -thirty#.

38. Operation Cast Lead killed 1,398 Palestinians (including 300 minors); nine Israelis (including three civilians) were also killed in the conflict. See both Amnesty International and the Israeli human rights organization B'Tselem: http://www.amnesty.ie/our -work/operation-cast-lead and http://www.btselem.org/statistics/fatalities/during-cast -lead/by-date-of-event.

39. http://docstalk.blogspot.com/2009/04/zoa-letter-to-chancellor-of-ucla-re .html.

40. In response to these attacks, a group of scholars including anthropologists formed the online network California Scholars for Academic Freedom in 2007. As we write, the network has over one hundred members, many of whom teach about MENA and/or Islam or are themselves Muslim and/or region-related scholars. http://cascholars 4academicfreedom.wordpress.com/.

41. http://www.pacbi.com/cms/rougesgallery.php?pid=22&id=226. Lavie's 2014 book amply demonstrates the kind of sexism and racism that many Mizrahi women face in Israel.

42. Her university administrators reassured her that nothing would happen. See Schrecker 2010: 25.

43. "The New Israel Campus Strategy," *New York Jewish Week*, Feb. 14, 2012. In Julie Wiener's interview with the executive director, he said, "Our goal is not to bolster Jewish students; it's to shape campus discourse, whether Jewish students are on campus or not. . . . We're going to be very active at a number of small liberal arts schools in the coming months and years. . . . Our new approach is to develop very in-depth ties to a set of schools where we can make the maximum difference. We will be in 12 by this fall and 25 by the following year." See http://www.thejewishweek.com/features/new_york_minute/ new_israel_campus_strategy.

44. Internal national politics also occasionally reared their head during the review process, especially in Iranian Studies—notorious among scholars in multiple disciplines for its political tensions. Scholars of Islam also noted reviews that could be interpreted as politically motivated, including comments rooted in assumptions about secularism and scholarship, and those that took Sunni Islam as normative and insisted that Shi'ism be treated as exceptional. Anthropologists of Islam also sometimes have to "denounce all the harm done by Islamic movements around the world" or be "accused of being . . .

apologist[s]" (Abu-Lughod 2013: 46). One interlocutor said she self-censors in her writing in order to be able to return to her fieldsite. And a few said that they had been told by various editors that there was "too much Arabic" in their texts and to use less of it. One scholar's response to this sort of request, understood to be anti-Arab, was, "I'm kind of trying to de-center the all-knowing Western reader." Some archaeologists told us about managing Israel politics by publishing only in disciplinary venues that attract less MENA interest, or simply *not publishing* certain findings because they feared political reprisals if they challenged the Israeli nationalist story.

45. The Committee for Accuracy in Middle East Reporting in America, a group started in 1992 that claims to be nonpartisan but consistently writes about reporting that it finds to be "anti-Israel," wrote a long criticism of BJ Fernea's film. See the original article at http://www.camera.org/index.asp?x_context=6&x_article=109. *The New York Times* reported on the subsequent official NEH retraction of its support for the film's production: http://www.nytimes.com/1983/06/25/movies/us-agency-calls-film-it -aided-propaganda.html.

46. This comment refers to controversies caused by Finkelstein's 2000 and 2005 books, both of which are critical of Israel. Prominent pro-Israel activist Alan Dershowitz threatened the University of California Press with a lawsuit after learning that the 2005 book charged him with plagiarism and lying about Israel's human rights record.

47. See the legal paper written by the assistant secretary entitled "Anti-Zionism as Racism" at http://scholarship.law.wm.edu/wmborj/vol15/iss3/4 as well the September 8, 2010 letter from Assistant Attorney General Thomas Perez to Assistant Secretary for Civil Rights Russlyn Ali, available at www.justice.gov/crt/about/cor/TitleVI/090810_ AAG_Perez_Letter_to_Ed_OCR_Title%20VI_and_Religiously_Identifiable_Groups .pdf. For more on the ways that post-9/11 proposed changes to Title VI legislation narrowly defined what kind of research should be funded within national security and military interests, see Laurie King-Irani, "Proposed Changes to Title VI Funding for Area Studies," *Anthropology News*, Jan. 2004: 7.

48. The petition is available here: http://www.columbiadivest.org/petition.html. A response to this interview by several of Dirks's former colleagues at Columbia (including MENA anthropologists) is available here: http://www.jadaliyya.com/pages/index/91 06/uc-berkeleys-new-chancellor-endorses-the-falsehood.

49. http://mondoweiss.net/2012/12/chancellor-falsehood-criticizing.html.

50. Since becoming chancellor, Dirks has presided over the intensified surveillance of Berkeley's SJP chapter as compared to other student organizations. This move is especially surprising for a historical anthropologist who is surely aware that Zionism began as a nationalist movement in the nineteenth century and that never in its history could it claim adherence by all Jews, and certainly not the thousands of Jews around the world who are critical of the actions that the Israeli state perpetrates in their names.

51. For a sensitive account of how anthropologists can speak to outside groups about Israel-Palestine, see Avram Bornstein's essay "Anthropologist as Middle East Expert" in *Anthropology News*, Oct, 2002: 22. One might also note that the conflict itself is not "balanced," considering the Israeli military's massive scale, weaponry, and international political and economic support.

Chapter 4

1. Boas 1919, reprinted in Gonzalez 2004a. Lucas 2009 takes issue with anthropological narratives that valorize Boas for this statement, suggesting that it does not in fact condemn secret research.

2. Fluehr-Lobban 2003b; Price 2004a. The "Council" included all members of the AAA who were eligible to vote. The AAA used to divide membership into "members" (anyone interested in anthropology) and "fellows" (those with PhDs in anthropology or were somehow prominent in the field, as determined by the board). Only fellows voted. Voting rights gradually expanded over time; by 1989, this structure no longer existed.

3. Price 2004a: 63.

4. Price 2008a details anthropology's participation in WWII. See also Fluehr-Lobban 2003b.

5. Price 2008a.

6. Kehoe and Doughty 2012b. This discourse of war as "opportunity" marked one of the ongoing tensions between academic versus applied anthropology.

7. See Mandler 2013 for a thorough study of Mead's involvement with WWII and the early Cold War.

8. See Price 2008a. While Price and others are staunchly critical of these involvements, Mandler contextualizes Mead's approach, suggesting that the idea that anthropological participation in WWII marked "the beginning of the slippery slope" that led to their participation in counterinsurgency operations in the 1960s was itself a product of the repoliticized post-Vietnam era. He argues that scholars viewing Mead through that prism do not allow for the very different context, of both anthropological climate and US geopolitical strategy, within which Mead was working (2013: 289). For a critique of Price's interpretations of the history of anthropology's intersections with US military and intelligence, see also Lucas 2009.

9. The Army Special Forces Special Services Division produced these guides, which included gems such as "not approaching Egyptian women" (Price 2008a: 42–43, 97–99).

10. Price 2008a.

11. Susan Slyomovics begins her account of US MENA cultural anthropology with Coon, but notes that Louise Sweet had instead suggested that E. E. Evans-Pritchard's *The Sanusi of Cyrenaica* was MENA's originary ethnography (Slyomovics 2013: 8–9).

12. Price 2008a: 248–259. Coon later wrote a book about his exploits that argued for the importance of anthropology's direct contributions to war: *A North Africa Story: The Anthropologist as OSS Agent, 1941–1943*. For a discussion of this text, see Slyomovics 2013 and Price 2008a.

13. Price 2008a: 122.

14. Price 2008a: 133.

15. Price 2008a: 133–134. Price argues that in this way, anthropologists' participation in the M Project both assisted "plans that would have used survivors of the Nazis' horrific genocidal campaigns as pawns in a global drive to expand American capitalism's developing global markets" and provided justification for the Zionist project because "the Israeli state used the same claims of 'empty lands' to justify its occupation of land" (2008a: 141–142).

16. Price 2008a: 267

17. Price 2004a; Fluehr-Lobban 2003b.

18. Nader 1997: 122.

19. The war also catalyzed the founding of the Society for Applied Anthropology in 1941. On these tensions, see Price 2008a and Kehoe and Doughty 2012b. Wax writes that WWII resulted in "a fully developed cohort of professional applied anthropologists holding firm notions of the role of anthropology in the running of the post-war government" (2008: 5). Many anthropologists also entered academia after WWII because of increased job openings due to government investment in education via the GI Bill (Salamone 2008: 90). See also Kehoe and Doughty's 2012a volume, which serves as a history of anthropology's post-WWII expansion, in part due to its applied aspects.

20. Price 2008a: 88–89.

21. Nader argues that not only were MENA projects spotty during this time, but money for studies of the region was "carefully channeled away from areas in conflict with Israel" (1997: 131).

22. Price 2011: 25.

23. Price credits a European sociologist that the project had tried to recruit for this exposure (2011: 23). See also Trencher 2012 on Project Camelot.

24. Price 2011. Lucas suggests that Project Camelot was never clandestine and that it was essentially a project that was unimportant, ill conceived, and short-lived and therefore not worthy of its place in anthropology's narratives about participation in secret research (2009).

25. On the effects of Project Camelot, the Beals Commission and Report, and the new emphasis on ethics in the AAA, see Trencher 2012; Hancock 2008; Price 2011; Nader 1997.

26. Letter dated Dec. 20, 1965, National Anthropology Archives (NAA) Box 218.

27. Letter dated Mar. 10, 1966, NAA Box 218. We also found a number of MENA anthropologists' responses to Beals's survey, including scholars who worked in Lebanon, Israel, and "North Africa." While some agreed with Fernea's assessment that government-related research was problematic, others did not. An anthropologist of North Africa noted that direct government research is not inherently more dubious than private research, and another person reported that he had remained in Israel for several years working for the Israeli government after completing his field research.

28. For more on Vidal's work with Aramco, see Jones 2010.

29. Letter dated July 11, 1966, NAA Box 223.

30. This statement is described in Hancock 2008.

31. The Radical Caucus formed in 1967 and reorganized as Anthropologists for Radical Political Action in 1972. See Price 2008b for more on these groups and the resolutions they introduced.

32. Price 2011; Mandler 2013.

33. The 1971 AAA business meeting and events leading to it are described in Wakin 1993; Price 2004b and 2011; Mandler 2013; and Fluehr-Lobban 2003b. Berreman 2003 is an account by someone who was on the Committee on Ethics at the time and involved in these events.

34. Jorgensen and Wolf 1970.

35. Mandler suggests that Mead's perspective was one "desperate to keep the profession united" (2013: 289).

36. One MENA anthropologist recalled that at the meeting, someone started reading aloud the titles of the studies revealed in the documents and one of them "had something to do with how fast you could be going and what altitude you have to be at to recognize a friendly from the air. . . . And this was, you know, stuff that some of these guys are being funded to do."

37. Wakin (1993) writes that the WWI generation was wary of government work, the WWII generation viewed it as a responsibility, and the Vietnam generation was staunchly against it. We add that this variation likely reflects broader generational differences in the US regarding attitudes to these wars.

38. Price 2008b notes that because the Mead Report was rejected via a motion from the floor of the business meeting, it was not sent out for a full membership vote.

39. Price 2008a: 277; Fluehr-Lobban 2003a.

40. This and subsequent AAA statements on ethics are available at http://www.aaa net.org/profdev/ethics.

41. Hancock 2008: 168.

42. Writing from the opposite perspective, Walter Goldschmidt (2012) suggests that an outcome of these tensions around government work was a deepening of tensions between academic and applied anthropology; anthropologists were discouraged from accepting government jobs, which precipitated an employment crisis for applied anthropologists. While these academic-applied tensions are significant, they did not emerge in our MENA anthropologist interlocutors' narratives. Others, including Goldschmidt and Price, have addressed those specific disciplinary tensions in greater depth.

43. Price 2011: 31.

44. Other scholars (e.g., Trencher 2012) suggest that some of the AAA impetus to create the PPR was the threat to anthropologists' ability to do fieldwork posed by local suspicions about US researchers, as in Fernea's concerns about scholars being viewed as spies. As Carolyn Fluehr-Lobban noted, "It was not the high crimes of anthropologists involved in Project Camelot that precipitated [this] crisis, but the effects that a bollixed operation had on future research in Latin America" (Fluehr-Lobban 2003b: 8).

45. Price 2011.

46. Price 2011: 30.

47. Ibid.

48. McAlister argues that the 1967 war had an "extraordinary, transformative effect" on American Jews such that "identification with Israel became a more important aspect of Jewishness" (2001: 111). She also shows that it produced a more muted pro-Israel stance among non-Jews (except among young Black liberationists). This broader context of American reactions certainly affected anthropologists' views.

49. The "Lebanese solution" refers to Lebanon's political-sectarian power-sharing system of government, whereby offices (president, prime minister, parliamentary positions, etc.) are allocated by sect.

50. Non-Arab Americans could join the association as "associate members."

51. See www.merip.org.

52. *MERA Forum* 1(1), 1977.

53. The rejoinder appeared in *MERA Forum* 4(3): 12–13, 1980. Newsletter content included letters prompting wider discussion (e.g., a letter from Walter Zenner calling for theoretical discussion of "critical anthropology" and the relationship of socialism and Marxism to anthropology, *MERA Forum* 2(4): 5–6, 1978), assessments of fieldwork possibilities in different countries, and reports on current research, with topics ranging from aesthetics to medical anthropology to regional systems. By the early 1980s, the topic "women in the Middle East" was a regular concern—timing that reflects the theoretical emergence of feminist anthropology and the spike in popular concern about Muslim women that stemmed from media images of the Islamic revolution in Iran.

54. This included lists of members' recent publications or accomplishments, calls for panels and papers, and announcements about informal gatherings (e.g., an Iran study group, a group of "female scholars interested in Middle East issues in southern California," etc.). Many issues had a "cooperation column" listing requests for assistance with various projects and calls to participate in edited volumes or collaborative research.

55. Beginning in winter 1977, *MERA Forum* was issued four times a year until the early 1980s, when it dwindled to two, then one annual issue. Eventually the Middle East Section column in *Anthropology Newsletter* replaced it. The last issue we were able to locate is from 1989.

56. *MERA Forum* 2(1): 1, 1978.

57. *MERA Forum* 1(1): 3, 1977. Suggested panel topics included what were then cutting-edge topics like immigration, verbal arts, and the state.

58. *MERA Forum* 1(1): 3, 1977.

59. This may well illustrate the initial effects of Talal Asad's 1973 *Anthropology and the Colonial Encounter*—a book by a MENA anthropologist well ahead of its time, appearing five years before Said's *Orientalism* and over a decade before the postcolonial and "writing culture" moments in anthropology writ large.

60. Slyomovics (2013) also corrects this impression, highlighting two 1977 "publishing landmarks, more accurately bombshells" that impacted anthropology: a preview chapter excerpted and prepublished from Said's *Orientalism* and Paul Rabinow's *Reflections on Fieldwork in Morocco*.

61. Membership among these organizations clearly overlapped. The newsletter consistently included announcements and reports about other conferences and groups, including MESA, AAUG, MERIP, AMESS, and the African Studies Association. It also addressed concerns common to interdisciplinary MENA Studies, such as how best to include scholars from the region in international networks, how to define the boundaries of the region, and how to conduct outreach about MENA beyond the academy.

62. *MERA Forum* 9(2–3): 6, 1986.

63. *MERA Forum* 3(2): 2, 1979. MERGA members were especially involved with AMESS in 1979, when it called on MESA members to boycott the 1979 conference because it was to be held in Utah, a state that had not ratified the Equal Rights Amendment, in support of the National Organization of Women's economic boycott of all such

states. They instead asked people to attend an "alternative conference" held in New York City that had women in the Middle East as its focal topic.

64. Our interlocutors often referred to "motions" and "resolutions" as though they are synonymous. The AAA created a procedural distinction between them for the 1973 business meeting, in response to Radical Caucus control of the agenda via motions from the floor: "motions" adopted in the business meeting went to the executive board, while "resolutions" were sent to the full membership in a mail ballot (Price 2008b). When we asked for clarification in 2014, the AAA executive director explained that a "motion" calls on an assembled body to do something, can be passed by a quorum at the AAA business meeting, and is not binding, whereas a "resolution" is a written statement that requires eventual adoption via ballot by the full AAA membership and is somehow "binding," though it is unclear what that means. It is unclear when these definitions shifted, and AAA minutes sometimes refer to written statements that fit the description of "resolution" as "motion" instead. We do our best to follow the definitions applicable for the statement in question, except when directly quoting an interlocutor or archival source.

65. These three resolutions were adopted by AMEWS in 1979 with MERIP support. See *MERA Forum* 4(1): 5–6, 1980.

66. Such discussions continued: in 1981, two petitions were discussed at the MERGA meeting: one supporting Egyptian feminist Nawal El Saadawi, who had been arrested that fall, and another protesting "infringements of academic freedom" at Bir Zeit University in the occupied Palestinian territories (*MERA Forum* 5(3): 2, 1982). The following year, Nancy Jabbra asked whether MERGA members wanted to take collective action against "biased treatments" of Middle Eastern subjects in media or textbooks (*MERA Forum* 6(1): 2, 1982).

67. Each newsletter ended with a questionnaire about research interests and contact information—information that was, at first, printed as a membership roster in the *Forum*, and later developed into a regularly updated directory. These rosters show that there have been many people active in MENA anthropology who contributed to the field primarily as educators or whose published work has not received significant attention. The field therefore comes to be defined and represented, internally and externally, by a much smaller number of scholars.

68. Another indication of sexism in academia at the time appears in the April 1979 AAA executive board minutes (NAA Box 137). In a vote about whether to censure five anthropology departments that were not in compliance with the AAA's 1972 resolution on fair practices and employment of women, three members voted no and one abstained. The measure passed.

69. The newsletter, other written records, and our interlocutors regularly mentioned the organizational work of Barbara Aswad, Dawn Chatty, Sondra Hale, Pat Higgins, Suad Joseph, Barbara Larson, Barbara Michaels, Emelie Olson-Prather, Barbara Pillsbury, and Lucie Wood Saunders, among others.

70. These were Roger Joseph (1976–1982), Laurence Michalak (1982–1988), and William Young (1988–1990).

71. *MERA Forum* 4(4), 1980.

72. Increasing bureaucratization can also be seen in how much time the AAA executive board spends dealing with matters like nominations, dues, membership categories, hotel reservations, and federal IRB regulations.

73. Especially Lucie Wood Saunders and Barbara Aswad.

74. It is possible that South Africa presented a similar exceptionalism; the AAA passed a resolution condemning apartheid but did not join the international cultural and academic boycott of that apartheid state. That said, it seems unlikely that any anthropologists would have defended South Africa's policies. We invite our Africanist colleagues to further explore this question.

75. NAA Box 137. A task force that had been charged with investigating the feasibility of such affiliation presented the report. The task force recommended that the AAA affiliate with three specific indigenous rights organizations.

76. NAA Box 136.

77. This report was made in November by the board liaison to groups working with indigenous people; the fact that such a liaison existed reflects the association's political commitments (NAA Box 136). The commission was initiated in December 1973.

78. These specifically concerned Colombia, Paraguay, and Mexico. NAA Box 137.

79. NAA Box 137.

80. While there exist many definitions of indigeneity, anthropologists generally use the category "indigenous peoples" to refer to people—including but not limited to those from the Americas, Australia, New Zealand, and the Pacific Islands—who have continuity with communities prior to (often but not always) European invasion and colonization. See Kauanui 2014 for a thorough discussion of the complexities of and historical contexts for defining the term indigenous. See also this overview posted by the United Nations Permanent Forum on Indigenous Issues: http://www.un.org/esa/socdev/un pfii/documents/5session_factsheet1.pdf. Many scholars recognize that Israel is a settler-colonial society. Some anthropologists also refer to Palestinians as "indigenous." Julie Peteet, in a paper titled "Framing, Naming and Linguistic Repertoires: Conceptualizing Palestine," presented at the Institute for Palestine Studies and the American University of Beirut on December 13, 2013, argued that indigeneity is a concept "capacious, or expansive, enough to be applicable in the colonial present" and therefore include Palestinians. Most MENA scholars who do not apply the term to Palestinians note that indigeneity is not the sole ground on which anticolonial politics rests.

81. This conclusion is based on a search of the (rather incomplete) National Anthropology Archives and our review of AAA EB minutes, *AN*, and *MERA Forum*. The executive board discussed the alleged death sentence of a US-trained Afghan anthropologist in April 1979; this was the impetus to authorize the executive director to contact "appropriate agencies and individuals to convey concern" in cases of "imminent threats to life" of anthropologists. Other board actions at that meeting included commending organizations committed to promoting the welfare of indigenous peoples in the Americas. NAA Box 137.

82. See Appendix B for the full text of the resolution.

83. The initial discussion group, self-named an Ad-Hoc Committee on Iranian-American Relations, decided to bring a statement to the full AAA. A smaller group then

"discussed the resolution until 2 AM in a coffee shop: this group included some Iranians and a reporter from the *Cincinnati Enquirer* . . . [Mary Catherine] Bateson, [Warren] Swidler, and [Sam] Beck then met at 7am for the actual drafting of the resolution" (*MERA Forum* 4(5): 3, 1979).

84. *MERA Forum* 4(5): 4, 1979.

85. *MERA Forum* 4(5): 5, 1979. The motion was also published in *Anthropology Newsletter* 5, Jan. 1980. At that time motions were not sent out for a full membership mail ballot vote.

86. This may sometimes have been unintentional, as non-MENA scholars may have been influenced by US foreign policy narratives to perceive "balance" as necessary to discussion of Israel-Palestine.

87. For an excellent analysis of how the notion of "balance" structures discussions about Israel-Palestine in ways that obscure the structural inequality of the situation, see Bishara 2013, especially chapter 1.

88. Our interlocutors agreed that writing these statements involved the collective effort of scholars of different backgrounds and research interests. Suad Joseph, Julie Peteet, and Laurence Michalak took the lead on the first resolution and recruited a broad coalition of colleagues to officially submit it to the AAA for the business meeting. Its signatories included Louise Sweet, Barbara Aswad, Hani Fakhouri, Michael Higgins, Lucie Wood Saunders, Eleanor Leacock, Rayna Rapp, Eva Friedlander, Suad Joseph, Nina Glick Schiller, Elizabeth Fernea, Robert Fernea, Stanley Diamond, Luis Loyola, Theresa Rubin, Alice James, Laurence Michalak, Randy Reiter, Karen Sacks, Henry Rosenfeld, Nabil Abraham, Elaine Combs-Schilling, and the Council for Marxist Anthropologists.

89. The exact numbers may never be known, and sources differ. The Israeli government gave the lower number; the higher numbers are from both the Palestinian Red Cross and Israeli journalist Amnon Kapeliouk in his carefully researched book (1982).

90. See Appendix B for the full resolution text. NAA Box 142.

91. Her statement is published in *MERA Forum* as "Witness to 'Peace for Galilee'" (*MERA Forum* 6(2–3): 9–10, 1982). The title refers to the Israeli operation and its justification.

92. The matter of a quorum is critical because if a resolution is approved without a quorum, the executive board decides how to proceed (e.g., send it out as a resolution for a full membership vote, do nothing, or use it as an executive board–only statement).

93. The signatories were Nabeel Abraham, Nicholas Hopkins, Frederick Huxley, Suad Joseph, Khalil Nakhleh, and Henry Rosenfeld. See Appendix B for the full motion text. NAA Box 142.

94. The first statement notes the AAA's historical opposition to "the destruction of peoples and cultures" and the second its history of "defending human rights and academic freedom."

95. The letter stated that "four additional motions" had been passed, "dealing with the situation in Lebanon, the internment of political refugees, CIA and military recruitment of anthropologists, and the apartheid policies of the union of South Africa and the murder of Ruth First." NAA Box 142. It is noteworthy that the AAA condemned the

government of South Africa for oppressing the rights of "indigenous peoples," given the parallels many scholars and activists make between the actions of apartheid South Africa toward Blacks and those of the Israeli state against Palestinians.

96. NAA Box 142.

97. Including letters by Stephen Pastner (*Anthropology Newsletter* 24(1): 2, 1983) and Laurence Loeb (*Anthropology Newsletter* 24(2): 9, 1983). A respondent reminded readers of the tactic employed by resolution opponents during the meeting to try to prevent a quorum, noting that this would have problematically denied people the opportunity to vote (Frederick Huxley, *Anthropology Newsletter* 24(5): 2, 1983.

98. *Anthropology Newsletter* 24(5): 2, 1983.

99. Ernst Wreschner, *Anthropology Newsletter* 24(5): 2, 1983. Other letters accused supporters of "one-sidedness" (including Stephen Pastner, *Anthropology Newsletter* 24(1): 2, 1983; Laurence Loeb, *Anthropology Newsletter* 24(2): 9, 1983; Ernst Wreschner, *Anthropology Newsletter* 24(5): 2, 1983) and questioned why they "singled out" Israel when other governments also violated human rights (including Saral Waldorf, *Anthropology Newsletter* 24(3): 2, 1983). We continue to see these arguments in the twenty-first century regarding the academic boycott of Israeli institutions, but notably they have typically not been raised in AAA discussion of human rights violations elsewhere.

100. Jacques Soustelle, *Anthropology Newsletter* 24(3): 2, 1983; Ernst Wreschner, *Anthropology Newsletter* 24(5): 2, 1983.

101. *Anthropology Newsletter* 24(1): 2, 1983.

102. *Anthropology Newsletter* 25(6): 7, 1984.

103. *Anthropology Newsletter* 24(3): 2, 1983.

104. *Anthropology Newsletter* 24(6): 6–7, 1983.

105. *Anthropology Newsletter* 25(3): 2, 1984.

106. *Anthropology Newsletter* 24(5): 2, 1983.

107. *Anthropology Newsletter* 24(6): 6–7, 1983. The quote continues, "when, in our day and age, its national liberation movement often represents the developing heart of a people's culture. It can be mentioned here that there are those among us, Jews, who are not prepared to deny to others what we ourselves value and fought for, our own historic liberation movement."

108. *Anthropology Newsletter* 25(5): 2, 1984.

109. Barbara Aswad and Louise Sweet, *Anthropology Newsletter* 24(6): 6–7, 1983.

110. Roselle Tekiner, *Anthropology Newsletter* 25(3): 2, 1984.

111. *Anthropology Newsletter* 24(3): 2, 1983.

112. *Anthropology Newsletter* 24(5): 2, 1983.

113. *Anthropology Newsletter* 25(5): 2, 1984.

114. One person suggested the standing ovation that greeted Edward Said during the twentieth-anniversary celebration panel for *Orientalism* (1979) marked the completion of this change.

115. AMEWS included several anthropologists among its founders, including Lucie Wood Saunders, Elizabeth (BJ) Fernea and Sondra Hale, with Suad Joseph playing a crucial leading role in envisioning and establishing it. On the founding of AMEWS, see Joseph 1988.

116. The MES mission and goals statement is available at http://www.aaanet.org/sections/mes/?page_id=65.

117. Incorporating into the AAA also meant instituting mechanisms like elections, peer review processes for panels, and prize selection, all of which increased gatekeeping in the subfield.

118. Records of the transition that we received from MERGA and early MES members show that in addition to Saunders and Aswad, Barbara Larson and William Young did much of that labor. Fadwa El Guindi served on the AAA executive board during this time (1994–1996) and provided information about AAA processes. Section officers spent significant time trying to understand and clarify AAA procedures for various activities.

119. To this academic, Eickelman and Rabinow represented high-profile MENA anthropologists.

120. See the full text of the 1998 code at http://www.aaanet.org/issues/policy-advocacy/upload/ethicscode.pdf.

121. For example, "strings attached" funding under the auspices of the National Security Education Program.

122. See David Price's 2000 *The Nation* article, available at http://www.anthropologiesproject.org/2013/07/anthropologists-as-spies.html. See also Berreman 2003. For a critique of such perspectives, see Lucas 2009.

123. Other 1990s statements addressed topics such as famine in Africa, a science-themed US postal stamp, war crimes in the former Yugoslavia, and internet sales of antiquities. The board also supported "rights to develop cultural and linguistic resources as communities see fit," participated in the Coalition on the Academic Workforce, promoted smoke-free meetings, began the RACE initiative, and added a requirement about nondiscrimination in hiring practices with regard to gays and lesbians for employment advertisements. NAA Box 144.

124. A decision to boycott Illinois was finally made in 2000.

125. NAA Box 43. For more discussion of this controversy, see Chapter 5.

126. David Price mentions other discussions related to the 1990–1991 Gulf War, namely "proposals by conservatives in the AAA that its members assist allied efforts against Iraq" which "provoked only minor opposition" (2004b: 67).

127. Specifically, it stated that US troop buildup was "leading to an escalation of tension without providing new opportunities for a diplomatic and peaceful resolution" and that the United States had no treaty obligations with Kuwait, was not in danger of attack, and had no mandate from the US population for an invasion.

128. See Appendix B for full text. NAA Box 224.

129. NAA Boxes 144 and 224. Beeman's recollection of this motion did not include his role in its revision; he instead explained that "balancing the general public policy concerns with the specific interests of the Association were very important, and that I think was the crux of the matter with the Executive Board."

130. Both the original and revised motions are in Appendix B.

131. NAA Box 224.

132. This hitch involved a rule about "timeliness" and resolutions; namely, some-

one asked why the AAA should make a statement at this time given that the sanctions had been in place for a while.

133. See the *AN* report of executive board actions for May 1997. Also at the 1997 AAA business meeting, someone suggested a potential motion "expressing public condemnation regarding the Taliban's treatment of women in Afghanistan, as well as for the women and children of Sudan and Algeria." She was asked to work with the CfHR to prepare a formal resolution; we found no later record of such a resolution.

134. They initially brought the statement to the MES board, which placed it on the section's business meeting agenda.

135. See Appendix B for the motion's text.

136. See Appendix B for the motion's text.

137. Email communications shared with us about this statement also highlighted the importance of bringing MENA anthropologists' "expert" voices to the discussion.

138. *Anthropology Newsletter*, Feb. 1998, p. 2.

139. Ferguson 1994 argues eloquently that depoliticization is a key effect of bureaucracy and mechanisms of administration (in relation to development, but also more broadly). For more on how bureaucracy, and associated technopolitics, can have depoliticizing effects, see Gupta 2012.

Chapter 5

1. Of course, this destruction began much earlier and was cemented by US sanctions in the 1990s.

2. See the AAA's most recent declaration in support of human rights at http://www.aaanet.org/about/Policies/statements/Declaration-on-Anthropology-and-Human-Rights.cfm.

3. During the early 2000s, senior white men held most public leadership positions in MES; four out of five presidencies). The twenty-first-century MES presidents have been Jon Anderson (2000–2002), Daniel Varisco (2002–2004), Jenny White (2004–2006), William Beeman (2006–2008), Gregory Starrett (2008–2010), Farha Ghannam (2010–2012), Lara Deeb (2012–2014), and Ilana Feldman (2014–2016). All terms begin at the *conclusion* of the AAA conference for the first year listed. The board's foci through 2006 included outreach to archaeologists, folklorists, and scholars in the region; internet presence; section prizes and elections; and future business meeting program content. These foci ensured that MES energy was often spent fulfilling the requirements of AAA bureaucracy (e.g., maintaining membership numbers; running nomination, program, and award committees; writing annual reports, etc.).

4. See Tierney 2000. For an anthropological perspective on the El Dorado controversy, see Fluehr-Lobban 2003b. Also see NAA Box 43.

5. http://www.haaretz.com/print-edition/opinion/more-than-a-million-bullets-1.127053.

6. See Appendix B.

7. The 2001 CfHR Annual Report states that it recommended "the EB, with the assistance of MES, revise the resolution."

8. All executive board minutes discussed in this chapter are found either in the Na-

tional Anthropology Archives (NAA) at the Smithsonian Institution or, for more recent years, at the AAA headquarters in Arlington, VA. Commission and section reports are from the AAA website: www.aaanet.org.

9. See http://www.btselem.org/statistics/fatalities/before-cast-lead/by-date-of-event.

10. The Middle East Section mission statement is here: http://www.aaanet.org/sections/mes/?page_id=65. The Task Force mission statement reads: "The Task Force is committed to increasing the public relevance, visibility, and application of anthropological perspectives on Middle Eastern peoples and cultures. It supports ending all acts of aggression and occupation in the Middle East, and all forms of prejudice against Middle Eastern and Muslim peoples. First and foremost, the Task Force works to ensure that conditions within the academy permit the open research and discussion of Middle East-related issues that are the foundation of a public Middle East anthropology. Second, the Task Force encourages anthropological participation in public discourse on Middle East issues by facilitating connections between anthropologists and media professionals, and by engaging in regular written and oral commentary in the public sphere. Third, the Task Force works to promote anthropological perspectives on the Middle East in K-12 and university classrooms, through teacher workshops and other activities. Finally, the Task Force works in concert with other academic organizations to create anthropologically informed conference panels, public statements, and reports on the various issues precipitated by conflicts involving the Middle East."

11. Similarly, that same year the MES president highlighted media outreach at the section business meeting and proposed creating an MES speakers and writers bureau called MESPEAK that would, according to the minutes, "provide resources and experts from the field of anthropology to community groups, journalists, editors, and newspapers." To our knowledge, MESPEAK never came to fruition.

12. It also created a listserv for anthropologists wanting to share discipline-related news about MENA and calls to action around issues affecting MENA anthropologists, wrote a proposal (that failed to receive MES funding) for a symposium to connect media professionals and MENA scholars, and created a website (www.meanthro.org) to document its activities and freely disseminate the handbook.

13. The adopted motion, passed during the 2002 nonquorum AAA business meeting, was to "assist the ad-hoc Latin American Studies Association delegates in supporting follow-up visits to Guatemala," to promote "scholarly activities with invited researchers from Guatemala" on US campuses, and to publish in *Anthropology News* "news of attacks on our Guatemalan colleagues." At this May 2003 meeting the board also discussed protecting artifacts in Iraq and the AAA's symbolic support for a lawsuit filed by the Association of American Publishers against the US Treasury Department's ruling that US-based scientific journals cannot edit papers submitted by Iranian scholars without US government permission. NAA Box 44.

14. See Bishara 2014.

15. "No action" was taken on the motion on marijuana laws, with no explanation in the minutes. NAA Box 42.

16. Executive Director Bill Davis apparently drafted these guidelines at the board's request. After agreeing that these guidelines should be posted online to "assist mem-

bers with information on how to construct motions" in the future, MENA anthropol-ogist William Beeman moved that they be adopted. They were, in a unanimous vote. NAA Box 42.

17. Resolution text in Appendix B. NAA Box 42.

18. Resolution text in Appendix B. Beeman moved to adopt "the spirit of the mo-tion" on academic freedom with the "proviso" that the president rewrite it "as a series of resolutions with a specific focus, one of which would deal with intimidation and censor-ship by the current administration" (NAA Box 42). This idea passed unanimously, but the resolution authors were told that the board had passed their original text.

19. Resolution text in Appendix B. NAA Box 42.

20. The resolution's authors received a rejection letter almost identical to the min-utes: "While the Board appreciated the spirit of the motion, and while it agrees that Iraq is an issue of critical importance, the Board decided that many of the specific issues raised in this motion are no longer relevant, given the passage of time and current events."

21. Resolution text in Appendix B. Again, MENA anthropologist William Beeman seems to have spearheaded this rejection, suggesting changes and that the resolution be vetted by the MES board, in what might have been an effort to reinscribe MES author-ity over the Task Force (we admit to personal frustration here as at-the-time junior Task Force members).

22. NAA Box 42.

23. Oddly, the rejection letter received by the scholars who submitted this resolu-tion referred instead to the resolution on civil liberties, stating, "While the Board be-lieves all citizens should be concerned about civil liberties in the aftermath of September 11, the statement itself was not crafted in a way to gain authority. I refer you to the guidelines to understand the criteria the Board will consider when making a public statement. It was determined that your statement in its current form did not meet these criteria." This suggests either administrative oversight or board antipathy to the entire group of linked resolutions.

24. NAA Box 49.

25. During the May 2004 meeting, the board also discussed a communication from the Israeli Anthropological Association about looking into a petition from Ahoti (Israel's Feminists of Color movement) about racism in the Israeli academy, again focusing on anthropologists themselves. NAA Box 45.

26. At that meeting, such work included establishing an online journal (*CyberOrient*) about internet usage in MENA, formulating nominations and award committees, dis-cussing the website, building the MES budget, and allocating one of the section's invited sessions to archaeology.

27. 2004 MES board meeting minutes.

28. A graduate student and junior faculty member ghostwrote this letter, which was eventually sent to leading members of Congress.

29. Resolution text in Appendix B.

30. Handwritten notes on an agenda from the May 2004 executive board meeting state, next to the agenda listing for the Palestine resolution: "Ask Bill Beeman what we want to do with this." NAA Box 45.

31. NAA Boxes 45–46 and emails shared with us.

32. This email, dated January 20, 2005, is from NAA, Box 43.

33. The meeting minutes state that it was decided that the resolution "did not follow the guidelines adopted previously by the board. They agreed it was not strategic, and not clearly association-related, and it doesn't demonstrate anthropological knowledge. It wasn't clear to the board what action was being sought and does not show a clear and succinct relevance to the AAA membership." NAA Box 46.

34. Starrett 2005: 12.

35. Ibid.

36. A former board member confirmed this impression, noting that Latin Americanists had made a concerted effort to nominate one another and populate both the board and the CfHR. We must also consider the sheer amount of volunteer labor that board members contribute to running the association and the time limits on what is possible to accomplish. A former board member noted, "I think, to be fair, for the people on the board, it's like, we're doing all this work, what's the point of doing it if we can't bring our interests to bear and use the association, right? And that's a fine balance."

37. A former executive board member also suggested to us that when MESA crossed the hotel picket lines in San Francisco in 2004 (AAA instead swallowed the costs of breaking the hotel contract), "the Middle East Studies people lost credibility with some Executive Board members" which "cost us" their support and "discredited Middle East anthropologists as a moral authority."

38. Some people made this assessment by contrasting MES with institutions: one scholar said of MES, "It is not MERIP, miraculously. It is not, to my knowledge, politicized, in the basic sense of the term." Another noted that MESA was "much worse" than MES on Israel-Palestine, with "outbreaks of real emotional expression."

39. Eickelman 2012: 213.

40. All of our interlocutors, including those who have submitted resolutions, expressed deep skepticism about their utility. One scholar who is critical of US and Israeli policy in MENA said, "Do you really think, you know, sending a letter to the president of the United States or Netanyahu from the American Anthropological Association . . . I'm not sure what it means. I think it makes the people who do it feel good about themselves."

41. Resolution texts are in Appendix B. In 2006, the board also adopted a resolution stating the association "supports the Colombian union SINALTRAINAL's call for a boycott of The Coca-Cola Company and its products, and calls its members to do the same, until Coca-Cola agrees in good faith to negotiate with workers."

42. Other motions at the 2007 meeting called for reinstating antisecrecy language into the ethics code, calling on the US Census Bureau to include a question about language proficiency other than English and asking for a task force to investigate issues related to rising global food prices.

43. Many of these are detailed in press releases, including a letter supporting the tenure review process for Nadia Abu El-Haj.

44. Another factor may be a broader renewed interest in anthropology as a publicly engaged discipline (Besteman and Gusterson 2005; Gonzalez 2004).

45. See articles by Seymour Hersh and Brian Whitaker. The latter points to Rafael Patai's 1973 book *The Arab Mind* as a key source for both US pro-war politicians and the military. http://www.newyorker.com/magazine/2004/05/24/the-gray-zone; http://www .theguardian.com/world/2004/may/24/worlddispatch.usa.

46. AAA press release on the resolutions, Dec. 11, 2006.

47. Gusterson has also worked in Russia. Inspired by the Union of Concerned Scientists pledge to refuse Star Wars funding, the network's first action was to circulate a pledge not to do counterinsurgency work for the United States. See Network of Concerned Anthropologists 2007.

48. Gonzalez 2004; Network of Concerned Anthropologists 2009. An exception is Kelly et al. 2010.

49. MESA has addressed secrecy issues frequently, but mainly in relation to transparency of funding. A 1982 MESA resolution stated that members must "disclose fully in any written results and also to all persons involved in its conduct (i.e., participants, contributors and subjects) all sources of support—other than personal—for that research" (see Dale Eickelman's letter to *Anthropology News*, Jan. 2001, 42(1): 3). In 1985, Harvard's Middle East Studies Center was expelled from MESA because its director, Nadav Safran, failed to disclose that he held a CIA research contract and that the CIA had sponsored a conference on Islamic fundamentalism at the university. It was the 1982 resolution that facilitated action against the center and pressured Harvard to release documents related to these CIA connections. (See Dale Eickelman's op-ed "Scholarly Ethics at Risk" in *The Washington Post*, Nov. 1, 1985, p. A24). This strategy of emphasizing transparency of funding and support essentially precludes clandestine or covert research without explicitly saying so.

50. Schrecker 2010 discusses the deliberate discrediting of academia that followed its opposition to the Vietnam War and the resulting government and corporate attempts to cultivate relationships with scholars, generally on the right politically, who support particular government policies. Kramer 2011 attempts precisely this sort of discrediting and calls for the government to cultivate relationships with scholars who will support US policy in the Middle East, including recruiting them for intelligence work. The Association for the Study of the Middle East and Africa (ASMEA) is an academic association that facilitates these relationships, established in 2008 by several politically conservative MENA scholars who had advised the Bush administration after 9/11.

51. To avoid recruitment, some interlocutors deliberately chose topics or fieldsites about which they thought they would not "be mined" for information.

52. Given both secrecy clauses and the environment of suspicion in anthropology around intelligence, security, military, and other government work, it is possible that people simply did not tell us about such work. Our discussion is limited to military, intelligence, and foreign policy work. Several of our interlocutors have done forms of development work, via government-related agencies or NGOs. There are also MENA anthropologists who work in corporations (e.g., the petroleum industry). Development and corporate work fall beyond the scope of this book.

53. See Luke and Kersel 2013 for a detailed history and discussion of archaeology's long-standing intersections with government.

54. Others noted that they welcomed policymakers and people in government, military, and intelligence agencies reading their published work.

55. Price noted the irony of this timing: "Although it came more than eighty-five years after the fact, this gesture represented an ambiguous statement of contemporary anthropology's view of its past, present, and future relationships to the intelligence community. . . . Even as the AAA passed this motion, President Bush's 'war on terror' found a chorus of AAA members calling for anthropologists to covertly contribute their skills to the Central Intelligence Agency (CIA) and other intelligence agencies, and new funding opportunities secretly connected anthropology's graduate students with intelligence agencies." This "chorus" consisted primarily of applied anthropologists and reminds us of long-standing differences between applied and academic anthropologists since WWII (Price 2008a: 16).

56. A November 15, 2005, memo from Executive Director Bill Davis to the executive board detailed the "CIA job ads" situation. Three times in prior months, the AAA had received job ads from the CIA for placement and posted them online and in *Anthropology News* (the print version included the note, "Publication of this advertisement does not signify endorsement by AAA.") The memo explained that AAA members had registered "moral, ethical, ideological, and/or political" concerns about the ads' posting. It also clarified existing AAA policy: employers must disclose their hiring practice regarding gay and lesbians and whether they are on the AAUP censure list and were "urged" "to comply with" the AAA Code of Ethics. There was, however, no systematic review of submitted ads. The memo also referred to a 1982 motion "to 'endorse' a resolution adopted earlier that year by the Northeastern Anthropological Association which stated that 'anthropologists should not engage (1) in work for the CIA and U.S. military intelligence, (2) in training students for work in these agencies, or (3) in assisting in the recruitment of anthropologists for work in these agencies.'" The memo stated that this motion was adopted at the 1982 business meeting and should have been sent out for a full membership mail vote, but that Davis was unable to locate any record of that vote and thus concluded that there was no effective policy preventing running CIA ads. He then detailed his concerns about instituting standards for recruitment ads, including a "slippery slope of censorship" and that it was unfair to practicing anthropologists to ban certain job ads. The memo recommended the board "take no action. Treat placement of job ads as a business transaction." In this case, the board did not listen to Davis. NAA Box 46.

57. We were told that NAPA published at least one such ad after the new policy was adopted to assert that AAA policy was not binding.

58. Another member, David Price, conducted his dissertation research in the region in the early 1990s, but his publications and work since have been about anthropology as a discipline and about the United States.

59. Articles about HTS appeared in the *New York Times*, the *Washington Post*, the *San Francisco Chronicle*, and the *Boston Globe*, among other venues.

60. King 2009: 16.

61. The CEAUSSIC report states that as of April 2009, only six held PhDs in anthropology (representing at least three subfields), and only five held MAs in anthro-

pology. For perspectives on HTS from such participants, see Griffin 2007; King 2009; Glenn 2007.

62. http://www.aaanet.org/issues/policy-advocacy/statement-on-HTS.cfm.

63. On the last point, the AAA noted that HTS was described as "a Department of Defense intelligence asset" and that the circumstances of its work "create a significant likelihood that HTS data will in some way be used as part of military intelligence, advertently or inadvertently."

64. The full report is available at http://www.aaanet.org/issues/policy-advocacy/CEAUSSIC-Releases-Final-Report-on-Army-HTS-Program.cfm. For a critique of both CEAUSSIC reports from the perspective of a philosophy professor at the US Naval Academy, see Lucas 2009. He notes that there is no evidence of actual ethical misconduct of HTS personnel, that HTS participation does not *require* clandestine research, and that the HTS job description fulfills AAA ethics code stipulations (2009). Fluehr-Lobban and Lucas (2015) also critique CEAUSSIC's handling of the HTS controversy. Note also that many in the military thought HTS was a bad idea because it was dangerous to have non-combat personnel around during operations.

65. The statement continued, "The AAA Executive Board concludes that the HTS program cannot produce beneficial and morally acceptable knowledge of local, social contexts. Furthermore, the HTS program operates in a context that is fundamentally incompatible with the Code of Ethics of the AAA and responsible social scientific research."

66. In 2007, Terence Turner introduced a motion to reinsert verbatim into the code the 1971 language prohibiting clandestine research. The motion passed without a quorum. The executive board did not implement it or send it out for a vote, but instead convened a committee to propose different modifications—including stronger language about doing no harm, transparency of research goals, and clandestine research—which passed in 2008. See http://www.aaanet.org/issues/policy-advocacy/Vote-on-Changes-to-the-AAA-Code-of-Ethics.cfm. On earlier revisions of the ethics code, see Fluehr-Lobban 2003b. The 2008 revision was followed by a major overhaul that reorganized the code into "principles," adopted in 2012. That version is available here: http://ethics.aaanet.org/category/statement.

67. MENA anthropologist Nancy Lindisfarne wrote that no anthropologist should work in any context of military occupation with any western NGO, military group, or NATO, because that is "in practice taking sides." If an anthropologist works in a war zone, they should "work for a local organization, on a local salary, and live at a standard similar to those of your neighbors and coworkers" (2008: 4).

68. 2011: 30.

69. A few CEAUSSIC members interviewed HTS participants individually, but the committee as a whole did not meet with any.

70. http://blog.aaanet.org/2009/06/08/ceaussic-anthropologists-and-analysts. See also his detailed critique of HTS and its deployment of the culture concept, as well as the AAA's focus on ethical practice (Albro 2010).

71. This was not the only CfHR letter on AAA letterhead in 2008; others addressed Thailand's war on drugs, the US Census linguistic classification, death threats to Guatemalan anthropologists, and protests in Tibet.

72. A MENA scholar involved with drafting the letter described email responses from the AAA that "made no sense . . . such gobbledygook," which prompted her to ask "Is it the case that the Executive Board changed the rules as a result of the Gaza letter?"

73. See Ferguson 1994 and Gupta 2012. After some outcry, the AAA quickly revised the Standard Operating Procedure in 2010 to allow room for sections or committees to make statements and write letters on their own, provided that they made clear that the statement was not coming from the AAA as a whole and that it was not on association letterhead. While this change gave subgroups some autonomy, it also ensured that the AAA remained depoliticized, especially on MENA issues, and reinforced a limited purview of political engagement that largely excluded MENA.

74. http://www.aaanet.org/sections/mes/?p=122.

Conclusion

1. See anthroboycott.wordpress.com. As we go to press, this petition has over one thousand signatures. Full disclosure: we are signatories. The first panel at the AAA annual meeting devoted to discussing the boycott took place in 2013.

2. As this book goes to press, the Critical Ethnic Studies Association, Peace and Justice Studies Association, the African Literature Association and the Association for Humanist Sociology have also endorsed the academic boycott. The full membership of the Middle East Studies Association voted down a resolution to suppress discussion of the boycott in February 2015. Discussions of the academic boycott will also continue at the American Historical Association , the National Women's Studies Association, and the Modern Languages Association in coming years; the last is scheduled to vote on a boycott resolution in 2017.

3. The international campaign to boycott Israeli academic institutions began in 2002 and grew rapidly over the following decade. See www.pacbi.org for the Palestinian boycott call. The US-specific campaign (http://www.usacbi.org) was launched in 2009 after Israel's Operation Cast Lead attack on Gaza, which was fully supported by the United States and enabled by US-supplied arms. Over 1,000 Palestinians were killed and 5,000 wounded (and 9 Israelis killed and 500 wounded), according to Israeli human rights organization B'Tselem: http://www.btselem.org/statistics/fatalities/during-cast -lead/by-date-of-event. See also http://www.amnesty.ie/our-work/operation-cast-lead. The academic boycott is part of a broader international boycott, divestment, and sanctions (BDS) campaign pressuring Israel to withdraw from Palestinian lands occupied in 1967, implement equal rights for Palestinian citizens of Israel, and respect the right of return for Palestinian refugees (see www.bdsmovement.net). For a comprehensive sixty-four-page report about how Israeli academic institutions abet the occupation, see Hever 2009, available at www.bdsmovement.net. See also http://elec tronicintifada.net/content/report-israeli-academic-institutions-role-occupation/3436.

4. http://www.amnesty.org/en/library/info/MDE15/029/2014/en. See also http://www.lrb.co.uk/2015/05/04/neve-gordon/the-day-after and http://www.breakingthesi lence.org.il/pdf/ProtectiveEdge.pdf.

5. Boycott supporters point out that Israel should be boycotted because it has violated more United Nations resolutions than any other country in the world and receives the most foreign aid of all countries supported by the United States.

6. Motion text available here: https://blacklivesmatteraaa.wordpress.com/2014/12 /08/section-assembly-motion-on-michael-brown-eric-garner-racialized-repression -state-violence.

7. http://www.ebony.com/news-views/the-fergusonpalestine-connection-403 #axzz3PgXeQS2t.

8. http://www.conferenceofpresidents.org/news/press/2013/dec24/presidents-con ference-welcomes-strong-rejection-american-academic-community. At least one such university president has been revealed to have financial ties to Israeli institutions that abet settlements: http://mondoweiss.net/2014/04/university-condemned-settlements.

9. See https://www.middleeastmonitor.com/blogs/politics/16395–israeli-think-ta nk-holds-anti-bds-hackathon; https://www.middleeastmonitor.com/news/europe/108 55–25–countries-attend-london-anti-bds-meeting. According to Liz Jackson, a lawyer for Palestine Legal, beginning in 2010 the Israeli state initiated a strategy to use "litigation and legislation" to repress discussion of BDS.

10. See an article on this very issue at http://www.anthropology-news.org/index .php/2014/11/05/debating-the-academic-boycott-of-israel-in-a-climate-of-fear. At least one anthropologist related that they did not sign onto the statement supporting the academic boycott of Israeli institutions, despite their personal support for the boycott, because they were concerned that such political stance-taking would paint the anthropology department negatively in the eyes of the administration, thereby harming untenured colleagues in the department. The concern was related to the administration's quick public condemnation of the American Studies Association's endorsement of the boycott.

11. See the statement at https://anthroantiboycott.wordpress.com, as well as links on that page to various letters written to the AAA from opponents to the boycott.

12. https://anthroboycott.wordpress.com.

13. http://blog.aaanet.org/2014/09/08/anthropologists-announce-new-task-force -on-aaa-engagement-with-israelpalestine.

14. Comments on the panel "What Is the Role of Academia in Political Change? The Case of Boycott, Divestment and Sanctions (BDS) and Israeli Violations of International Law," Dec. 4, 2014.

15. A senior scholar suggested to us that the AAA was seeking to avoid some of the conflicts that arose in other task forces between regional specialists; perhaps there was an additional presumption that there would inevitably be conflicts in such a task force on Israel-Palestine.

16. http://blog.aaanet.org/2014/11/13/format-for-december-4th-members-open -forum-on-engagement-with-israel-and-palestine.

17. For critiques of the dialogue model, see Kosmatopoulos 2014 and Saguy, Tropp, and Hawi 2012, as well as: http://electronicintifada.net/content/can-we-talk-middle -east-peace-industry/8402 and http://www.aljazeera.com/indepth/opinion/2011/08/20 1188976675245.html.

18. In the academic realm, the Association of Arab American University Graduates is perhaps the best example of this.

19. We learned of the subfield's vibrancy via the work we did for an *Annual Review of Anthropology* article (Deeb and Winegar 2012).

Appendix A

1. Deeb and Winegar 2012.
2. See Langness and Frank 1981; Ochs and Capps 1996; Ochs and Capps 2001.

Appendix B

1. Submitted to the AAA membership at the 20 November 1979 business meeting by Mary Catherine Bateson, Warren Swidler, and Sam Beck. The resolution text appears in the January 1980 *AN*.

2. Submitted to the AAA membership at the 5 December 1982 business meeting by Louise Sweet, Barbara Aswad, Hani Fakhouri, Michael Higgins, Lucie Wood Saunders, Eleanor Leacock, Rayna Rapp, Eva Friedlander, Suad Joseph, Nina Glick Schiller, Elizabeth Fernea, Robert Fernea, Stanley Diamond, Luis Loyola, Theresa Rubin, Alice James, Lawrence Michalak, Randy Reiter, Karen Sacks, Henry Rosenfeld, Nabil Abraham, Elaine Combs-Schilling, and the Council for Marxist Anthropologists. This is the text of the resolution as it passed, printed in the January 1983 issue of *AN*. It contains minor modifications from the originally proposed motion text, which specified the withdrawals of each national military (e.g., US, Israeli, French, Italian) as separate points.

3. Submitted to the AAA membership at the 5 December 1982 business meeting by Nabeel Abraham, Nicholas Hopkins, Frederick Huxley, Suad Joseph, Khalil Nakhleh, and Henry Rosenfeld. This is the text available in the report about the meeting in *AN* 24(1): 6. The report noted that this text was "passed." An almost identical text appears in *MERA Forum* 6(2/3), summer/fall 1982, page 4.

4. Submitted to the AAA membership at the 14 November 1990 business meeting by Carol Shepherd McClain. Text from the NAA.

5. This text was revised by Ronald Cohen and William Beeman and sent by the AAA in letters to President Bush, Vice President Quayle, and Speaker of the House Foley.

6. Submitted to the AAA membership at the November 1997 business meeting by Soheir Morsy. Text from the February 1998 *AN*.

7. Submitted to the MES membership at its 1997 business meeting by Ann Bragdon and Barbara Aswad. This text is in a letter dated November 24, 1997, from MES President Barbara Larson to executive director of the AAA, Bill Davis.

8. Submitted to the AAA membership at the 16 November 2000 business meeting by the MES board.

9. Submitted to the AAA membership at the November 2003 business meeting by Olga Sooudi. Adopted in a nonquorum meeting. Adopted in a unanimous vote by the executive board in May 2004.

10. Submitted to the AAA membership at the November 2003 business meeting by Lara Deeb, Smadar Lavie, and Jessica Winegar. Adopted in a nonquorum meeting. Adopted by the executive board in May 2004.

11. Submitted to the AAA membership at the November 2003 business meeting by Rochelle Davis. Adopted in a nonquorum meeting. Rejected by the executive board in May 2004.

12. Submitted to the AAA membership at the November 2003 business meeting by

Nadine Naber, David Chaudoir, and Anthony Shenoda. Adopted in a nonquorum meeting. Rejected by the executive board in May 2004.

13. Submitted to the AAA membership at the November 2003 business meeting by Ted Swedenberg. Adopted in a nonquorum meeting. Rejected by the executive board in May 2004.

14. Submitted to the AAA membership at the 2004 business meeting by a group of anthropologists including Lila Abu-Lughod, Michael Gilsenan, Brinkley Messick, and Catherine Lutz. Adopted in a nonquorum meeting. Rejected by the executive board in May 2005.

15. This letter was dated 12 December 2004, addressed and sent to the chair of the House International Relations Subcommittee on International Terrorism, Nonproliferation and Human Rights (Elton Gallegly), and signed by the chair of the AAA Committee for Human Rights (Sam Martinez) and the president of the AAA Middle East Section (Daniel M. Varisco).

16. Submitted to the AAA membership at the 2006 business meeting. Adopted in a full membership vote in spring 2007.

17. Submitted to the AAA membership at the 2006 business meeting by Roberto Gonzalez and Kanhong Lin. Adopted in a full membership vote in spring 2007. We received this text directly from the AAA office.

18. http://www.ochaopt.org/gazacrisis/admin/output/files/ocha_opt_gaza_humanitarian_situation_report_2009_01_19_english.pdf.

19. Numerous international and Israeli news outlets have documented the use of white phosphorus on Palestinian civilians. See, among others, http://www.timesonline.co.uk/tol/news/world/middle_east/article5556027.ece; http://news.bbc.co.uk/1/hi/world/middle_east/7848768.stm; http://www.haaretz.com/hasen/spages/1054947.html; and stories in *The Guardian* (UK) on January 16, 2009, and *Los Angeles Times*, January 13, 2009.

20. International human rights organizations, including Human Rights Watch, have denounced Israeli use of white phosphorus in Gaza; see, for example, http://www.hrw.org/en/news/2009/01/22/incendiary-idf-kenneth-roth and http://www.hrw.org/en/news/2009/01/10/israel-stop-unlawful-use-white-phosphorus-gaza.

21. http://www.amnesty.org.uk/actions_details.asp?ActionID=551.

22. This statement was dated February 1, 2009; signed by the Committee for Human Rights, American Anthropological Association; and addressed and sent to Israeli Prime Minister Ehud Olmert, US Secretary of State Condoleezza Rice, and Middle East Envoy for the Quartet Tony Blair. It is available here: http://www.aaanet.org/cmtes/cfhr/upload/CfHR-Gaza-Statement-020509.pdf.

Bibliography

Abowd, Thomas. 2014. "The BDS Movement and Violations of Academic Freedom at Wayne State University." In *The Imperial University: Academic Repression and Scholarly Dissent*, edited by Piya Chatterjee and Sunaina Maira, 169–186. Minneapolis and London: University of Minnesota Press.

Abraham, Matthew. 2008. *Out of Bounds: Academic Freedom and the Question of Palestine*. New York: Pluto Press.

Abraham, Nabeel. 1989. "Arab-American Marginality: Mythos and Praxis." In *Arab Americans: Continuity and Change*, edited by Baha Abu-Laban and Michael Suleiman, 17–44. Belmont, MA: Association of Arab-American University Graduates Press.

Abu El-Haj, Nadia. 2001. *Facts on the Ground: Archaeological Practice and Territorial Self-Fashioning in Israeli Society*. Chicago: University of Chicago Press.

Abu-Lughod, Lila. 1986. *Veiled Sentiments: Honor and Poetry in a Bedouin Society*. Berkeley: University of California Press.

———. 1989. "Zones of Theory in the Anthropology of the Arab World." *Annual Review of Anthropology* 18: 267–306.

———. 1990. "Can There Be a Feminist Ethnography?" *Women and Performance* 5 (1): 7–27.

———. 1991. "Writing against Culture." In *Recapturing Anthropology: Working in the Present*, edited by Richard G. Fox, 137–162. Santa Fe, NM: School of American Research Press.

———. 2002. "Do Muslim Women Need Saving?" *American Anthropologist* 104 (3): 783–790.

———. 2013. *Do Muslim Women Need Saving?* Cambridge, MA: Harvard University Press.

Adely, Fida J. 2009. "Educating Women for Development: The Arab Human Development Report 2005 and the Problem with Women's Choices." *International Journal of Middle East Studies* 41 (1): 105.

Ahmed, Sara. 2006. *Queer Phenomenology: Orientations, Objects, Others*. Durham, NC: Duke University Press.

Albro, Robert. 2010. "Anthropology and the Military: AFRICOM, 'Culture' and Future of Human Terrain Analysis." *Anthropology Today* 26 (1): 22–24.

Ali, Kamran Asdar. 2007. "Rounding off Our Space on Anthropology and the Middle East." *Anthropology News* (May): 13–14.

Anderson, Jon W. 2013. "Anthropology's Middle Eastern Prehistory: An Archaeology of Knowledge." In *Anthropology of the Middle East and North Africa: Into the New Millennium*, edited by Sherine Hafez and Susan Slyomovics, 47–62. Bloomington: Indiana University Press.

Anthony, Constance G. 2012. "The Port Hueneme of My Mind: The Geography of Working-Class Consciousness in One Academic Career." In *Presumed Incompetent: The Intersections of Race and Class for Women in Academia*, edited by Gabriella Gutiérrez y Muhs, Yolanda Flores Niemann, Carmen G. González, and Angela P. Harris, 300–312. Boulder: University Press of Colorado.

Aruri, Naseer H. 1985. "The Middle East on the U.S. Campus." *The Link (published by Americans for Middle East Understanding)* 18 (2): 1–14.

Asad, Talal, ed. 1973. *Anthropology and the Colonial Encounter*. Ithaca, NY: Ithaca Press.

Beinin, Joel. 2006. "The New McCarthyism: Policing Thought about the Middle East." In *Academic Freedom after September 11*, edited by Beshara Doumani, 237–266. New York: Zone Books.

Berreman, Gerald D. 2003. "Ethics versus 'Realism' in Anthropology: Redux." In *Ethics and the Profession of Anthropology: Dialogue for Ethically Conscious Practice*, 2nd ed., edited by Carolyn Fluehr-Lobban, 51–83. Walnut Creek, CA: AltaMira Press.

Besteman, Catherine, and Hugh Gusterson, eds. 2005. *Why America's Top Pundits Are Wrong: Anthropologists Talk Back*. Berkeley: University of California Press.

Bishara, Amahl. 2013. *Back Stories: U.S. News Production and Palestinian Politics*. Stanford, CA: Stanford University Press.

Blackwell, Maylei, and Nadine Naber. 2002. "Intersectionality in an Era of Globalization: The Implications of the UN World Conference against Racism for Transnational Feminist Practices—A Conference Report." *Meridians* 2 (2): 237–248.

Boas, Franz. 1919 [2004]. "Scientists as Spies." *The Nation*, Oct. 16.

Bok, Derek. 2004. *Universities in the Marketplace: The Commercialization of Higher Education*. Princeton, NJ: Princeton University Press.

Bourdieu, Pierre. 1988. *Homo Academicus*. Stanford, CA: Stanford University Press.

Boyer, Dominic, and Claudio Lomnitz. 2005. "Intellectuals and Nationalism: Anthropological Engagements." *Annual Review of Anthropology* 34: 105–120.

Brodkin, Karen, Sandra Morgen, and Janis Hutchinson. 2011. "Anthropology as White Public Space?" *American Anthropologist* 113 (4): 545–556.

Butler, Judith. 2012. *Parting Ways: Jewishness and the Critique of Zionism*. New York: Columbia University Press.

Cable, Umayyah. n.d. *Cinematic Activism: Palestinian Cultural Politics in the United States*. Dissertation in progress. Department of American Studies and Ethnicity, University of Southern California.

Caton, Steven C. 1999. *Lawrence of Arabia: A Film's Anthropology*. Berkeley: University of California Press.

Chatterjee, Piya, and Sunaina Maira, eds. 2014a. *The Imperial University: Academic Repression and Scholarly Dissent.* Minneapolis: University of Minnesota Press.

———. 2014b. "Introduction: The Imperial University: Race, War, and Nation-State." In *The Imperial University: Academic Repression and Scholarly Dissent,* edited by Piya Chatterjee and Sunaina Maira, 1–52. Minneapolis: University of Minnesota Press.

Chomsky, Noam, and Ilan Pappe. 2010. *Gaza in Crisis: Reflections on Israel's War against the Palestinians.* New York: Penguin Books.

Christiansen, Christine, Mats Utas, and Henrik Vigh, eds. 2006. *Navigating Youth, Generating Adulthood: Social Becoming in an African Context.* Uppsala, Sweden: Nordic Africa Institute.

Clifford, James. 1988. *The Predicament of Culture: Twentieth-Century Ethnographic Literature and Art.* Cambridge, MA: Harvard University Press.

———, and George E. Marcus, eds. 1986. *Writing Culture: The Poetics and Politics of Ethnography.* Berkeley: University of California Press.

Cole, Jennifer, and Deborah Durham, eds. 2007. *Generations and Globalization: Youth, Age, and Family in the New World Economy.* Bloomington: Indiana University Press.

———. 2008. *Figuring the Future: Globalization and the Temporalities of Children and Youth.* Santa Fe, NM: School for Advanced Research.

Collins, Patricia Hill. 2000. "It's All in the Family: Intersection of Gender, Race, and Nation." In *Decentering the Center: Philosophy for a Multicultural, Postcolonial, and Feminist World,* edited by Uma Narayan and Sandra Harding, 156–176. Bloomington: Indiana University Press.

Constantine, Madonna G., and Cristina Dorazio. 2008. "Racial Microaggressions." In *Encyclopedia of Counseling,* edited by Frederick T. L. Leong, 1291–1292. Thousand Oaks, CA: Sage.

Crenshaw, Kimberlé. 1991. "Mapping the Margins: Intersectionality, Identity Politics, and Violence against Women of Color." *Stanford Law Review* 43: 1241–1299.

Darnell, Regna. 2001. *Invisible Genealogies: A History of Americanist Anthropology.* Omaha: University of Nebraska Press.

The David Project. 2012. *A Burning Campus? Rethinking Israel Advocacy at America's Universities and Colleges.* Boston: The David Project.

Dean, Jodi. 2009. *Democracy and Other Neoliberal Fantasies: Communicative Capitalism and Left Politics.* Durham, NC: Duke University Press.

Deeb, Lara, and Mona Harb. 2013. *Leisurely Islam: Negotiating Geography and Morality in Shi'ite South Beirut.* Princeton, NJ: Princeton University Press.

Deeb, Lara, and Jessica Winegar. 2012. "Anthropologies of Arab-Majority Societies." *Annual Review of Anthropology* 41: 537–558.

———. 2013a. "The Post Cold-War Politics of Middle East Anthropology: Insights from a Transitional Generation Confronting the War on Terror." In *Anthropology of the Middle East and North Africa: Into the New Millennium,* edited by Sherine Hafez and Susan Slyomovics, 79–102. Bloomington: Indiana University Press.

———. 2013b. "Anthropology's 'Regions': The View from Middle East Anthropology." *Comparative Studies of South Asia, Africa, and the Middle East* 33 (2): 139–141.

Deloria, Philip. 1999. *Playing Indian.* New Haven, CT: Yale University Press.

di Leonardo, Micaela. 2000. *Exotics at Home: Anthropologies, Others, and American Modernity*. Chicago: University of Chicago Press.

———. 2008. "Introduction: New Global and American Landscapes of Inequality." In *New Landscapes of Inequality: Neoliberalism and the Erosion of Democracy in America*, edited by Jane L. Collins, Micaela di Leonardo, and Brett Williams, 3–19. Santa Fe, NM: School for Advanced Research Press.

Dirks, Nicholas B. 2004. *Edward Said and Anthropology*. Berkeley: University of California Press, for the Institute for Palestine Studies.

Donoghue, Frank. 2008. *The Last Professors: The Corporate University and the Fate of the Humanities*. New York: Fordham University Press.

Doumani, Beshara, ed. 2006a. *Academic Freedom after September 11*. New York: Zone Books.

———. 2006b. "Between Coercion and Privatization: Academic Freedom in the Twenty-First Century." In *Academic Freedom after September 11*, edited by Beshara Doumani, 11–57. New York: Zone Books.

Edwards, Brian. 2005. *Morocco Bound: Disorienting America's Maghreb, from Casablanca to the Marrakech Express*. Durham, NC: Duke University Press.

Eickelman, Dale F. 1985. "Scholarly Ethics at Risk." *Washington Post*, Nov. 1, A24.

———. 1992. "The Re-Imagination of the Middle East: Political and Academic Frontiers." *Middle East Studies Association Bulletin* 26 (1): 3–12.

———. 2012. "Social Science under Siege: The Middle East." In *Serendipity in Anthropological Research: The Nomadic Turn*, edited by Haim Hazan and Esther Hertzog, 213–228. Surrey, UK: Ashgate.

Emberling, Geoff. 2008. "Archaeologists and the Military in Iraq, 2003–2008: Compromise or Contribution?" *Archaeologies: Journal of the World Archaeological Congress* 4 (3): 445–459.

Fabian, Johannes. 1983. *Time and the Other: How Anthropology Makes Its Object*. New York: Columbia University Press.

Farsakh, Leila. 2002. "Palestinian Labor Flows to the Israeli Economy: A Finished Story?" *Journal of Palestine Studies* 32 (1): 13–27.

Feldman, Ilana. 2008. *Governing Gaza: Bureaucracy, Authority, and the Work of Rule, 1917–1967*. Durham, NC: Duke University Press.

Ferguson, James. 1994. *The Anti-Politics Machine: 'Development,' Depoliticization, and Bureaucratic Power in Lesotho*. Minneapolis and London: University of Minnesota Press.

Finkelstein, Norman G. 2000. *The Holocaust Industry: Reflections on the Exploitation of Jewish Suffering*. New York: Verso.

———. 2005. *Beyond Chutzpah: On the Misuse of Anti-Semitism and the Abuse of History*. Berkeley: University of California Press.

Fluehr-Lobban, Carolyn, ed. 2003a. *Ethics and the Profession of Anthropology: Dialogue for Ethically Conscious Practice*, 2nd ed. Walnut Creek, CA: AltaMira Press.

———. 2003b. "Ethics and Anthropology 1890–2000: A Review of Issues and Principles." In *Ethics and the Profession of Anthropology: Dialogue for Ethically Conscious Practice*, 2nd ed., edited by Carolyn Fluehr-Lobban, 1–28. Walnut Creek, CA: AltaMira Press.

Fluehr-Lobban, Carolyn, and George R. Lucas, Jr. 2015. "Assessing the Human Terrain Teams: No White Hats or Black Hats Please." In *Social Science Goes to War: The Human Terrain System in Iraq and Afghanistan*, edited by Montgomery McFate and Janice H. Laurence. London: Hurst.

Ghosh, Amitav. 1993. *In an Antique Land*. New York: Knopf.

Ginsburg, Benjamin. 2011. *The Fall of the Faculty: The Rise of the All-Administrative University and Why It Matters*. Oxford, UK: Oxford University Press.

Glenn, David. 2005. "Cloak and Classroom." *The Chronicle of Higher Education*, Mar. 25, A14.

———. 2007. "Former Trainee in Human Terrain System Describes a Program in Disarray." *The Chronicle of Higher Education*, Dec. 14, A8.

———. 2009. "New Pentagon-NSF Grants Draw Criticism from Social Scientists." *The Chronicle of Higher Education*, Oct. 12.

Goldschmidt, Walter. 2012. "Anthropology and the Business Cycle." In *Expanding American Anthropology, 1945–1980: A Generation Reflects*, edited by Alice Beck Kehoe and Paul L. Doughty, 110–122. Tuscaloosa: University of Alabama Press.

Gonzalez, Roberto J. 2009. *American Counterinsurgency: Human Science and the Human Terrain*. Chicago: Prickly Paradigm Press.

———, ed. 2004. *Anthropologists in the Public Sphere: Speaking Out on War, Peace, and American Power*. Austin: University of Texas Press.

Gordon, Neve. 2008. *Israel's Occupation*. Berkeley: University of California Press.

Griffin, Marcus B. 2007. "Research to Reduce Bloodshed." *The Chronicle of Higher Education*, Nov. 30, B10.

Gualtieri, Sarah M. 2009. *Between Arab and White: Race and Ethnicity in the Early Syrian American Diaspora*. Berkeley: University of California Press.

Gumport, Patricia J., ed. 2007. *Sociology of Higher Education: Contributions and Their Contexts*. Baltimore, MD: Johns Hopkins University Press.

Gupta, Akhil. 2012. *Red Tape: Bureaucracy, Structural Violence, and Poverty in India*. Durham, NC: Duke University Press.

Gutiérrez y Muhs, Gabriella, Yolanda Flores Niemann, Carmen G. González, and Angela P. Harris, eds. 2012. *Presumed Incompetent: The Intersections of Race and Class for Women in Academia*. Boulder: University Press of Colorado.

Hafez, Sherine, and Susan Slyomovics, eds. 2013a. *Anthropology of the Middle East and North Africa: Into the New Millennium*. Bloomington: Indiana University Press.

———. 2013b. "Introduction: Power and Knowledge in the Anthropology of the Middle East and North Africa." In *Anthropology of the Middle East and North Africa: Into the New Millennium*, edited by Sherine Hafez and Susan Slyomovics, xiii–xxiv. Bloomington: Indiana University Press.

Hagopian, Elaine C. 2004. *Civil Rights in Peril: The Targeting of Arabs and Muslims*. London: Pluto Press.

Hancock, Robert L. A. 2008. "Afterword: Reconceptualizing Anthropology's Historiography." In *Anthropology at the Dawn of the Cold War: The Influence of Foundations, McCarthyism and the CIA*, edited by Dustin Wax, 166–178. London: Pluto Press.

Hanieh, Adam. 2013. "The Oslo Illusion." *Jacobin* https://www.jacobinmag.com/2013/04/the-oslo-illusion/.

Haraway, Donna. 1988. "Situated Knowledge: The Science Question in Feminism and the Privilege of Partial Perspective." *Feminist Studies* 14 (3): 575–599.

Harvey, David. 2005. *A Brief History of Neoliberalism.* Oxford, UK: Oxford University Press.

Heineman, Kenneth J. 1994. *Campus Wars: The Peace Movement at American State Universities in the Vietnam Era.* New York: New York University Press.

Hever, Shir. 2009. "Academic Boycott of Israel and the Complicity of Israeli Academic Institutions in Occupation of Palestinian Territories." *The Economy of the Occupation: A Socioeconomic Bulletin* 23.

Hirschkind, Charles, and Saba Mahmood. 2002. "Feminism, the Taliban, and Politics of Counter-Insurgency." *Anthropological Quarterly* 75 (2): 339–354.

Hollinger, David A. 1996. *Science, Jews, and Secular Culture: Studies in Mid-Twentieth-Century American Intellectual History.* Princeton, NJ: Princeton University Press.

Honig, Emily. 1997. "Striking Lives: Oral History and the Politics of Memory." *Journal of Women's History* 9 (1): 139–157.

hooks, bell. 1992. *Black Looks: Race and Representation.* Boston: South End Press.

Horowitz, David. 2006. *The Professors: The 101 Most Dangerous Academics in America.* Washington, DC: Regnery.

Jamal, Amaney, and Nadine Naber, eds. 2008. *Race and Arab Americans before and after 9/11: From Invisible Citizens to Visible Subjects.* Syracuse, NY: Syracuse University Press.

Jarmakani, Amira. 2008. *Imagining Arab Womanhood: The Cultural Mythology of Veils, Harems, and Belly Dancers in the U.S.* New York: Palgrave Macmillan.

Jones, Toby Craig. 2010. *Desert Kingdom: How Oil and Water Forged Modern Saudi Arabia.* Cambridge, MA: Harvard University Press.

Jorgensen, Joseph, and Eric Wolf. 1970. "A Special Supplement: Anthropology on the Warpath in Thailand." *New York Review of Books,* Nov. 19. http://www.nybooks.com/articles/archives/1970/nov/19/a-special-supplement-anthropology-on-the-warpath-i.

Joseph, Suad. 1988. "The Founding of AMEWS." *AMEWS NEWS* 1 (1): 10–14.

Kapeliouk, Amnon. 1982. *Enquête sur un massacre: Sabra et Chatila.* Paris: Seuil.

Kaplan, Amy. 2013. "Zionism as Anticolonialism: The Case of Exodus." *American Literary History* 25 (4): 870–895.

Karp, Ivan, and Corinne A. Kratz. 2014. "The Interrogative Museum." In *Museum as Process: Translating Local and Global Knowledges,* edited by Raymond Silverman, 279–298. New York: Routledge.

Kates, Charlotte. 2014. "Criminalizing Resistance." *Jacobin.* https://www.jacobinmag.com/2014/01/criminalizing-resistance.

Kauanui, J. Kēhaulani. 2014. "Indigenous." In *Keywords for American Cultural Studies,* edited by Bruce Burgett and Glenn Hendler, 133–137. New York: New York University Press.

Kehoe, Alice Beck, and Paul L. Doughty, eds. 2012a. *Expanding American Anthropology, 1945–1980: A Generation Reflects.* Tuscaloosa: University of Alabama Press.

———. 2012b. "Breaking Ground: Postwar Anthropologists." In *Expanding American*

Anthropology, 1945–1980: A Generation Reflects, edited by Alice Beck Kehoe and Paul L. Doughty, 1–13. Tuscaloosa: University of Alabama Press.

Keller, John M., and Maritheresa Frain. 2010. "The Impact of Geo-Political Events, Globalization, and National Policies on Study Abroad Programming and Participation." In *A History of U.S. Study Abroad: 1965–Present*, edited by William W. Hoffa and Stephen C. DePaul, 15–54. A Special Publication of *Frontiers: The Interdisciplinary Journal of Study Abroad*.

Kelly, John D., Beatrice Juaregui, Sean T. Mitchell, and Jeremy Walton, eds. 2010. *Anthropology and Global Counterinsurgency*. Chicago: University of Chicago Press.

Kennedy, Michael D. 2015. *Globalizing Knowledge: Intellectuals, Universities, and Publics in Transformation*. Stanford, CA: Stanford University Press.

Kessler, Jonathan, and Jeff Schwaber. 1984. *The AIPAC College Guide: Exposing the Anti-Israel Campaign on Campus*. Washington, DC: The American-Israel Public Affairs Committee.

Khalidi, Rashid. 2013. *Brokers of Deceit: How the U.S. Has Undermined Peace in the Middle East*. Boston: Beacon Press.

Khuri, Fuad I. 2007. *An Invitation to Laughter: A Lebanese Anthropologist in the Arab World*. Chicago and London: University of Chicago Press.

King, Christopher. 2009. "Managing Ethical Conflict on a Human Terrain Team." *Anthropology News* 50 (6): 16.

Kluckhohn, Clyde. 1949. *Mirror for Man*. New York: McGraw-Hill.

Knopf-Newman, Marcy Jane. 2011. *The Politics of Teaching Palestine to Americans: Addressing Pedagogical Strategies*. New York: Palgrave Macmillan.

Kosmatopoulos, Nikolas. 2010. "The Gaza Freedom Flotilla: Ethnographic Notes on 'Othering Violence.'" *Anthropology Today* 26 (4): 26–29.

———. 2014. "The Birth of the Workplace: Technomorals, Peace Expertise, and the Care of the Self in the Middle East." *Public Culture* 26 (3): 529–558.

Kramer, Jane. 2008. "The Petition: Israel, Palestine, and a Tenure Battle at Barnard." *The New Yorker*, Apr. 14. http://www.newyorker.com/magazine/2008/04/14/the-petition.

Kramer, Martin. 2011. "Rules of Engagement: How Government Can Leverage Academe." *Washington Institute for Near East Policy, Policy Focus #113* (June).

Langness, L. L., and Gelya Frank. 1981. *Lives: An Anthropological Approach to Biography*. Novato, CA: Chandler and Sharp.

Lavie, Smadar. 2014. *Wrapped in the Flag of Israel: Mizrahi Single Mothers and Bureaucratic Torture*. New York: Berghahn Books.

Lévi-Strauss, Claude. 1955. *Tristes Tropiques*. Translated by John Weightman and Doreen Weightman. New York: Atheneum.

Lindisfarne, Nancy. 2008. "Culture Wars." *Anthropology Today* 24 (3): 3–4.

Liss, Julia E. 1998. "Diasporic Identities: The Science and Politics of Race in the Work of Franz Boas and W.E.B. Du Bois, 1894–1919." *Cultural Anthropology* 13 (2): 127–166.

Little, Douglas. 2003. *American Orientalism: The United States and the Middle East Since 1945*. London: I.B. Tauris.

Lockman, Zachary. 1996. *Comrades and Enemies: Arab and Jewish Workers in Palestine, 1906–1948*. Berkeley: University of California Press.

———. 2004. *Contending Visions of the Middle East: The History and Politics of Orientalism*. Cambridge, UK: Cambridge University Press.

Lucas, George R., Jr. 2009. *Anthropologists in Arms: The Ethics of Military Anthropology*. Lanham, MD: AltaMira Press.

Luke, Christina, and Morag M. Kersel. 2013. *U.S. Cultural Diplomacy and Archaeology: Soft Power, Hard Heritage*. New York: Routledge.

Lutz, Catherine. 1995. "The Gender of Theory." In *Women Writing Culture*, edited by Ruth Behar and Deborah A. Gordon, 249–266. Berkeley: University of California Press.

Mahdavi, Pardis. 2013. *From Trafficking to Terror: Constructing a Global Social Problem*. New York: Routledge.

Mandler, Peter. 2013. *Return from the Natives: How Margaret Mead Won the Second World War and Lost the Cold War*. New Haven, CT: Yale University Press.

Mamdani, Mahmood. 2004. *Good Muslim, Bad Muslim: America, the Cold War, and the Roots of Terror*. New York: Random House.

Mannheim, Karl. 1952. "The Problem of Generations." In *Essays on the Sociology of Knowledge*, edited by Paul Kecskemeti, 276–320. New York: Oxford University Press.

Mansour, Camille. 1994. *Beyond Alliance: Israel and U.S. Foreign Policy*. New York: Columbia University Press.

Marcus, George E., and Michael M. J. Fischer, eds. 1986. *Anthropology as Cultural Critique: An Experimental Moment in the Human Sciences*. Chicago: University of Chicago Press.

McAlister, Melani. 2001. *Epic Encounters: Culture, Media, and U.S. Interests in the Middle East, 1945–2000*. Berkeley: University of California Press.

Mearsheimer, John J., and Stephen M. Walt. 2008. *The Israel Lobby and U.S. Foreign Policy*. New York: Farrar, Straus and Giroux.

Messer-Davidow, Ellen. 1993. "Manufacturing the Attack on Liberalized Higher Education." *Social Text* 36: 40–80.

Michener, James A. 1965. *The Source*. New York: Random House.

Mirsepassi, Ali, Amrita Basu, and Frederick Weaver, eds. 2003. *Localizing Knowledge in a Globalizing World: Recasting the Area Studies Debate*. Syracuse, NY: Syracuse University Press.

Mitchell, Timothy. 2002. *Rule of Experts: Egypt, Techno-Politics, Modernity*. Berkeley: University of California Press.

Naber, Nadine. 2000. "Ambiguous Insiders: An Investigation of Arab American Invisibility." *Ethnic and Racial Studies* 23 (1): 37–61.

———. 2008. "Introduction: Arab Americans and U.S. Racial Formations." In *Race and Arab Americans before and after 9/11: From Invisible Citizens to Visible Subjects*, edited by Amaney Jamal and Nadine Naber, 1–45. Syracuse, NY: Syracuse University Press.

———. 2014. "Imperial Whiteness and the Diasporas of Empire." *American Quarterly* 66 (4): 1107–1115.

Nader, Laura. 1997. "The Phantom Factor." In *The Cold War and the University: Toward an Intellectual History of the Postwar Years*, edited by Noam Chomsky et al., 107–146. New York: The New Press.

———. 2002. "Breaking the Silence: Politics and Professional Autonomy." *Anthropological Quarterly* 75 (1): 160–169.

Navarro, Tami, Bianca Williams, and Attiya Ahmad. 2013. "Sitting at the Kitchen Table: Fieldnotes from Women of Color in Anthropology." *Cultural Anthropology* 28 (3): 443–463.

Network of Concerned Anthropologists. 2007. "The Network of Concerned Anthropologists Pledges to Boycott Counterinsurgency." *Anthropology News* (Dec.): 4–5.

———. 2009. *The Counter-Counterinsurgency Manual, or, Notes on Demilitarizing Anthropology.* Chicago: Prickly Paradigm Press.

Ochs, Elinor, and Lisa Capps. 1996. "Narrating the Self." *Annual Review of Anthropology* 25: 19–43.

———. 2001. *Living Narrative: Creating Lives in Everyday Storytelling.* Cambridge, MA: Harvard University Press.

Ogden, Anthony C., Heidi M. Soneson, and Paige Weting. 2010. "The Diversification of Geographic Locations." In *A History of U.S. Study Abroad: 1965–Present,* edited by William W. Hoffa and Stephen C. DePaul, 161–198. A Special Publication of *Frontiers: The Interdisciplinary Journal of Study Abroad.*

Pappé, Ilan. 2006. *The Ethnic Cleansing of Palestine.* London: One World.

Pomeranz, Kenneth, and Daniel A Segal. 2012. "World History: Departures and Variations." In *A Companion to World History,* edited by Douglas Northrop, 15–31. Oxford, UK: Blackwell.

Powdermaker, Hortense. 1966. *Stranger and Friend: The Way of an Anthropologist.* New York: Norton.

Pratt, Mary Louise. 2007 [1992]. *Imperial Eyes: Travel Writing and Transculturation,* 2nd ed. New York: Routledge.

Price, David. 2004a. "Anthropologists as Spies." In *Anthropologists in the Public Sphere: Speaking Out on War, Peace, and American Power,* edited by Roberto J. Gonzalez, 62–70. Austin: University of Texas Press.

———. 2004b. *Threatening Anthropology: McCarthyism and the FBI's Surveillance of Activist Anthropologists.* Durham, NC: Duke University Press.

———. 2008a. *Anthropological Intelligence: The Deployment and Neglect of American Anthropology in the Second World War.* Durham, NC: Duke University Press.

———. 2008b. "Limiting Democracy and Reining-in ARPA at the Annual Business Meeting: Or, Rules for Radicals (as Interpreted and Enforced by the Old Guard)." Paper presented at the Annual Meeting of the American Anthropological Association, San Francisco.

———. 2011. *Weaponizing Anthropology.* Petrolia, CA: Counterpunch and AK Press.

———. 2014. "Counterinsurgency by Other Names: Complicating Humanitarian Applied Anthropology in Current, Former, and Future War Zones." *Human Organization* 73 (2): 95–105.

Puar, Jasbir. 2007. *Terrorist Assemblages: Homonationalism in Queer Times.* Durham, NC: Duke University Press.

Rabinow, Paul. 1977. *Reflections on Fieldwork in Morocco.* Berkeley: University of California Press.

Rana, Junaid. 2011. *Terrifying Muslims: Race and Labor in the South Asian Diaspora*. Durham, NC: Duke University Press.

Rossiter, Margaret W. 1995. *Women Scientists in America: Before Affirmative Action, 1940–1972*. Baltimore, MD: Johns Hopkins University Press.

Roy, Sara. 2002. "Living with the Holocaust: The Journey of a Child of Holocaust Survivors." *Journal of Palestine Studies* 32 (1): 5–12.

Rubinstein, Robert A., Kerry B. Fosher, and Clementine K. Fujimura, eds. 2012. *Practicing Military Anthropology: Beyond Expectations and Traditional Boundaries*. Sterling, VA: Kumarian Press.

Saguy, Tamar, Linda R. Tropp, and Diala Hawi. 2012. "The Role of Group Power in Intergroup Contact." In *Advances in Intergroup Contact*, edited by G. Hodson and M. Hewstone, 113–132. New York: Psychology Press.

Said, Edward. 1978. *Orientalism*. New York: Vintage.

———. 1980. *The Question of Palestine*. New York: Routledge.

———. 1993. "Intellectual Exile: Expatriates and Marginals." *Grand Street* 47: 112–124.

Salaita, Steven. 2006. *Anti-Arab Racism in the USA: Where It Comes from and What It Means for Politics Today*. London and Ann Arbor: Pluto Press.

———. 2014. "Normatizing State Power: Uncritical Ethical Praxis and Zionism." In *The Imperial University: Academic Repression and Scholarly Dissent*, edited by Piya Chatterjee and Sunaina Maira, 217–236. Minneapolis and London: University of Minnesota Press.

Salamone, Frank A. 2008. "In the Name of Science: The Cold War and the Direction of Scientific Pursuits." In *Anthropology at the Dawn of the Cold War: The Influence of Foundations, McCarthyism and the CIA*, edited by Dustin Wax, 89–107. London: Pluto Press.

Saliba, Therese. 1999. "Resisting Invisibility: Arab Americans in Academia and Activism." In *Arabs in America: Building a New Future*, edited by Michael Suleiman, 304–319. Philadelphia: Temple University Press.

Samhan, Helen Hatab. 1999. "Not Quite White: Race Classification and the Arab American Experience." In *Arabs in America: Building a New Future*, edited by Michael Suleiman, 209–226. Philadelphia: Temple University Press.

Sawalha, Aseel. 2010. *Reconstructing Beirut: Memory and Space in a Postwar Arab City*. Austin: University of Texas Press.

Schrecker, Ellen. 2010. *The Lost Soul of Higher Education: Corporatization, the Assault on Academic Freedom, and the End of the American University*. New York: The New Press.

Segal, Daniel A. 2005. "Worlding History." In *Looking Backward and Looking Forward: Perspectives on Social Science History*, edited by Harvey J. Graff, Leslie Page Moch, and Philip McMichael, 81–100. Madison: University of Wisconsin Press.

Shaheen, Jack. 2014. *Reel Bad Arabs: How Hollywood Vilifies a People*. Northampton, MA: Olive Branch Press.

Sharma, Aradhana. 2013. "State Transparency after the Neoliberal Turn: The Politics, Limits, and Paradoxes of India's Right to Information Law." *PoLAR: Political and Legal Anthropology Review* 36 (2): 308–325.

Slyomovics, Susan. 2013. "State of the State of the Art Studies: An Introduction to the

Anthropology of the Middle East and North Africa." In *Anthropology of the Middle East and North Africa: Into the New Millennium*, edited by Sherine Hafez and Susan Slyomovics, 3–22. Bloomington: Indiana University Press.

Smith, Tony. 2005. *Foreign Attachments: The Power of Ethnic Groups in the Making of American Foreign Policy*. Cambridge, MA: Harvard University Press.

Spiegel, Steven L. 1985. *The Other Arab-Israeli Conflict: Making America's Middle East Policy from Truman to Reagan*. Chicago: University of Chicago Press.

Starn, Orin. 2011. "Here Come the Anthros (Again): The Strange Marriage of Anthropology and Native America." *Cultural Anthropology* 26 (2): 179–204.

Starrett, Gregory. 2005. "The Spirit of Your Resolution, or, Political Culture and the AAA." *Anthropology News* (Feb.): 11–12.

Stocking, George W., Jr. 1968. *Race, Culture, and Evolution: Essays in the History of Anthropology*. Chicago: University of Chicago Press.

———. 1992. *The Ethnographer's Magic and Other Essays in the History of Anthropology*. Madison: University of Wisconsin Press.

Stockton, Ronald. 1994. "Ethnic Archetype and the Arab Image." In *The Development of Arab American Identity*, edited by Ernest McCarus, 119–153. Ann Arbor: University of Michigan Press.

Strathern, Marilyn. 1987. "An Awkward Relationship: The Case of Feminism and Anthropology." *Signs* 12 (2): 276–292.

Strong, Pauline Turner. 2004. "Representational Practices." In *A Companion to the Anthropology of American Indians*, edited by Thomas Biolsi, 341–359. Oxford, UK: Blackwell.

Taylor, Mark C. 2010. *Crisis on Campus: A Bold Plan for Reforming Our Colleges and Universities*. New York: Knopf.

Terry, Janice. 2005. *U.S. Foreign Policy in the Middle East: The Role of Lobbies and Special Interest Groups*. Ann Arbor, MI: Pluto Press.

Tierney, Patrick. 2000. *Darkness in El Dorado: How Scientists and Journalists Devastated the Amazon*. New York: Norton.

Tochluk, Shelly. 2007. *Witnessing Whiteness: First Steps Toward an Antiracist Practice and Culture*. New York: R&L Education.

Toensing, Chris. 2013. "A Dishonest Umpire." *Jacobin*. https://www.jacobinmag.com/2013/04/a-dishonest-umpire.

Trencher, Susan R. 2012. "American Anthropology and the Opening of the Ethnographic 'I.'" In *Expanding American Anthropology, 1945–1980: A Generation Reflects*, edited by Alice Beck Kehoe and Paul L. Doughty, 131–144. Tuscaloosa: University of Alabama Press.

Varisco, Daniel Martin. 2005. *Islam Obscured: The Rhetoric of Anthropological Representation*. New York: Palgrave Macmillan.

Wagner, Donald E. 1995. *Anxious for Armageddon: A Call to Partnership for Middle Eastern and Western Christians*. Scottsdale, PA: Herald Press.

Wakin, Eric. 1993. *Anthropology Goes to War: Professional Ethics and Counterinsurgency in Thailand*. Madison: University of Wisconsin Press.

Wax, Dustin, ed. 2008. *Anthropology at the Dawn of the Cold War: The Influence of Foundations, McCarthyism and the CIA*. London: Pluto Press.

Weber, Devra. 1989. "*Raiz Fuerte:* Oral History and Mexicana Farmworkers." *Oral History Review* 17 (2).

Weber, Timothy P. 2004. *On the Road to Armageddon: How Evangelicals Became Israel's Best Friend*. Grand Rapids, MI: Baker Academic.

Winegar, Jessica. 2006. *Creative Reckonings: The Politics of Art and Culture in Contemporary Egypt*. Stanford, CA: Stanford University Press.

Index